THE ESSEX LANDSCAPE:
IN SEARCH OF ITS HISTORY

The 1996 Cressing Conference

edited by

L. S. Green

ACKNOWLEDGEMENTS

The editor would like to thank all the speakers who made the conference on which this collection of papers is based a success, Martin Wakelin who was persuaded to write a postscript to the other contributors, David Andrews for suggesting the event and Terry Staplehurst, Andrew Westman, Charlotte Harding and Annie Hooper for their help in producing this volume. The editor dedicates this volume to her colleagues in the former Environmental Services Branch of Essex County Council Planning Department whose enthusiasm and knowledge provided the climate in which such a conference as this could take place.

M. BURCHELL BA, MA, MRTPI
Head of Planning
Essex County Council
County Hall
Chelmsford
Essex CM1 1QH

CONTRIBUTORS

Dr David Andrews
Historic Buildings and Design,
Essex County Council, Planning Division, Chelmsford

Nigel Brown
Archaeology Section,
Essex County Council, Planning Division, Chelmsford

Fiona Cowell
Hatfield Priory, Hatfield Peverel, Essex

Sarah Green
Landscape Consultancy,
Essex County Council, Planning Division, Chelmsford

John Hunter
The Market Cross, Thaxted, Essex

Peter Murphy
Centre of East Anglian Studies, University of East Anglia, Norwich

Dr Oliver Rackham
Corpus Christi College, University of Cambridge

Dr Stephen Rippon
Department of Archaeology, School of Geography and Archaeology, University of Exeter

Pat Ryan
Danbury, Essex

Professor Robert Tregay
Landscape Design Associates, Peterborough

Martin Wakelin
Landscape Consultancy,
Essex County Council, Planning Division, Chelmsford

Dr Stuart Wrathmell
West Yorkshire Archaeology Service, Wakefield

ISBN 185281 190 0

Printed in England by Essex County Council, County Hall, Chelmsford, Essex, CM1 1QH

CONTENTS

LIST OF FIGURES & TABLES

FIGURES

TABLES

PREFACE

Essex is a relatively large county with an interesting diversity of physical form and an intricate coastline. A long and rich history can be seen in the county's landscape and coast, in the pattern of its woods and fields, banks and hedges, roads and waterways, and in the layout of boundaries and buildings. This history, ingrained in the physical fabric of Essex, was the subject of a one-day conference at Cressing Temple in September 1996. The present volume contains all but one of the papers presented on that occasion, subsequently revised and updated by their authors, as well as one additional contribution.

The conference was sponsored by Essex County Council Planning Division as one of a series of annual conferences on a theme relevant to the Division's work. The conferences started in 1992 and are usually held in the celebrated medieval barns at Cressing Temple, acquired by the County Council in 1987 and since refurbished. The 1996 Cressing Conference was the first to be devoted wholly to the historical aspects of the county's landscape and, as the subtitle of the conference (and of this volume) suggests, it was intended very much to be a starting point rather than the last word on the subject.

About 200 people attended the conference. The intended audiences for this record of the papers presented and discussed at the conference are (1) everyone who lives or works in Essex, especially all those who live and work in the countryside, (2) archaeologists and historians of the landscape, and (3) conservationists, planning professionals, administrators, architects, civil engineers and developers, who have a hand in shaping the landscape of the future.

The idea of 'historic landscape' is not new, but until relatively recently the idea was not taken very far nor very seriously. The landscape tended to be regarded as if it were a somewhat blank space in between individual monuments and archaeological sites, or else as forming the setting for such monuments and sites, a secondary consideration; it was not regarded as being a fully-formed historical artefact in its own right, in which individual sites are embedded. Appreciation of the history that is integral to virtually every landscape has moved from being the cause of a few enthusiasts, as was the case perhaps 20 years ago, to being the received wisdom of many and a desirable, if not mandatory, consideration in planning and development.

The papers were presented at the conference and are reproduced here in a chronological sequence, and touch upon every period from prehistory to the 21st century. An introductory paper (by John Hunter) provides a basic analysis of the county's landforms and an afterword (by Martin Wakelin) considers ways in which the public perception of the landscape and its historical testimony is itself subject to change through time. The chronological divisions are self-explanatory, although it is worth emphasising here what most contributors also alluded to, that the landscape is a physical unity, in which continuity from one period of human history to another is at least as important as any change that takes place. It is a truism, of course, that the landscape we enjoy is the sum of what survives from the past, in all its richness and variety, as well as what we add to it, and it is a finite, irreplaceable and often vulnerable resource.

The conference aimed to examine a range of themes in this chronological framework, and to explore some of the factors that have influenced the form of the landscape. In the coastal zone of Essex (described by Peter Murphy and Nigel Brown) many activities have evidently continued or recurred over millennia; an instance was keeping cattle and sheep to graze the salt marshes as suggested by Brown (1988). These ideas were subsequently developed as part of a wider consideration of the economy of east Essex based on archaeological evidence, including that of the Roman period (Wymer & Brown 1995, 151-73). Local case studies of factors at work in forming the landscape include the different interests of landowners great and small, at Hadleigh and Rayleigh (by Stephen Rippon), the purpose and uses of various kinds of woodland and Forest (by Oliver Rackham), and the first appearance of brick mansions and their parks (by David Andrews and Pat Ryan). Many such factors could be at work. Soils are suggested (by Stuart Wrathmell) as an important influence in the pattern of settlement dispersal–varying between dense and

Fig 1 Reconstruction painting of the Romano-British farmstead excavated recently at Great Holts Farm, Boreham, as it might have looked early in the 4th century AD (by Peter Froste).

sparse–as shown by comparison with corresponding patterns in other parts of England. The country-wide mapping of settlement patterns provides a useful interpretative framework for local studies.

Other aims of the conference included reviewing what elements of the landscape survive from different periods. For example, the importance of the county's comparatively long total coastline is enhanced by the survival in the intertidal zone of features that would have been destroyed on dry land. This matter of survival and understanding of different elements of the landscape is addressed (by Robert Tregay) from the point of view of a modern architectural and landscape design practice, with an eye to the future. The deliberate design of the rural landscape on a large scale, for pleasure as well as profit, began in the 18th century (outlined by Fiona Cowell). Particular features of the Essex landscape are identified by many contributors, including unique assets of European-wide importance such as the Forests of Hatfield and Writtle, the coastal wetlands, and ancient woods; and Hill Hall, Theydon Mount, is possibly one of the earliest and most remarkable Renaissance houses to survive in Britain.

The chronological coverage is not complete, the pre-Saxon landscape for example being discussed only in relation to the coast (by Murphy and Brown). A wide range of evidence exists throughout the county for these earlier periods, however (Bedwin 1996), and attempts have been made to describe the orientation of the landscape during the Neolithic (Brown 1997). It has not been possible unfortunately to include the conference paper given by Chris Going, 'From Iron Age Britain to Saxon England: perceptions of the Roman legacy', and a brief account is supplied here. In his paper Going emphasised the difficulty of confirming claims of a Roman, or earlier, origin for large expanses of field systems. At Little Waltham there is good evidence for pre-Roman organisation of the land (Drury 1978). Certain local studies appear to have produced positive results as at Rivenhall (Rodwell & Rodwell 1986), Grays (Wilkinson 1988), Rochford (Rippon 1991) and Stansted (Brooks & Bedwin 1989).

These do not, however, suggest a single origin for rectilinear field systems in Essex. The large area excavated at Mucking (Clarke, A 1993) provides a relatively complete and evocative picture of the local Roman and later landscape. This points to radical change, rather than overall decline, in the local economy towards the end of the Roman period, in the 4th century (when 'Britain became a land of sheep', as an anonymous contemporary Latin chronicler wrote, prefiguring England's medieval development). It seems that the wealth earned by the production for export of wool, beef and hides was not returned here. The eastern part of Britain may have suffered very greatly from taxation and other forced exactions for the supply of Gaul in the 3rd and 4th centuries.

The high point of Roman life in Essex was apparently in the 2nd century AD or a little later. This is substantiated by an excellent example of a Romano-British farmstead excavated recently over an area of nearly 9 hectares at Great Holts Farm, Boreham (information by courtesy of the excavator, Mark Germany). Excavation in advance of gravel extraction began in the expectation of uncovering a fairly humble farmstead. In the event the farm proved to have grown in affluence from its foundation in the 2nd century AD. In the 3rd century the farmstead was enlarged and equipped with a bath-house, a variety of evidence suggesting that the farm obtained its wealth from raising livestock. Pollen in waterlogged deposits indicates the presence of damp, weedy grassland and trees and shrubs, notably oak, pine, birch, hawthorn, beech and elder (Fig 1). By the mid 4th century, however, the farm was in rapid decline and the site was soon abandoned. Other recent investigations of the prehistoric, Roman and Saxon landscape in Essex are reported by Wallis and Waughman (1998), and in Bedwin (1996).

An understanding of the history and development of the Essex landscape is of crucial importance to the County Council's Planning Division, and awareness of the practical setting and consequences of historical knowledge was evident in several papers. It is clear, for example, that these days the overwhelming majority of archaeological work in the county is occasioned by commercial or public sector redevelopment and is therefore 'rescue' archaeology rather than true research. Funding follows suit, in accordance with national planning policy guidance 'PPG 16', *Archaeology and planning* (DoE 1990). The other planning guidance usually considered in this context, 'PPG 15', *Planning and the historic environment* (DoE 1994), although often perceived to be of relevance mainly for the built historic environment in fact specifically mentions the wider historic landscape, recommending in paragraph 2.26 that 'authorities should take account of the historical dimension of the landscape as a whole [and] should assess the wider historic landscape at an early stage in development' plans. In addition, paragraph 6.40 endorses systematic assessment of the historic landscape.

Maps, written records and other documentary sources contribute greatly to understanding the historic landscape, but purely documentary research cannot be funded in the same way as archaeology. Essex has excellent resources, notably the good cartographic and documentary collections in the County Record Office. The 1777 map by Chapman and André, for instance, is mentioned by nearly every contributor and, as will be seen from the bibliography in the present volume, reference is made continually to the many works on the history of the county and its landscape that have been sponsored by the County Council and County Record Office. The County Council also makes many technical and advisory documents available to those who live and work in the countryside, or whose work impinges on the historic landscape.

The subject of landscape history has been touched on by previous conferences, but nothing has been said before in this context about such matters as landscape character analysis and historic landscape conservation, which have immediate utility for planning purposes as well as intrinsic interest, and also relate to recent regional and national initiatives. The Countryside Commission's and English Nature's joint *Countryside Character Map* was launched in December 1996, forming a basis for a series of regional descriptions and countryside character maps. English Heritage has published a discussion paper, *Sustaining the historic environment* (1997) and is funding an Historic Landscape Character Project in East Anglia, currently underway in Suffolk and beginning in Essex at the end of 1999. Essex County Council has played a leading role in creating a Regional Research Framework for the Eastern Counties to support and guide the setting of archaeological priorities in the region (Glazebrook 1997; Brown & Glazebrook forthcoming).

Sarah Green
Essex County Council, Planning Division

1

Regions and subregions of Essex

by John Hunter

Essex is a woodland county–a long established term to describe those parts of the lowland zone of England with enclosed fields, as distinct from 'champion' landscapes where open field farming was the rule. William Harrison, the rector of Radwinter, writing in the reign of the first Elizabeth, put it thus:

> 'It is so that, our soil being divided into champaign ground and woodland, the houses of the first lie uniformly builded in every town, together with streets and lanes, whereas in the woodland countries (except here and there in great market towns) they stand scattered abroad, each one dwelling in the midst of his own occupying' (Edelen 1994, 217).

With the enclosure of the open fields across the country in the 18th and 19th centuries the difference became, superficially at least, less distinct; a better terminology would seem to be Oliver Rackham's 'ancient' and 'planned' countryside (Rackham 1976, 17). Of course, there is a wide range of variation–we will encounter ancient planned landscapes–but the terms are useful as they include the pattern and processes which underlie the landscapes we observe and seek to understand. If we except a few parishes in the extreme north-west of the county, Essex belongs firmly in the category of ancient countryside.

This conference is most welcome and reflects the progress made over the last 25 years. When I joined the County Council in 1971, shortly before the Archaeology Section came into being, Essex was a Cinderella in landscape terms–pretty but neglected. We had Ken Newton's fine studies of Writtle and Thaxted, but that was all. Essex was not included in the series of county books edited by Professor Hoskins, and I think that was just as well; although there were great resources waiting to be tapped –the Essex Record Office and the Victoria County History –there was not then the fieldwork or detailed survey that could support a worthwhile volume. But those years in the early 1970s were auspicious: archaeologists were looking at landscapes as a whole rather than at the sites within them, and interest was extending beyond the Midland open-field landscapes that had dominated studies for so long. Within the County Council, landscape planners worked in the same team as archaeologists and historic buildings specialists with obvious benefits in encouraging a holistic approach. Oliver Rackham's studies of woodlands were becoming available to us, and were a revelation. We were fortunate in the Nature Conservancy's Officer for Essex, the late Colin Ranson, who imparted his great knowledge of the historic dimension of the familiar countryside. Essex had begun late and there was much to discover.

This paper seeks to define the character of different areas within Essex; a difficult task as the variety, even between adjacent parishes, can be bewildering. Three broad regions are apparent (Fig 3), arising from geology and topography (Fig 4), and the influence these factors have had on settlement, communications and farming. Two other major factors are proximity to the North Sea and the Thames Estuary, and the growth of London. The three regions are:

1. Coastal or maritime Essex. This zone consists of the estuaries and their hinterlands, mostly on the heavy London Clays, and productive marshlands formed of marine and fluvial silts. Distinct subregions are the Thames Terraces, the South Essex Hills, and the Tendring Plain.
2. The mid-Essex zone. Mostly composed of acid soils deriving from the Bagshot and Claygate Beds, glacial outwash, fluvial deposits and some areas of London Clay. The area divides into two subregions I have termed the 'wooded hills' and the 'former heathlands'.
3. The Essex till. This region was directly affected by the Anglian cold phase, when an ice sheet covered most of the area leaving a thick deposit of boulder clays, made fertile by their chalk content. Two subregions are the 'chalk uplands' and what I have called the 'Copped Hall Hills'.

THE COASTAL ZONE

Coastal Essex relates to the North Sea and the Thames Estuary; until relatively recently its people and goods travelled mostly by water, and it is difficult now to imagine how active this maritime life still was in the first half of the 20th century. Since the later Middle Ages there was a symbiosis with London, which received the produce of farmland, marshland pastures, fisheries, decoy ponds and oyster beds, and exported its mountains of manure to fertilise the fields. Pleasure steamers bringing Londoners to Southend Pier for a day out and the diaspora of Londoners settling along the Fenchurch Street railway lines are only a recent phase in a long relationship.

While the seascape has been impoverished with the virtual disappearance of coastal craft, and the fleets of sailing barges are now only a memory for a few, the inland landscapes have been stricken by the loss of standing trees. Over the London Clays that cover much of the area elm was the dominant hedgerow tree, and the rapid spread of an imported strain of Dutch Elm disease in the early 1970s destroyed this tree cover. Areas such as the Dengie Peninsula, once regarded as beautiful with trees arching over the roads, now look dismal in landscape terms. The root systems of the elm hedgerows remain alive but subsequent growth becomes reinfected when the stems become woody, and for the time being, therefore, there is no prospect of promoting new trees from the root stocks, as was the former practice.

The coastal zone is diverse, and before describing the historic landscapes of the coastal marshes and London Clays we will consider the subregions of the Tendring Plain, Thames Terraces and the South Essex Hills.

The **Tendring Plain** consists mainly of fertile loams, the basis of productive farmland, but of a somewhat flat, bleak aspect. Early fluvial deposits are to be seen in the sandy cliffs of the Stour Estuary and in the bluffs above Brightlingsea, where the sites of a Bronze Age cemetery and a Neolithic ring monument overlook the Colne. The whole area contains much of archaeological interest; the extensive Palaeolithic deposits of struck flints at Clacton have given the name Clactonian to this type of artefact. Along the North Sea coast lie sandy beaches, a scarce asset in Essex, that have given rise to coastal resorts ranging in character from sedate Frinton to jolly Jaywick.

The **Thames Terraces** form the eastern end of a much larger area that was part of the county of Essex before the boundary changes of 1965. The fluvial deposits are free-draining and have always supported arable farming. Early settlement gave rise to the construction of a causewayed enclosure near Orsett, which lies on a broad eminence looking southwards to the Thames and the North Downs beyond. A long history of mineral extraction has left many scars, and an outcrop of chalk appears mainly in a series of former quarries. As on the London Clays elm dominance has led to the loss of tree cover, and with the effects of urbanisation the landscape is under stress. But it has its moments: the Mar Dyke Valley resembles a wooded combe with mixed woodland on the slopes and a grazed floor; its 'river' now flows in an artificial channel but careful analysis of samples taken during bridge construction have revealed the complex landscape history of this small stream over the last 7,000 years (Wilkinson 1988).

The **South Essex Hills** are composed mainly of Bagshot and Claygate Beds over London Clay, and comprise two groups of hills: the larger based in Rayleigh, Hockley and Hadleigh, and the smaller, some distance to the west, forming the Langdon Hills. With their extensive tree cover and wooded outlines both groups form an agreeable contrast to the surrounding plain. The Rayleigh group contains 47 woods. They have been studied by Oliver Rackham, who knows of no group of rural woods that has suffered as little deterioration in the last 40 years as these; 'in particular, they have entirely escaped the replanting that ruined a third of the ancient woodland of England in the 1950s and 1960s'

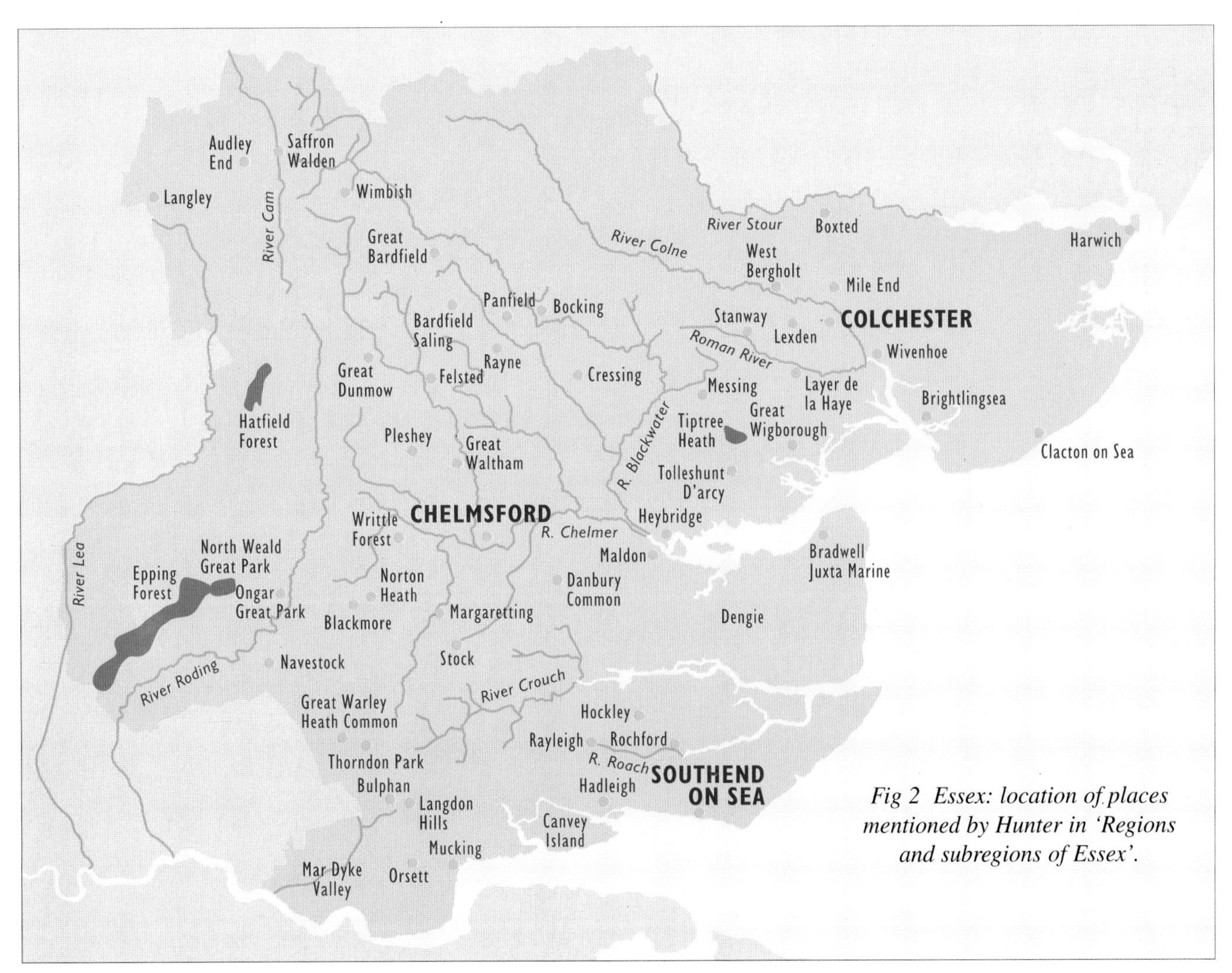

Fig 2 Essex: location of places mentioned by Hunter in 'Regions and subregions of Essex'.

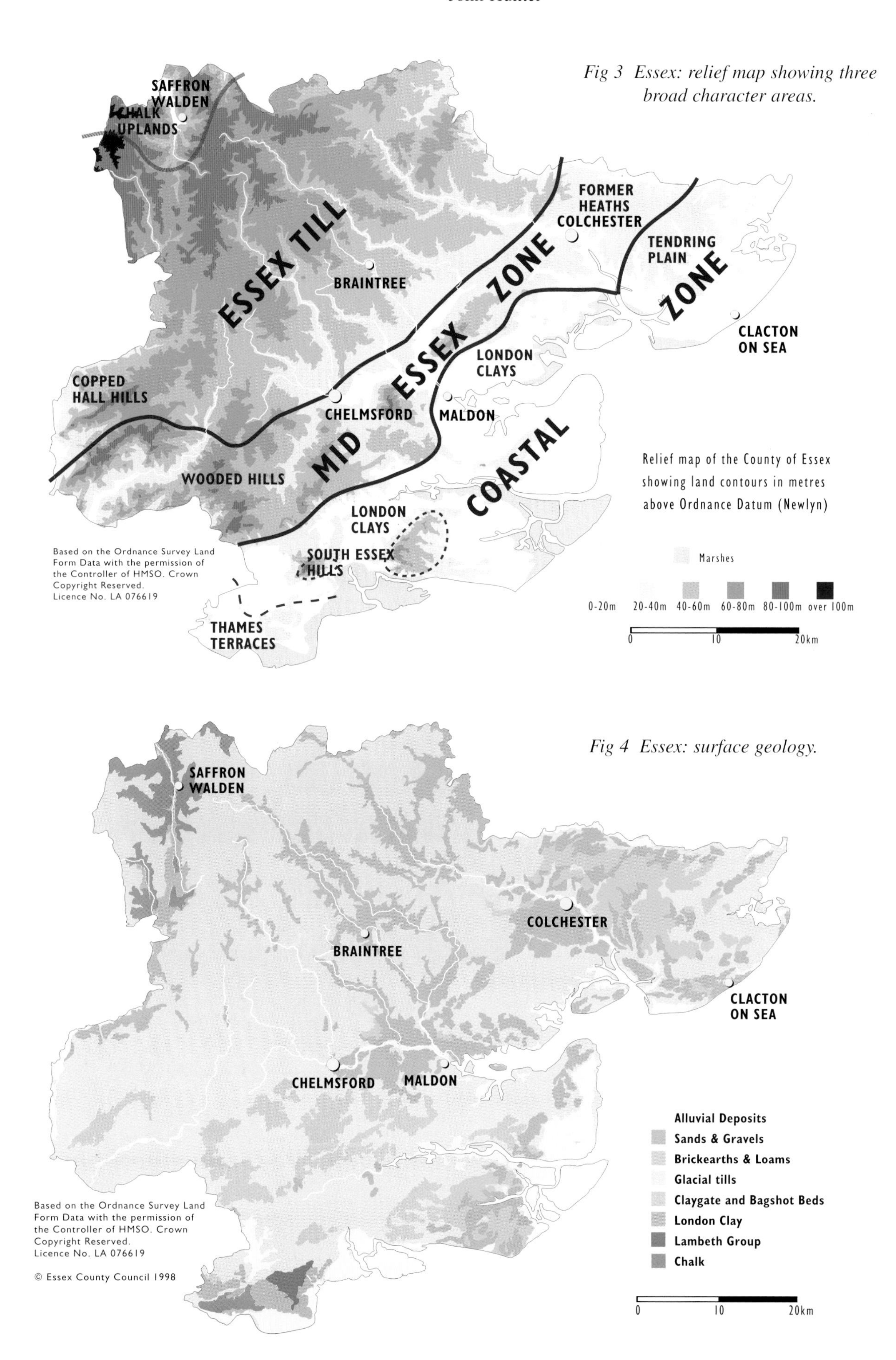

Fig 3 Essex: relief map showing three broad character areas.

Fig 4 Essex: surface geology.

(Rackham 1986, 1). Saxon clearings in the woods, evident in names ending *-leah*, gave rise to heaths and later, small fields. Rayleigh Park, created before 1086, lay in the upper Roach Valley between the two main areas of woodland. Many of the woods were enclaved and linked to manors in the area around, which otherwise lacked woodland resources.

The **Coastal Marshes** consist of the traditional grazing marshes, now mostly arable, with saltmarsh, mudflats and shingle banks beyond the seawalls. They have always been valued as a productive resource and more recently recognised as an internationally important area for overwintering birds. Despite the artificiality of the sea defences and arable crops, the marshes convey a sense of wildness and the power of natural forces. The walls have been raised since the disastrous floods of 1953, but new problems have arisen: the loss of saltmarsh that helped to protect the seawalls from the force of the waves, and the possibility of an accelerating increase in sea level. While the latter is a national problem it is particularly a problem for Essex, which has a coastline nearly 400 miles in length.

At the end of the last cold phase of the Ice Age the coastline was far out in the North Sea. By the Neolithic the high tide line was not far from that of the present low tide, and a land surface at The Stumble in the Blackwater Estuary, exposed for short periods at low tide, has preserved a record of early human activity. This has formed part of an extensive archaeological study of the intertidal zone of the whole Essex coastline, which has yielded most impressive results and has recently been published (Wilkinson & Murphy 1995). Aerial and cartographical study of the grazing marshes continues, revealing a far higher density of features such as 'red hills' and decoy ponds than previously known.

In the Iron Age and Roman periods there was an extensive salt-making industry, leaving its record in the 'red hills' that were formed by an accumulation of briquetage, the debris of pottery containers in which brine was evaporated. Most have been levelled and ploughed but can be detected by field walking, and a few survive. Later they were to become refuges for sheep at exceptionally high tides, and hillocks on which the sheep could be milked. Sheep pasturage was widespread on the marshes by Roman times, at least, and by 1086 was a source of wealth; Domesday Book assessed the marshlands in terms of sheep grazing, all owned by inland manors, most of them abutting the marshland edge or lying close to the coast. Sir Clifford Darby saw the characteristic enclaving of coastal pastures by inland manors as having originated in earlier systems of intercommoning, such as have been noted in the Fenlands and elsewhere (1971, 243). Besides wool, hides and meat, the value of sheep farming may already by this time have lain in the huge cheeses that were noted by later writers. By the 14th century a rise in sea level led to the construction of seawalls which defined the division between fresh and salt-water marsh. Dairying began to decline in the 16th century, and by the 18th had given way to beef-fattening and conversion to arable. In the 1930s the marshes were once again grazed by sheep, but in the post-war years most of the marshes were ploughed and now only a few precious areas remain of the original grazing marsh. It has now become clear that a serious problem exists in the rapid loss of the saltings and shingle banks that protected the seawalls from the force of the waves and tides, and the solution does not lie in further raising and fortifying the sea defences. One would like to envisage a future in which the marshes are once more grazed, for sheep and cattle will tolerate salt.

It is only along the Thames that development has taken place below the level of high tide. Despite the floods of 1953, Canvey Island has been built over and defended by massive seawalls. At Coryton and Shellhaven, oil refineries bring incident and interest within the broad scale of the estuary.

The **London Clays** are the hinterland of the marshes and divide into three main areas, which have in common the heavy and difficult nature of their soils, known traditionally as 'three-horse land'. No arable farmer, given a choice, would have chosen such land before the introduction of modern equipment, and historically these clay lands were pastured and sparsely populated. There is virtually no woodland, but the medieval manors had enclaves in adjoining wooded areas such as the South Essex Hills, as they did on the rich marshland pastures, and the economy should be seen as broadly based with a ready market in London.

The area of coastal clays which lies north-east of Maldon, between the Blackwater and Colne estuaries, differs from the others in showing no evidence of early planned landscapes, and the soils merge into the sands and gravels of the adjacent heathlands. Tiptree Heath extended onto the clays, even in its reduced state depicted on Chapman's and André's map of 1777.

The South Essex Plain lies to the south of the Thorndon -Billericay ridge and the Southend arterial road, extending eastwards below the Crouch to the Rochford and Shoebury area, where the clay soils give way to brickearths, and to fluvial deposits left by early courses of the Medway and Thames-Medway. Throughout the Plain field patterns are reticulated and governed by long parallel axes but, despite a superficial homogeneity, the axes have different foci and possibly different dates. Both a Roman and an Iron Age origin have been mooted, but Middle or Late Saxon now seems more likely in much of the area (Rippon 1991). The parallel parishes show the integration of the heavy claylands with adjacent areas. Running roughly north-south, these parishes include the former commons and heaths of the Thorndon ridge, with the manors and churches sited on the break of slope, then descending to the plain and extending to the fens of Bulphan and Orsett.

The Dengie Peninsula, lying between the Crouch and the Blackwater, is gently undulating with the clays merging into fluvial deposits around Southminster; the contours then descend onto the flat expanse of the Dengie marshes. The field pattern is markedly rectilinear, the area being sparsely populated and traditionally pasture. Although the field systems have been regarded as Roman there is no hard evidence that this is so and the matter of their date must remain open. At the eastern extremity, at Bradwell-juxta-Mare, stands the church built by St Cedd and the scant remains of a Roman fort of the Saxon Shore, mostly lost to the sea. Not far off, the simple geometry of Bradwell power station provides an imposing but not unattractive landmark.

Lacking cliffs, the Essex coastline is attractive to invaders and defensive measures have been taken at various periods beginning with the large ringwork at Mucking, below which lies Coalhouse Fort, a fortress of the Napoleonic Wars, later re-equipped by Gordon of Khartoum. Coalhouse superseded Tilbury Fort, built in the 17th century and adorned by a gateway designed in Wren's office, itself superseding a Tudor fort. On a spur above the marshes Hubert de Burgh built Hadleigh Castle, which William of Wykham later rebuilt, perhaps more as a stylish royal residence than a powerful defence. At Harwich, the Redoubt survives, restored with loving care by the Harwich Society.

THE MID-ESSEX ZONE

The area defined as the **wooded hills** contains some of the most attractive and historically interesting landscapes in Essex, while lying on soils least attractive to arable farming. A ridge of Bagshot and Claygate formations partially withstood the assault of the ice sheet, which thrust through in places depositing a stony outwash and turning the ridge into a series of hills. Erosion in river valleys has revealed the underlying heavy London Clays. It is a landscape conducive to woodland and to pasture farming, and accommodating to systems of commoning. A remarkable relic is the wood-pasture, pollard Forest of Epping, formerly a part of the larger Waltham Forest, which survived due to the tenacity of intercommoners in the face of enclosing landlords, leading to a celebrated legal battle towards the end of the 19th century which helped awake public opinion to the value of the remaining commons, then everywhere under threat. Commons survive at Danbury, Norton Heath, Great Warley and Childerditch–the latter incorporated into Thorndon Great Park, latterly Thorndon Country Park. Chapman's and André's map of 1777 shows many areas as heaths and commons, subsequently enclosed when these came to be seen by agricultural improvers as retrograde and unproductive. The parallel parishes of the Thorndon ridge have already been noted, reflecting an organisation of resources that had taken place before the fragmentation of ownership recorded in Domesday Book.

Another remarkable survival is Writtle Forest, far smaller than Epping and of a similar scale and type to Hatfield. Common rights continued, as at Hatfield, after the wood-pastures were embanked and converted to coppice woodlands. The boundaries to two deer parks remain, an assart, the site of a hermitage, a length of Roman road and relict greens; it has been described by Dr Rackham as 'a wild and lovely place. Nearly everything one sees there is of the 14th century or earlier' (Rackham 1976, 165).

To the east of North Weald lay Ongar Great Park, the earliest known deer park in England with a reference of 1045. Its enclosing bank can be seen in the remaining fragment of Ongar Park Wood, and elsewhere its boundary is preserved in hedgerows. Weald, imparked by the abbots of Waltham, is now a country park and a valued historic landscape. While later generations have made alterations, adding to its interest, a substantial area of medieval wood-pasture remains. Mention must be made of a unique, but local, architectural form–the 'pagoda' timber belfries to be seen at Stock, Navestock, Margaretting and Blackmore.

Northwards, the wooded hills merge into the area of light, often sandy, soils described as the **former heathlands,** which surround Colchester and extend to the parishes bounding the River Stour. Extensive heaths were mapped by Chapman and André at Boxted, Bergholt, Mile End, Lexden and Stanway; a necklace to the east of Colchester from Wivenhoe northwards to Dedham; and to the south, along the valley of the Roman River from Layer through the Donylands to the River Colne. A great ramified network, Tiptree Heath, stretched northwards from Heybridge to Messing and eastwards to the Tolleshunts and Wigborough. Tiptree was intercommoned by the inhabitants, whose rights extended to estovers of trees and underwood. An inquisition taken in 1401 defined the rights and noted that manors in adjoining parishes had 'grievously incroached upon a great part of the waste'. Common of Pasture was affirmed by an order of council in Henry VIII's reign, adding further parishes to make a total of 17. Estovers and grazing were again carefully defined; goats were banned and 'hog must be ringed'.

The map of 1777 shows farms and smallholdings abutting the heathland, much as they do elsewhere along the margins of greens and common land. This, I suggest, defines limits of cultivation reached on the eve of the Black Death, and it is probable that, allowing for some encroachments, Chapman and André depict the landscape of the early 14th century. It was not to last much longer. 'Agrimania' and record prices for corn in the closing years of the 18th century and during the French Wars swept the heaths away and now only a sad fragment, styled Tiptree Heath, lies to the south of the village, which itself did not exist in 1777.

While the boundary between the light heathlands and the heavy London Clays of the coastal zone is blurred, excavations at Slough House, Lofts and Chigborough farms, together with archaeological fieldwork in the Blackwater Estuary, are revealing landscapes of far greater antiquity than those discussed above. These link to the Chelmer Valley to the east of Chelmsford where a Neolithic causewayed enclosure, a cursus, and two Bronze Age ring monuments have been excavated. Long and patient work has paid remarkable dividends, and the enclosure at Springfield has given its name to this type of monument.

In many parts of Essex it is not difficult to envisage the landscape of 1600, and many features would be familiar to someone transported from the 16th century and even earlier.

This is not the case with the former heathlands, which appear not to be have been recorded pictorially. John Constable, influenced by Dutch painters in his youth, would have liked them, but he had to go to Hampstead to depict an existing working heath. The great Dutch painters of the 17th century, Jacob van Ruisdael and Meindert Hobbema, favoured areas of infertile sandy soils in the Netherlands, which supported rough pasture, occasional crops, scrub and windblown trees; parts of the Essex heaths may have been much like this.

THE ESSEX TILL

This region comprises at least one third of Essex and consists of a thick till of chalky boulder clays deposited by the Anglian ice sheet over a series of terraces (Kesgrave Sands and Gravels) left by earlier courses of the River Thames. The melting occurred around 430,000 BP and gave rise to a new drainage system; this was governed by a slight south-east downward tilt and formed a network of rills and water-courses flowing into the Rivers Stour, Colne and Blackwater, and Chelmer, which debouch into the North Sea, and the River Roding which joins the Thames. The Cam is an exception, flowing northwards to join the Great Ouse. Initially the rivers flowed 20-30m above their present heights, gradually cutting through the underlying Kesgraves, sometimes down to the London Clay, and forming the familiar river valleys and floodplains. The resulting topography is one of dissected plateaux, with occasional deposits of glacial gravel and loess to be found on watersheds, clothed by ancient woodland. Although the soils vary they are highly fertile, their fertility being reflected in an ear of bearded wheat depicted on Late Iron Age coins, and the large number of villa sites scattered over the region attest to its prosperity in Roman times.

The settlement pattern is scattered and diverse although not sparse. It consists of farmsteads, small villages and hamlets usually in the form of ends, greens and tyes. Charters for markets in the early Middle Ages led to some successful towns, as noted by Harrison, and others that eventually failed and are now perceived as villages, such as Pleshey and Great Bardfield.

Landscape features relate to topography and soil type, and suggest evolution and change over a very long period of time. Roads and lanes, where unimproved, are rarely straight; they have variable verges, wide on flat land and becoming banked on the slope. Sunken lanes are to be found on valley sides, sometimes enhanced by lynchets, and former roads often survive as 'green lanes'. Hedges tend to be sinuous and species-rich; pollards occur in areas where they formed a part of local custom. The older hedges tend to follow changes in soil type as well as highways and property boundaries. Unfortunately factors other than productivity were not considered in the rush to improve following the post-war Agriculture Acts, and much unnecessary damage was caused. A correlation was evident between field sports and conservation of the landscape, for farmers who valued their game birds were far less likely to sacrifice all natural cover for the alternative inducements on offer.

An attractive feature of the area are the long views across the plateau, in which individual trees and spinneys may merge with woodlands in the distance to give the impression of a wooded horizon. Another feature is that churches lie below the plateau, almost always beside a late Saxon manor, above a river crossing or on a spring line. South of the A12, churches are frequently sited on hill tops.

Land use patterns reflected in farm and field boundaries are as diverse as the settlement patterns, and where lost to modern depredations can still be studied from that epitome of cartographical achievement (for the landscape student), the first edition of the Ordnance Survey map at a scale of six inches to the mile. Leaving aside a few, relatively small-scale reorganisations of the 18th and 19th centuries, the landscape depicted on these maps is generally that of the Essex till in 1600. Many of the boundaries in that landscape go back much further and it is sometimes possible to detect the landscape of the early 14th century, before the Black Death removed the pressures of population for several centuries to come. At Cressing, Felsted, Great Waltham and Writtle there is evidence for a dispersed pattern of small-scale peasant farming related to hamlets, often beside a green (Hunter 1995, 138-44). There appear to have been individual crofts and tofts, and small–sometimes very small –common fields beside the hamlet, rather than parish or manor. In contrast to the peasant pattern the fields of a compact demesne, around or beside the capital manor, could be huge, sometimes well over 100 acres in size (Hunter 1993b, 34). As far as this can be called a system, it is clearly wholly different from that of most Midland parishes with a nucleated village containing church, manor and farms, surrounded by common fields extending to the parish boundary and governed by a manorial court or parish assembly. It would seem likely that these Essex examples reflect a system predating the development of the Midland system, and parallels may be sought further afield, perhaps in the Irish townland and *clachan.*

There are elements in common between the parishes described above and those with extensive networks of both linear and focal greens. Examples are Felsted, Wimbish and parts of Great Dunmow, Rayne, Panfield and Bardfield Saling, where farms and smallholdings are sited characteristically on the edges of the greens. It seems likely, as with the heathlands, that these are instances where the community succeeded in securing and protecting the last areas of common grazing before population pressure was eased by the plague.

In marked contrast is the Tabor Estate, located largely in the parish of Bocking, where the hedgerows–of which a large number survive–date mostly from 1350 to 1600, many being even older (Hunter 1993a). Across its 2,000 acres there are no hamlets or greens, and holdings comprise home farms around the manors and tenant farms of reasonable size. This is clearly a different system from the ones already described and it is not untypical. It would seem, then, that we have two broad models that have evolved differently, although there is no apparent logic for this difference in situation, topography or soil type.

Two subregions occur within the area defined here as the Essex till. The first I have termed the **Copped Hall Hills,** after the noble shell that dominates the landscape seen from the M25. It is of relatively small extent, consisting of dissected London Clays between the Epping Forest Ridge and the River Lee–attractive rolling country with planted spinneys and a late estate character, rather more Middlesex than Essex. Yet in Upshire an area survives of small farms and irregular hedges, indicative of an earlier landscape, with the character of Boulder Clay landscape.

The chalk uplands, around and to the north of Saffron Walden, have a distinct character more akin to the late-enclosure, former open-field landscapes of adjacent Cambridgeshire, and it is here that one finds enclosure awards of arable land by act of parliament. The chalk emerges in the Cam Valley and in the escarpment close to the county boundary, but elsewhere a skim of clays maintains similarities to the till. Dispersed greens and hamlets occur, many ancient woods survive, lanes were not straightened, and at Langley, where a pre-enclosure map survives to be compared with the award, the extent of early enclosure by agreement is apparent. It should be noted that the great park at Audley End is a post-Dissolution creation, mainly of the 18th century; in the Middle Ages all land above the floodplain in the Cam valley was strip-farmed. The medieval park lay on the Boulder Clay plateau in the north of the parish.

Of all landscapes in Essex Hatfield Forest must take pride of place, a living and functioning medieval landscape which any serious student of the subject should visit. Oliver Rackham describes the Forest in his paper in this volume, and I can only add that, while we may not have a Durham Cathedral or York Minster in Essex, in Hatfield Forest we have a monument of equivalent importance (Fig 5).

Fig 5 Hatfield Forest: pollarded hornbeams.

2

Archaeology of the coastal landscape

by Peter Murphy and Nigel Brown

'...Eastward and landward it is all flat pasture, once marsh, except for a few gardens, and there are very few permanent dwellings there: scarcely anything but a few sheds, and cots for the men who come to look after the great herds of cattle pasturing there. But however, what with the beasts and the men and the scattered red-tiled roofs and the big hayricks, it does not make a bad holiday to get a quiet pony and ride about there on a sunny afternoon of autumn, and look over the river and the craft passing up and down, and on to Shooters Hill and the Kentish uplands, and then turn round to the wide green sea of the Essex marshland, with the great domed line of the sky, and the sun shining down in one flood of peaceful light over the long distance.' (William Morris *News from Nowhere*)

INTRODUCTION

Writing an account of the archaeology of the Essex coast in 1996, the centenary of the death of that great Essex man, William Morris, it is appropriate to begin with what is arguably the best known literary description of the Essex marshes: particularly so given the profound importance of landscape and sense of place on his life and work (MacCarthy 1994, 13-14). However much Morris' description may seem an accurate account of the appearance of the coastal zone as, in some part, it still is and as much of it was in the not too distant past, it is actually taken from a fantasy of the future. This paradox is entirely appropriate. There is an equivocation about the Essex coast, a curious amalgam of land, sea and sky with a numinous quality difficult to escape (Fig 6); the past seems very close (Schama 1995, 3-5). In common with many apparently wild and largely unoccupied landscapes, the remoter parts of the Essex coast evoke a sense of timelessness, which belies the profound changes that have formed and transformed the landscape. Despite these changes, the human activities which have taken place in, and shaped the landscape of, the coastal zone, have often been if not actually continuous then at least recurrent over millennia. The present paper attempts a brief account of the development of the Essex coast over the past 10,000 years. It concentrates on the intertidal zone but occasionally strays inland and offers some reflections on the way in which the coastal landscape and its human uses related to the wider world.

Fig 6 Early morning at the Neolithic site at The Stumble in the Blackwater Estuary.

ARCHAEOLOGICAL INVESTIGATIONS IN THE COASTAL ZONE

The recent publication of *England's coastal heritage: a statement on the management of coastal archaeology* by English Heritage and the Royal Commission on the Historical Monuments of England (1996) is a clear indication that coastal and intertidal archaeology has at last been fully integrated into the mainstream of archaeological study. For too long intertidal archaeology was seen by many as the marginal preserve of a few eccentric enthusiasts. The publication of this document marks the recognition, now widespread, that coastal sites are exceptionally informative but also exceptionally vulnerable. There is a chronic resource loss due to erosion and human activities.

Essex has always been in the forefront of coastal studies in archaeology. In the late 19th century Spurrell (1889), working on the Thames Estuary, recorded prehistoric peat beds and Roman occupation surfaces. His work was followed by that of Reader (1911) and Warren (1911) at the intertidal Mesolithic site at Hullbridge on the Crouch. Warren's later extensive studies of the pre-transgression land surface and the associated Mesolithic to Beaker sites at Dovercourt, Clacton, Walton and Jaywick were summarised in a collaborative paper in the *Proceedings of the Prehistoric Society* (Warren *et al* 1936). This was one of the earliest papers in the archaeological literature in which integration of archaeology and palaeoecology was attempted.

Thereafter, until the 1980s, most archaeological fieldwork (as opposed to study of artefact collections) on the Essex coast was undertaken by skilled amateurs, particularly Vincent and George (1980), who recorded numerous prehistoric sites, and De Brisay and the Colchester Archaeological Group (1978; Fawn *et al* 1990), who provided a number of useful studies on 'red hills'.

Systematic survey of the intertidal archaeology of the Essex coast, the Hullbridge Survey, began in 1982 (Wilkinson & Murphy 1995, and forthcoming), culminating in sample excavation of a Neolithic settlement and later prehistoric to early modern wooden structures on a mudflat known as The Stumble (Fig 6), to the north of Osea Island, in 1986-8. During the later 1980s and 1990s further discoveries and recording continued apace. Perhaps the most impressive recent achievement has been the recognition of very extensive complexes of fish-traps, some of Anglo-Saxon date, in the Blackwater Estuary. The amateur archaeologists, Kevin Bruce, Ron Hall and Barry Pierce, first drew attention to these, and they have subsequently been recorded and sampled by Essex County Council staff, particularly

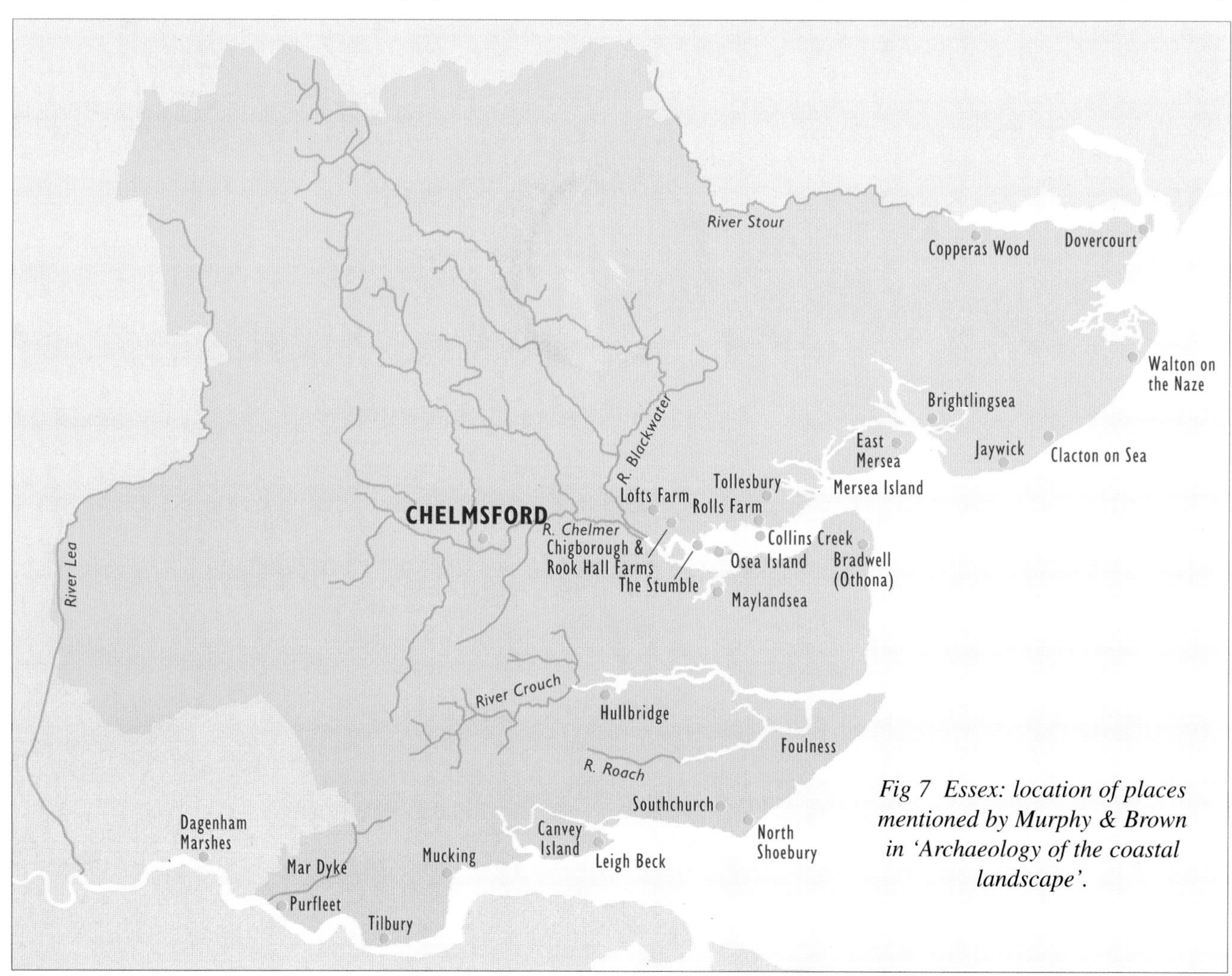

Fig 7 Essex: location of places mentioned by Murphy & Brown in 'Archaeology of the coastal landscape'.

the examples at Collins Creek, Sales Point and The Naze (Clarke, C P 1993; Strachan 1998). More recently aerial photography by Strachan (1996) has drawn attention to relict early modern to 19th-century features on the saltmarshes, including decoy ponds and various features, structures and vessels associated with the oyster industry.

New sites certainly remain to be discovered, both by ground-based and by aerial survey, but the pioneering phase of site detection is nearing its close. Some suggestions on potentially profitable areas of further search are made below. However, the main categories of site comprising the archaeological resource have probably now been defined. In the climate of the 1990s this naturally leads to consideration of site management, explanation and synthesis. In the Blackwater Estuary, a programme of site monitoring and evaluation is already underway (Strachan 1996) and a coherent approach to understanding the archaeology of the intertidal zone is now being developed (Essex County Council, Kent County Council, English Heritage and RCHME forthcoming).

THE PRE-TRANSGRESSION LANDSCAPE: EARLIER PREHISTORIC DRYLAND SITES

From the end of the last glacial stage (Devensian) around 10,000 years ago, rising global sea levels and subsidence of the southern North Sea basin led to progressive submergence of former lowlands now lying off the Essex coast. Sites submerged in the final stages of this process are still visible between tides, though the Mesolithic coastal sites which must lie offshore are now inaccessible. A sequence of transgressive overlaps (when the sea advanced inland) and regressive overlaps (when there was a retreat of marine conditions, permitting development of freshwater peat or even terrestrial surfaces on estuarine sediments) was first defined by Devoy (1979) in the Thames Estuary. Of particular archaeological significance is the Thames III transgression, which resulted in submergence of a fringe of land all round the coast, now lying in the intertidal zone, from around 4,000 BP (uncalibrated). A series of dates from archaeological deposits and peats provides a *terminus post quem* for this event (Wilkinson & Murphy 1995, table 18). The latest dates from archaeological sites on the land surface exposed in the modern intertidal zone are from a 'burnt flint mound' at The Stumble (3885 ±70 BP: Cal., one sigma 2490-2285 BC (OxA-2297) and from a Beaker pit at Jaywick (3830 ±80 BP: Cal., one sigma 2460-2144 BC (HAR-8154)).

The effect of this transgressive overlap was to seal the land surface, and sites on it, under sediments: peats, estuarine detritus muds and estuarine clay. These sites had been on dry land when occupied, so there is no preservation of organic materials there by waterlogging (apart from recalcitrant organic materials, such as oak tree stumps). However, the sedimentary cover sealed and protected the sites from processes of weathering, disturbance and truncation, which have obliterated many similar sites still in terrestrial locations, leaving only unstratified lithic scatters.

MESOLITHIC

Lithic scatters of this period were noted at a number of locations, but major sites are known at Hullbridge and Maylandsea. Both are in modern estuaries, but when occupied would have been inland, well above their contemporary sea level, located on the banks of freshwater rivers. The very large lithic assemblages from these sites imply repeated occupation over a long period. They may represent inland bases from which the coastal lowlands were exploited (Fig 8). By the Late Mesolithic pollen data from boreholes at Bradwell and the Mar Dyke (Wilkinson & Murphy 1995, 212) indicate that the dryland slopes bordering the coastal zone were well wooded with oak and lime the dominant trees.

EARLIER NEOLITHIC

Artefact scatters indicate the presence of settlements notably within the Blackwater Estuary and the Jaywick/Walton area. By this time high water mark would have been around -3 to -4m OD: the intertidal sites located would have had large areas of their resource catchments on dry land though the coast would have been readily accessible (Fig 9). One site, The Stumble, in the Blackwater Estuary has been sampled in detail. Structural features, pits and large quantities of lithics and pottery were recorded, on an extensive area of old land surface developed on silt or sandy clay head. Pollen analysis of these soils pointed to a predominantly wooded landscape of lime, oak and hazel, with similar results from soils at the contemporary site of Rolls Farm further east in the Blackwater Estuary (Scaife 1995, 47-51). The Stumble site would have lain on the low-lying neck of a small promontory, between areas of higher ground represented by the present shore and Osea Island, with small watercourses to east and west flowing into the main estuary to the south. Until recently, the presence of extensive Neolithic occupation in well-wooded, low-lying locations with clayey soil, such as The Stumble, would have been unthinkable.

Although Neolithic charred plant remains from the gravels adjacent to the Blackwater Estuary are very poorly preserved, by contrast such remains from the protected conditions of submerged sites within the estuary are plentiful. Charred remains of crops from The Stumble were abundant (mainly emmer wheat, with einkorn, bread wheat, naked barley and flax) but charred fruit stones, nuts and tubers of wild species were just as common (Wilkinson & Murphy 1995, and forthcoming). This is thought to indicate substantial reliance on plant food foraging in woodland, and that there was no sudden switch from a Mesolithic foraging economy to a Neolithic agricultural economy.

Further south in what is now the Bradwell, Burnham, Wallasea and Foulness area, the coastline was radically different from that of today. The tidal limit appears to have been inland of the present range, and the whole area must have formed a complex environment of tidal sand flats, upper tidal silt flats, and occasional beach ridges of sand, gravel and shell with intervening estuaries (Wilkinson & Murphy 1995, 215). Shell ridges at depths of -5.5m to -8.3m OD and dated

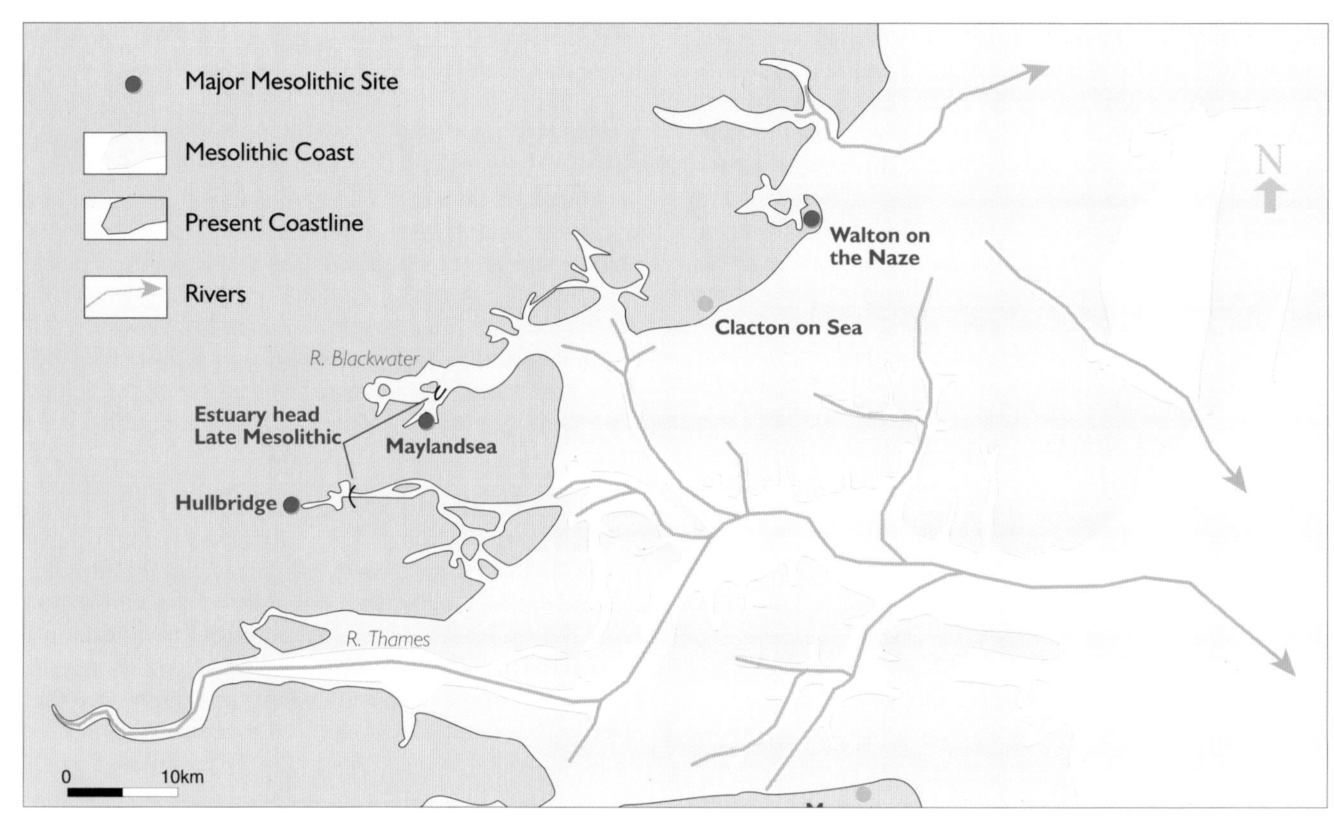

Fig 8 The coastline of Essex during the Mesolithic (after Wilkinson & Murphy 1995). This map gives only an approximate indication of the high-water mark of 9,000-8,500 BP. Nevertheless it is evident that the proto-Thames swung north to join the proto-Crouch and Blackwater and form a broad estuarine area. Extensive lowlands north of this estuary would have been available for human occupation during the Mesolithic, but would have been inundated as the Mesolithic progressed. The approximate locations of the heads of the Crouch and Blackwater estuaries during the Late Mesolithic are indicated.

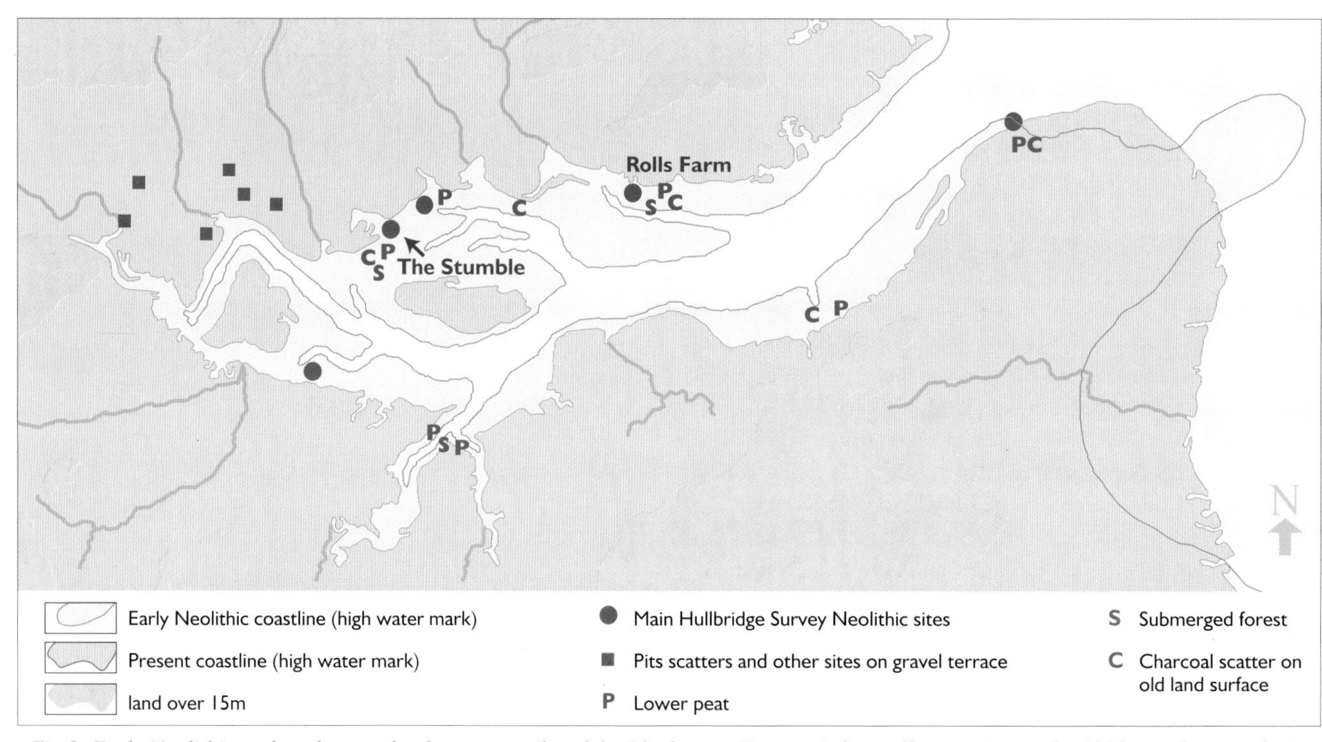

Fig 9 Early Neolithic archaeology and palaeogeography of the Blackwater Estuary (after Wilkinson & Murphy 1995). At this time high-water mark appears to have been roughly equivalent to the modern low-water mark. The location of major sites and deposits in the inter-tidal zone are shown, together with pit scatters and other sites revealed during excavation on the gravels to the north.

between 4265 and 3580 BP (Lake *et al* 1986, table 6), show that by the Late Neolithic/Early Bronze Age these features were established at the mouth of the Roach/Crouch estuary. These ridges are clearly a recurrent feature of the Essex coast. Today small examples occur at various points around Tollesbury Wick, at Bradwell and, most importantly, off Foulness, where the largest examples of such ridges in Britain extend for c. 20 hectares (Corke 1986).

LATE NEOLITHIC/EARLY BRONZE AGE

An extensive settlement complex once existed in the intertidal zone of the Jaywick/Walton area (Warren *et al* 1936). However, little of this remained when the area was resurveyed in the 1980s. Settlement here apparently took place in an area protected by an offshore barrier or spit (Wilkinson & Murphy 1995, 217). Late Neolithic occupation at The Stumble was represented by a low burnt flint mound, which by then would have been quite close to the edge of the tidal estuary. Also present were pits, with charcoal, burnt flint, Grooved Ware and Beaker pottery. These features were essentially similar to the 'cooking holes' recorded on the coast of north-east Essex (Warren *et al* 1936). No cereal remains were recovered from these features although hazelnut and apple fragments were frequent, possibly indicating a specialised site, processing woodland products. Several types of later Neolithic submerged woodland were recorded, including the stumps of oak trees growing on the pre-transgression land surface and wet valley woods of alder, oak and sometimes yew and ash, associated with peat development. At Purfleet a buried soil, formed on former mud-flats and later sealed by peat, produced a woodland mollusc fauna, polished axes and other lithics. A butchered femur of aurochs came from the site. Again, some form of activity in woodland, but not involving wholesale clearance or settlement, is indicated. Widespread and sometimes dense spreads of charcoal recorded at many locations in the intertidal zone may relate to woodland activity, possibly a late stage of clearance (Wilkinson & Murphy 1995, 87-90). It thus appears that many areas of the Essex coast were wooded, with trees running down close to the water's edge, something which, with the possible exception of Copperas Wood on the Stour Estuary, is alien to the present landscape of the Essex coast.

THE POST-TRANSGRESSION LANDSCAPE

Following the Thames III transgression the Essex coast took on something approaching its present form. Archaeological evidence relates to a range of human activities mostly familiar from the relatively recent past, including transport, fisheries, shell-fisheries, grazing, salt production, ritual and religion. The first period for which this is clearly apparent is the Middle and Late Bronze Age (c. 1500-800 BC).

LATER BRONZE AGE

Shellfish were no doubt exploited by the inhabitants of the Essex coast during the Mesolithic and Neolithic. However, the earliest archaeological evidence for their use comes from the Bronze Age. A Beaker burial from Thorpe Hall, Southchurch, was apparently accompanied by a heap of cockle shells (Clark 1970, 414), while domestic refuse in the Middle Bronze Age settlement at North Shoebury included dumps of mussel shell (Wymer & Brown 1995). Similarly the earliest salt production site from the Essex coast, at Fenn Creek near Woodham Ferrers, is of Middle Bronze Age date (Wilkinson & Murphy 1995, 157-65). Salt production equipment is known from a number of Late Bronze Age sites, particularly Mucking (Barford 1988b). Numerous later Bronze Age settlements of various kinds are known throughout Essex, particularly along the Thames and Blackwater estuaries (Brown 1996). In the latter area wells are a particular feature of the settlements, and may reflect a pastoral economy, ensuring adequate supplies of water for livestock. Most notable of the Blackwater settlements is an enclosed site at Lofts Farm (Brown 1988) situated about 1.5km north of the present shore of the Blackwater Estuary. Charred plant remains indicate that processed crops were brought to the site and it appears to have had a primarily pastoral economy (Fig 10). Plant macrofossils from a well at this site and pollen from other wells at Chigborough and Slough House Farms nearby indicate a locally open landscape of damp grassland with some evidence for nutrient enrichment by dung from grazing animals (Murphy 1988; Wiltshire & Murphy 1998). However, compared to later periods, the pollen data indicates relatively high percentages of tree pollen (almost 30% in some deposits). Therefore, the Blackwater terraces still supported areas of woodland dominated by oak. The Lofts Farm site was well placed to exploit the grassland not only of the surrounding low-lying gravel terrace but also of the marsh pasture provided by the

Fig 10 Lofts Farm: reconstruction of a Late Bronze Age enclosure looking north, as it may have appeared c. 800 BC. The site was located just south of the 10m contour, on the gravels about 1.5 km north of the modern shore of the Blackwater Estuary. Data from this site and others nearby indicate a landscape of open, damp grassland, with some indication of woodland and of scrub growth, possibly hedges.

saltmarshes fringing the Estuary. This was a particularly valuable resource during periods of summer drought, which would have reduced productivity of the grasslands on the gravels. The importance of wetland pasture during the Bronze Age elsewhere in eastern England has recently been emphasised by Pryor (1996). The generally open pastoral landscape of the Essex coastal zone during the Bronze Age thus presented a marked contrast with the densely wooded Neolithic landscape. Certain of the Bronze Age wooden structures recorded in the Essex estuaries (Wilkinson & Murphy 1995) have been interpreted by analogy with medieval and later periods as sheep bridges placed to provide safe access for livestock. More extensive trackways preserved within deeply buried peat deposits in north-east London/south-west Essex have similarly been interpreted as allowing access to marshland for grazing (Meddens 1996).

Other later Bronze Age wooden structures from around the Essex coast include a variety of platforms and possible landing stages. The latter reflect the great importance of the estuaries for transport. During drainage works in the later 19th and early 20th centuries on the marshes fringing the Thames and the Lea, a number of supposed boats and canoes were recorded which may have been prehistoric (part of one is preserved in Chelmsford Museum). Similar finds have been reported from the Clacton/Walton coast (Warren *et al* 1936, 184). More recently a Bronze Age wooden paddle 2m long has been recovered from Canewdon, radiocarbon dated to 2900 ± 70 BP (BM-2339) (Fig 11). The paddle lay in estuarine muds, associated with a mass of plant debris from saltmarsh; the whole appears to represent a strand-line, where the lost paddle came to rest. Boat finds from the Humber Estuary and the recent discovery of the Dover boat emphasise the potential of areas like the Essex coast. Persistent inspection of eroding sections is likely to be rewarding.

Fig 11 A Bronze Age paddle from Canewdon. This remarkable object was recovered during survey work in the intertidal zone of the Essex coast (Wilkinson & Murphy 1995). It was identified eroding out of the base of the saltmarsh, where it lay on a Bronze Age strand line, deeply buried by later alluvium.

Such boats plying the numerous creeks and estuaries of the Essex coast would not only have linked local communities but also have enabled contact across the southern North Sea and the Dover Straits. Imported items of continental metalwork and occasional ceramics testify to these contacts (Brown 1996).

The numinous qualities of the Essex coast were no doubt apparent in earlier periods. The earliest and most famous evidence for ritual or religious activity in the coastal zone is the wooden idol from the Dagenham marshes, now shown to be of Late Neolithic date (Coles 1990). Ritual deposition in wet locations is a well-attested phenomenon in the Bronze Age (e.g. Pryor 1992; Bradley & Gordon 1988). The Thames in particular was a focus of deposition and there is some evidence to suggest that the Blackwater may have received similar offerings (Wilkinson & Murphy 1995, 190; Brown 1996). At Fenn Creek two human skulls were apparently deliberately placed on a wooden platform, which yielded a radiocarbon date of 2730 ± 60BP (HAR-5222) 927-823 Cal BC (one sigma) (Wilkinson & Murphy 1995). Similar practices clearly took place on dryland sites (e.g. Needham 1993) but it is the particular, often waterlogged, conditions of areas like the Essex coastal zone that have led to superior preservation of fragile remains. This is clearly demonstrated by comparing possible shrine structures from inland sites in Essex (Brown 1996) with, perhaps similar, remains in wetland contexts (Waterbolk & Van Zeist 1961).

IRON AGE AND ROMAN

Wooden structures of Iron Age and Roman date are less frequent than those of the Bronze Age. This may reflect an episode of marine regression. Extensive areas of Roman activity on now submerged land surfaces have been recorded in the Thames Estuary (Wilkinson & Murphy 1995, 219-20). 'Red hills' are the most distinctive sites of this period in the Essex coastal zone. These are the remains of extensive salt-working, and fringe the Essex coast and estuaries particularly in the north-east of the county. Considerable numbers are known and are listed in a recently published gazetteer (Fawn *et al* 1990). Significant numbers of new sites (Fig 12) are still being reported (Strachan 1996). When in operation, perhaps seasonally in late summer and early autumn, numerous fires must have produced an effect in the coastal zone (Rodwell 1979) not unlike that of the seasonal stubble burning commonplace in recent decades.

At The Stumble a line of posts across a palaeochannel, radiocarbon dated to 2380 ± 70BP (HAR-8458), may be a simple Iron Age fish-trap, and represents the earliest known example from the county of a method of fishing which continued in Essex until about twenty years ago (Crump & Wallis 1992). At North Shoebury there is possible evidence for management of oyster beds (Murphy 1995), and whelks appear in the archaeological record; this may reflect intensification and diversification of fishing. Whelks cannot be gathered from the foreshore; traditionally they have been caught in baited pots rather like lobster (Murphy 1995, 145). At Leigh Beck, Canvey Island, a possible fish-processing site has been recorded (Wilkinson & Murphy 1995). Animal bone from this site was dominated by sheep/goat, perhaps indicating that the marshland was important for pasture during the Roman period (Wymer & Brown 1995, 160). The coast and estuaries of Essex are particularly exposed to attack from across the North Sea, as the establishment of a Saxon Shore fort at Bradwell indicates. The palaeogeography of this site has recently been investigated (Wilkinson & Murphy 1995); it appears to have occupied a promontory between two creeks, the southern creek coming almost to the walls of the fort. Defensive installations of various kinds have been a prominent part of the Essex coastal landscape well into the 20th century.

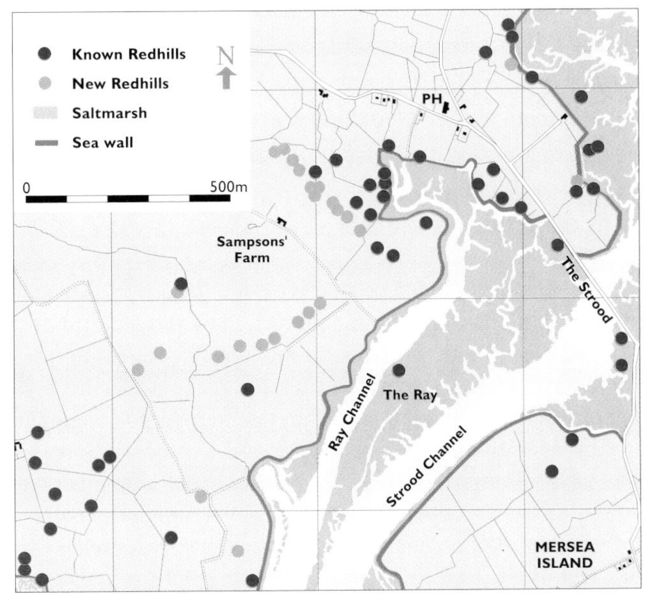

Fig 12 'Red hills' around the Ray and Strood channels, Mersea Island, showing previously recorded sites and those revealed by aerial photography in 1995.

SAXON

Most striking of the sites of this period on the Essex coast is St Peter's Church at Bradwell. Now starkly isolated on the edge of the marshes (Fig 13), its dramatic location is peculiarly affecting and has no doubt helped to establish it in its present role as a place of pilgrimage. However, its original position was far from isolated. It was built within the remains of the Roman shore fort; such a location was frequently chosen for the establishment of religious institutions (as at Reculver, Kent, and possibly Burgh Castle, Norfolk), providing a link with royal authority (Hinton 1991). A shell ridge ran across the mouth of the creek south of the Bradwell fort. A southern extension of this ridge has been dated to the 6th or 7th centuries AD, and its existence may have either blocked access to the creek or helped to provide sheltered anchorage (Wilkinson & Murphy 1995). The church lay across the Blackwater from the important estates on Mersea (Crummy 1982) and the royal vill at Brightlingsea (Rippon 1996a). In the estuary itself massive amounts of timber were apparently used to build large fish-

Fig 13 The Saxon church of St Peter's, Bradwell, from the air, looking out to sea: the church is visible in the centre of the photograph, isolated at the edge of the marshes, and a shell ridge separating the salt marsh from the open sea shows as a white line in the middle distance.

traps, notably around Collins Creek, Sales Point and The Naze, where radiocarbon dating has established a Middle Saxon date (Strachan 1998). Similarly large quantities of wood went into constructing the causeway linking Mersea to the mainland, which is also of Middle Saxon date (Crummy *et al* 1982). Evidence for relatively extensive ironworking has been recovered from the gravels north of the Blackwater

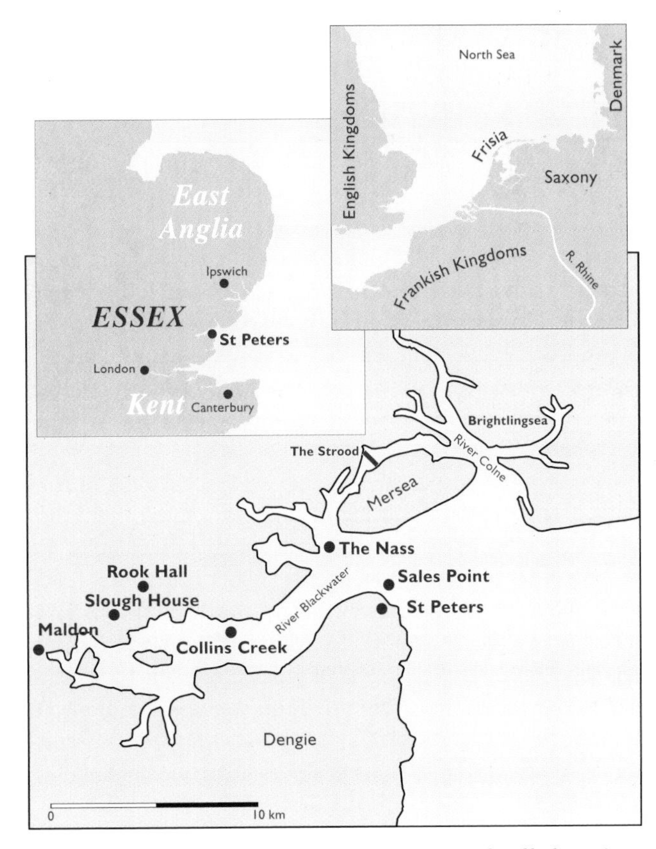

Fig 14 The Saxon church of St Peter's, Bradwell: location in a pivotal position on the North Sea coast.

at Rook Hall and Slough House Farms (Wallis & Waughman 1998). Pollen and plant macrofossils indicate either intensification or better management of pasture, or both, and increased crop production during the Early/Middle Saxon period: pollen from a 7th-century well at Slough House Farm included up to 14% cereal pollen (Wiltshire & Murphy 1998). St Peter's was thus an integral part of a thriving landscape centred on the Blackwater Estuary. Moreover, its coastal location would have facilitated contacts with the kingdoms of East Anglia to the north and Kent to the south, the important trading centres of Ipswich and London, and the coastal areas of Europe around the North Sea basin (Fig 14). The Blackwater area is indicative of the importance of the coastal zone of Essex in general. In particular the importance of the creeks and estuaries in facilitating trade may be reflected in the remarkable range of coins and other objects now known from Canvey (Crowe 1996).

Fig 15 Cropmark of a backfilled and ploughed decoy pond, with a highly distinctive starfish shape.

MEDIEVAL AND POST-MEDIEVAL

The importance of coastal trading, fish, shellfish and marsh pasture in the medieval and post-medieval periods is well known (e.g. Emmison 1976; Ward 1987). Seawalls which protected large areas of grazing marsh, much of it now ploughed, around the Essex coast appear to be largely of medieval or post-medieval origin. Taken together the seawalls represent the most substantial timber and earthwork structure in the county, and are one of the most striking and characteristic features of the coastal landscape. Despite this they have received remarkably little archaeological study (Allen 1997). Some work has been done particularly on Foulness, where the timber framework of a former seawall, inland of the present one, has been dated by dendrochronology to the 15th century (Crump 1981). Radiocarbon dates for a site in the Crouch date seawall construction at that location to the post-medieval period. The timber substructures of seawalls are exposed where they have been breached, as at North Fambridge, or undercut and then eroded, for example, at Tollesbury Creek, where a 400m length of vertical posts with diagonal braces is visible. The latter site is probably the largest medieval or post-medieval timber structure currently visible in Essex, though comparable but more eroded lengths are also visible on the foreshore at Rolls Farm, Tollesbury.

Some of the best archaeological evidence for the importance of grazing on the marshes comes from the 'red hills' which seem to have provided convenient raised areas for temporary occupation by shepherds (Wymer & Brown 1995, 169). A 'red hill' on Canvey Island (Rodwell 1965) produced, above the Roman levels, a series of medieval midden deposits almost 1m thick, which yielded remains of hearths and ceramics of the 12th to 15th centuries. Camden's description of Canvey (1607) fits well with these archaeological deposits (the hillocks he refers to are presumably the 'red hills'):

> '...So low lying, that often it is all overflown, except for the higher hillocks, on which there is a safe retreat for the sheep. For it pastures about 4,000 sheep of very delicate flavour, which we have seen youths carrying out a womanly task, milk, with small stools fastened to their buttocks and make ewes cheese in those sheds which they call Wickes.'

The Canvey midden produced oyster, mussel, cockle and winkle shells and these are common finds in medieval and post-medieval sites (e.g. Murphy 1995), reflecting the importance of shellfish production. Large areas of saltmarsh are covered with the remains of oyster storage pits, a graphic demonstration of the importance of the oyster industry in the 19th century. Unsurprisingly sheep bone dominated the animal bone assemblage from the Canvey middens, as they do from the assemblage from a medieval fish-processing site at Leigh Beck, Canvey (Wilkinson & Murphy 1995). Small-scale sampling of this site has produced remains of shark, thornback ray, ?shad, herring/sprat, conger eel, whiting, cod, haddock, grey mullet, mackerel and indeterminate flatfish. This site, apparently unique in the east of England, presumably represents a once common type of site, where fish were processed for local consumption and shipment to supply the London market. In the medieval and post-medieval periods documentary evidence for the importance of fishing and fish-traps is plentiful (Emmison 1976; Ward 1987; Crump & Wallis 1992; Wymer & Brown 1995, 169-70).

In the early 18th century Defoe's description of the Blackwater Estuary (1724-6) provides an evocative picture of the Essex coast and the exploitation of its resources:

> '...There is nothing for many miles together remarkable, but a continued level of unhealthy marshes, called the Three Hundreds, till we come before Leigh, and to the mouth of the River Chelmer, and Black-water. These rivers united make a large firth, or inlet of the sea, which by Mr Camden is called Idumanum Fluvium; but by our fishermen and seamen, who use it as a port, 'tis called Malden-Water. In this inlet of the sea is Osey or Osyth Island, commonly called Oosy Island, so well known by our London men of pleasure, for the infinite number of wild-fowl, that is to say, duck, mallard, teal and widgeon, of which there are such vast flights, that

they tell us the island, namely the creek, seems covered with them, at certain times of the year, and they go from London on purpose for the pleasure of shooting; and indeed often come home very well loaden with game. But it must be remembered too, that those gentlemen who are such lovers of the sport, and go so far for it, often return with an Essex ague on their backs, which they find a heavier load than the fowls they have shot.

''Tis on this shore, and near this creek, that the greatest quantity of fresh fish is caught, which supplies not this country only, but London markets also. All along, to the mouth of Colchester Water, the shore is full of shoals and sands, with some deep channels between; all of which are so full of fish, that not only the Barking fishing-smacks come hither to fish, but the whole shore is full of small fisher-boats in very great numbers, belonging to the villages and towns on the coast, who come in every tide with what they take; and selling the smaller fish in the country, send the best and largest away upon horses, which go night and day to London market.'

While archaeological evidence for fishing in the form of fish-traps and bone deposits is relatively plentiful, the remains of wildfowling, no doubt important from earliest times, have proved elusive. The medieval fish processing site on Canvey produced remains of a dunlin, perhaps merely a chance occurrence. Thereafter there is no archaeological evidence for wildfowling until the development of clearly distinguishable structures. Most striking of these are the decoy ponds, often starfish-shaped in plan, which were once a common feature of the Essex marshes. Relatively few survive, many having been destroyed in the 1950s and 60s when so much traditional grazing marsh was converted to arable. Early aerial photographs often show decoy ponds in some detail and still in use. More recent air survey has revealed the distinctive cropmarks produced by these features when backfilled (Fig 15) (Strachan 1995).

Defensive structures became a prominent part of the coastal landscape in the medieval period. Hadleigh Castle was established at the mouth of the Thames (Fig 16), commanding wide views of the estuary. Throughout the post-medieval period defensive installations proliferated, from small earthworks like the 16th-century example at East Mersea (Priddy 1983) to elaborate forts like Tilbury, the Martello Towers, later 19th-century forts like Coalhouse, and the wide variety of 20th-century defences from both World Wars. Over the last couple of centuries the coastal landscape of south Essex, along the Thames, became increasingly built-up with a wide variety of industrial installations, docks, factories, refineries and power stations (RCHME 1995).

CONCLUSIONS

There is a wide variety of archaeological evidence preserved around the Essex coast which can be used to attempt to understand the past landscape and its human exploitation. Much of the coastal area, particularly the marshes and the intertidal zone, preserves deposits and remains that do not survive at inland locations. These sites are highly fragile and subject to a number of threats, notable amongst which are erosion, ploughing of grazing marsh and a rise in sea level. These are problems familiar from the way they adversely affect the rich diversity of plant and animal communities of the Essex coast. However, there is an important and fundamental difference. It might be possible to allow saltmarsh regeneration by managed retreat; it may be possible to encourage particular plants and animals by the creation and management of particular habitats; by contrast it is impossible to regenerate a Neolithic land surface or establish a breeding programme for Saxon fish-traps. Having begun with one quotation from William Morris it is appropriate to end with another:

'Whatever else happens, whatever glories or happiness befalls the English people in the future, these things, if we ever lose them, we can never get back again...'

Fig 16 Hadleigh Castle: conjectural reconstruction as seen from the Thames Estuary in the late 14th century. This view shows three recurrent elements of the Essex coast: defences, grazing and trade or transport (by Frank Gardiner)

3

The Rayleigh Hills in south-east Essex: patterns in exploitation of a woodland

by Stephen Rippon

This paper examines certain aspects of landscape evolution in south-east Essex, where three broad topographical areas can be identified: the low-lying London Clay basin east of Basildon, an outcrop of the Bagshot Beds forming the Rayleigh Hills at the centre, and lower-lying gravels and brickearths to the east. The Rayleigh Hills are currently well wooded and a range of evidence shows this to have been the case since the Saxon period, though later prehistoric and Roman settlement had been extensive. Following post-Roman woodland regeneration and later Saxon clearance, the establishment of an extensive royal estate, which included three deer parks, transformed part of the region. In contrast, the remaining areas were exploited in a piecemeal fashion as individual smallholders and great monastic landlords alike created a landscape through gradual assarting. The abundance of woodland and common pasture on the Rayleigh Hills was in sharp contrast to surrounding, lower-lying areas and, though land on the Hills had the lowest value in the 11th century, by 1334 they were more highly valued than the London Clay area to the west.

INTRODUCTION

The medieval landscape of Essex was very different from the open fields and nucleated villages of Midland England, and during the 16th century the terms 'woodland' (as in south-east England) and 'champion' (as in the Midlands) were given for these contrasting areas (Rackham 1986a, 1-5; Williamson 1988). Essex typifies a 'woodland' landscape: the mainly enclosed fields were often held in severalty, and the abundant hedgerows gave the countryside a very bosky appearance. The settlement pattern was largely dispersed, with farmsteads and cottages sprawling around greens and commons throughout the parish.

Rackham (1986a) has used the terms 'ancient' countryside (south-east England) and 'planned' countryside (the Midlands) for these same two areas, though this broad classification has rather misleading chronological overtones and fails to recognise the wide range of processes that led to the creation of 'ancient' landscapes. Some areas in the 'ancient' zone were in fact planned with great precision during the Iron Age (Drury 1976), and the Roman (Rodwell 1978), Saxon (Rippon 1991, 55-8), and medieval periods (Hunter 1995, 138), while other areas of 'ancient' countryside were created through the gradual and piecemeal assarting of woodland. It is the last process that is explored in this paper.

While Essex has benefited from a long history of archaeological and documentary research on the Saxon and medieval periods, there has been relatively little enquiry as to the origins of its present landscape. Notable exceptions have included the work of Bassett (1982), Drury (1976), Rackham (1986b) and Rodwell (1978; 1993) on the surviving planned landscapes of prehistoric and Roman date, while research in south-east Essex has suggested a later Saxon origin for a similarly regular pattern of fields and roads (Rippon 1991), a hypothesis which has received support from the publication of large-scale excavations at North Shoebury (Wymer & Brown 1995). A number of other studies have also shed new light on the medieval field systems of certain Essex parishes, notably Cressing (Hunter 1993b; 1995), Havering (McIntosh 1986), Rivenhall (Rodwell & Rodwell 1985; 1993), Saffron Walden (Cromarty 1966), Thaxted (Newton 1960), Witham (Britnell 1983; Rodwell 1993) and Writtle (Newton 1970). Such work shows a marked bias towards central and northern Essex (see Gray 1915 and Roden 1973 for more general discussions of Essex field systems).

This paper will examine the previously neglected south-east corner of the county, in which the role of a number of major landlords and the local peasant community in shaping the landscape can be compared. It will show how powerful estate owners could radically reshape the countryside, though it was not always possible nor desirable for them to do so. This paper will also show how smallholders in this area tended not to cooperate in creating planned field systems, but worked individually in the clearance of woodland, creating distinctive, irregular landscapes.

THE STUDY AREA

The Rayleigh Hills, between Southend and Basildon, stretch from Hockley in the north, through Rayleigh and Thundersley, to Hadleigh and South Benfleet in the south. The Hills comprise a complex sequence of clays, sands and gravels of the Claygate and Bagshot series, which in places give rise to podsolized heaths, contrasting sharply with heavy London Clays to the west and lighter terrace gravels and brickearths to the east (Scarfe 1942, 448; Wymer &

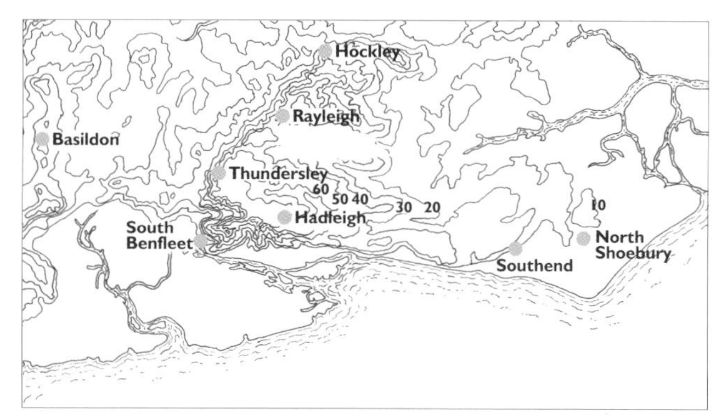

Fig 17 South-east Essex: relief, and location of places referred to by Rippon in 'The Rayleigh Hills in south-east Essex...'.

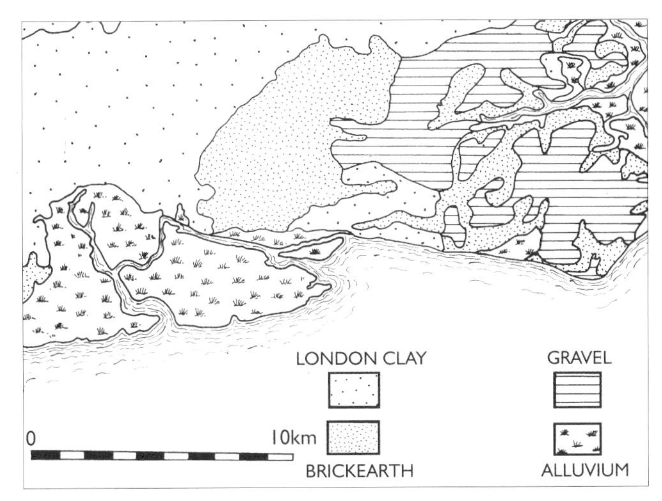

Fig 18 South-east Essex: simplified geology.

Brown 1995, 3). The southern edge of the Hills is marked by a relatively steep degraded cliff, fringed by post-glacial estuarine alluvium along the margins of the Thames Estuary (Figs 18 and 19). The western and northern edge of the Hills is marked by a steep scarp slope, with a much gentler dip slope to the east.

Landscape character on the Rayleigh Hills was summed up by Woodward (1903, 9): 'The land is less cultivated than on other formations, and commons, village greens and much woodland help to diversify the scenes'. At the end of the 18th century there was a great abundance of woodland (Fig 20) and soils were agriculturally less productive than on the adjacent lowlands, such as Shoebury and Wakering to the east (Table 1).

Table 1 Agricultural productivity in Hadleigh, Shoebury and Wakering in 1795 (based on Vancouver 1795, table facing 76).

parish	value (shillings) enclosed arable	value (shillings) enclosed pasture	yields (bushels per acre) wheat	yields (bushels per acre) barley	yields (bushels per acre) oats
Hadleigh	12s	12s	24	32	32
Shoebury	16s	16s	28	34	40
Wakering	16s	16s	28	34	40

THE ANTIQUITY OF 'ANCIENT WOODLAND': PREHISTORIC AND ROMAN SETTLEMENT

The well-wooded landscape and lower agricultural productivity in the post medieval period might lead to the assumption that the Rayleigh Hills have never been extensively settled and are a marginal landscape: an area not ideally suited to agriculture and only settled at times of high population pressure (Bailey 1989; Dyer 1990b; Rippon 1997). This impression is certainly confirmed by the report of the Land Utilisation Survey carried out in the 1930s, when it was argued that 'much of the sandy soil turned out to be too poor to cultivate after clearance and became heath and common' (Scarfe 1942, 448).

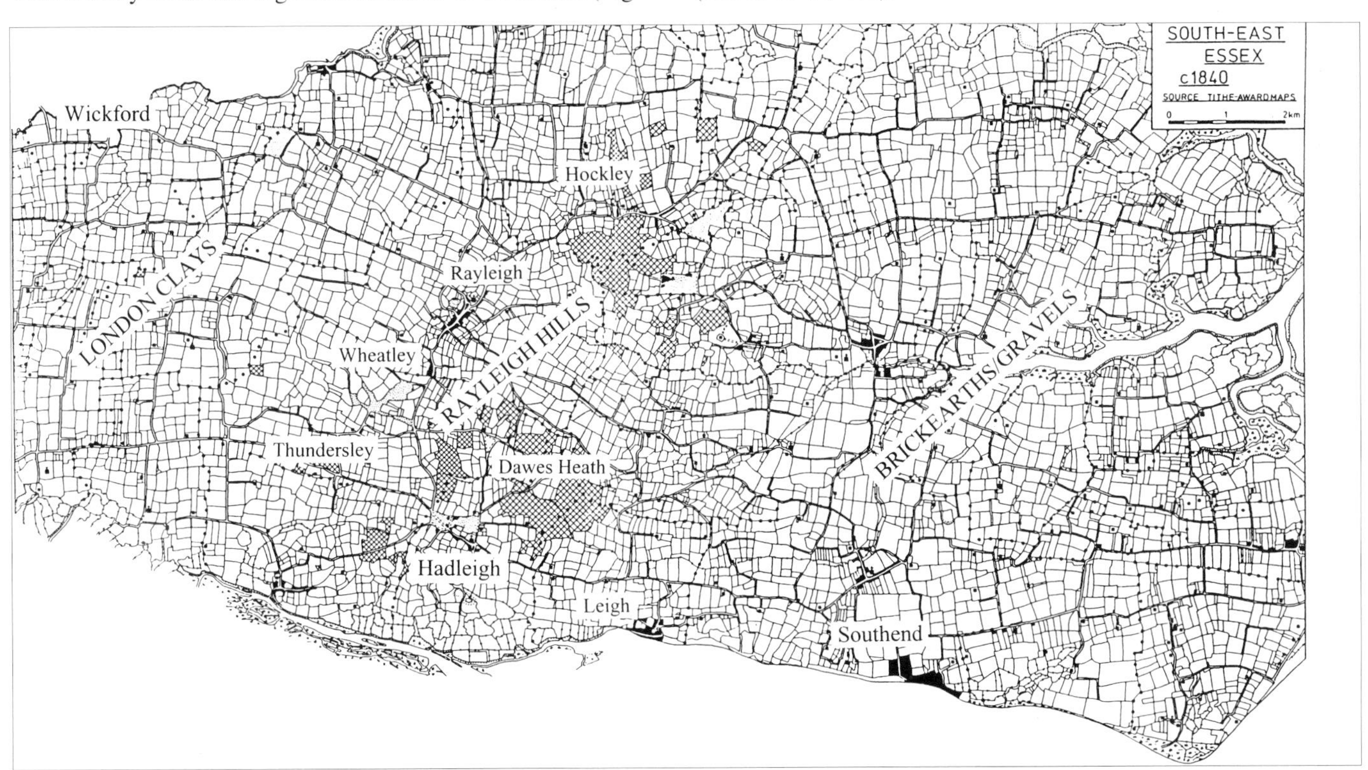

Fig 19 Field boundary patterns in south-east Essex (based on the Tithe Award maps of c. 1840). Note the regularly laid-out landscapes on the London Clay (south of Wickford) and brickearths and gravels (north of Southend), which contrast with the more irregular landscape on the Rayleigh Hills.

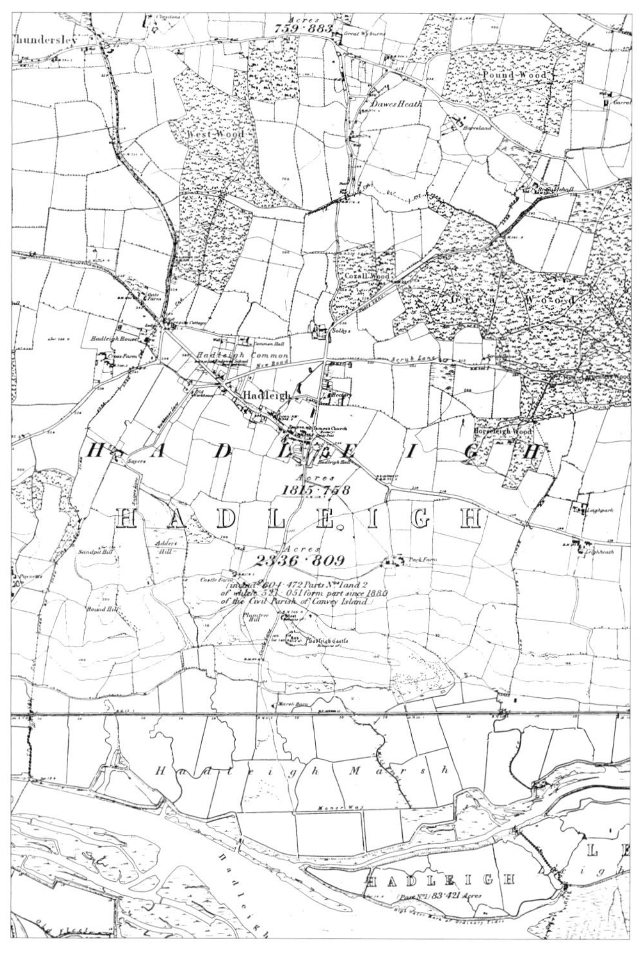

Fig 20 Extract from the Ordnance Survey first edition six-inch map of south-east Essex (surveyed in 1876). This forms the basis for the landscape analysis in Figure 21. For example, recent enclosures, such as the woodland assart from West Wood north-west of Solby's (compare Fig 21) and Hadleigh Common, have a far more regular layout than the earlier fields around the village.

Key issues are the date when this clearance was undertaken and the age of the surviving woodland. If the Land Utilisation Survey was correct then we should expect an abundance of woodland and less settlement on the Rayleigh Hills compared to the adjacent areas (except at times of high population pressure). Unfortunately there has been relatively little archaeological work on the Hills, though bearing in mind that the vast majority of archaeological discoveries are, therefore, antiquarian and other chance finds, there is in fact a remarkable number (Buckley 1980; Pollitt 1953). For example, taking just one parish, Hadleigh (Fig 21), later prehistoric finds include an Early Iron Age enclosure off Chapel Lane (Brown 1987), several Late Iron Age burial urns from Sayer's Farm (ECC SMR 7208-9, 9610; SM TQ 88 NW 74), and the cropmarks of a substantial double-ditched enclosure of a type dated elsewhere in Essex to the Late Iron Age and the Roman periods (Priddy & Buckley 1987, 61-6). Other examples of this type of enclosure are at Mucking (Clarke, A 1993, 20-1), Orsett (Toller 1980), Rainham (Greenwood 1982) and Stansted (Brooks & Bedwin 1989). A substantial Roman settlement existed to the north of Hadleigh at Dawes Heath, at the centre of what is still one of the most wooded parts of the Rayleigh Hills (see below; Delderfield & Rippon 1996; Drury *et al* 1981). A number of unstratified finds have also been found throughout the parish, including a mortar of Purbeck marble from Great Wood (SM TQ 88 NW 7, pottery and a bronze statue from Hadleigh Castle (ECC SMR 9533-4; SM TQ 88 NW 13; Drewett 1975, 135-8), and coins from six locations: Bilton Road (ECC SMR 9754; SM TQ 88 NW 37), Castle Farm (SM TQ 88 NW 21), Church Road (SM TQ 88 NW 39), Meadow Road (SM TQ 88 NW 87), Scrub Lane (ECC SMR 9724; SM TQ 88 NW 51) and West Wood (SM TQ 88 NW 68).

The coastline was also an important focus of activity (Fig 21). To the south of the Rayleigh Hills lay an extensive area of saltmarsh which, in the Roman period, was the setting for at least three 'red hills' used for salt production (Fawn *et al* 1990, 52). On the adjacent fen edge Roman material has been found at the eastern end of the Castle Saddleback (ECC SMR 9579), while a large amount of very

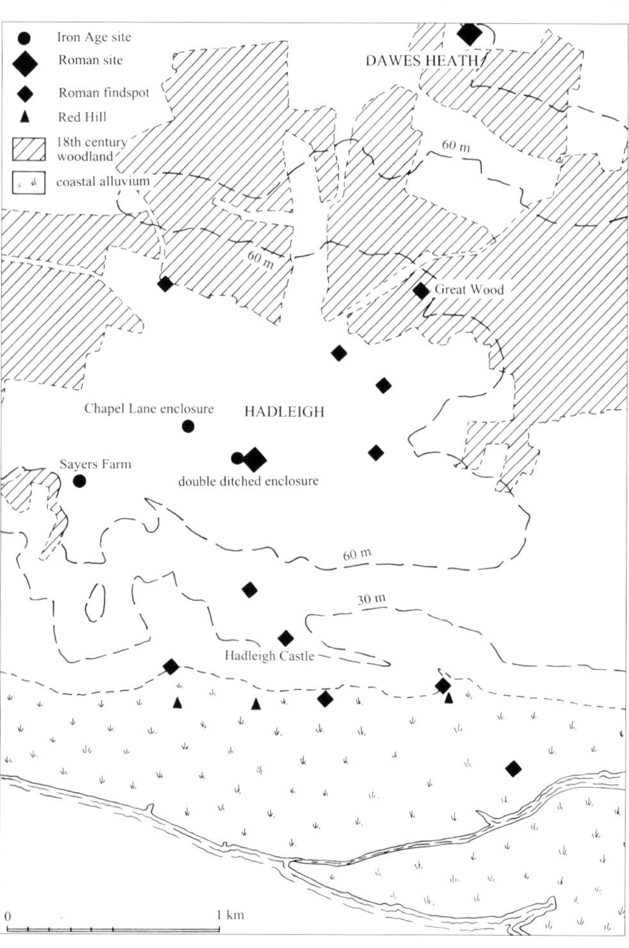

Fig 21 Hadleigh: findspots marking late prehistoric and Roman settlement. The density of findspots is greatest in the southern part of the parish, because this area has seen the greatest urban development. Note that several findspots occur in or on the edge of areas known to have been wooded in the late 18th century (source: ECC SMR and Southend Museum).

poorly fired tile (*tegula, imbrex,* and comb-decorated box flue tile), though curiously no pottery, has been discovered on the edge of the marshes at the southern end of Chapel Lane, south of Sayer's Farm (ECC SMR 9718).

This density of late prehistoric and Roman sites and findspots is repeated over much of the Rayleigh Hills and is comparable to most of the surrounding lower-lying areas (Pollitt 1953); this does not appear to have been marginal land. In contrast, however, there is just one findspot of Early Saxon date on all of the Rayleigh Hills: a possible burial from Plumberow Mount in Hockley (Jones 1980, 92; Pollitt 1953, 74) the suggestion that an iron spear and knife point from Dawes Heath are Saxon (Pollitt 1953, 76) is regarded by Jones (1980, 92) as doubtful. This lack of Saxon findspots contrasts sharply with the Southend area to the east of the Rayleigh Hills, which has an abundance of Saxon settlement and burial sites (Crowe 1996, fig 1; Wymer & Brown 1995, figs 99-100).

THE ORIGINS OF THE PRESENT LANDSCAPE: POST-ROMAN REGENERATION

It would seem, therefore, that the Rayleigh Hills were settled by the Roman period, but during the Early Saxon period activity was much less intense. This leads to the critical question of whether the present, well-wooded character of the area derives from a post-Roman regeneration (Day 1993). Botanically, most woodland on the Rayleigh Hills is regarded as 'ancient', though this only proves that it is at least several hundred years old (Rackham 1986b).

In southern England as a whole palaeoenvironmental evidence for post-Roman woodland regeneration is very limited; overall, the landscape appears to have remained open (Bell 1989, 273-7; Murphy 1994; Williamson 1993, 58-9). The closest pollen sequence to south-east Essex, from the Mar Dyke in Thurrock, suggests that there may have been limited regeneration in the post-Roman period in that area (Wilkinson 1988, 125), but too much should not be read into this one diagram.

Several fragments of evidence, however, suggest that some at least of the woodland on the Rayleigh Hills is indeed post-Roman. A possible Roman villa at Dawes Heath was first identified in the 1970s (Drury *et al* 1981). The structure's character is unclear, though the presence of ceramic roof tiles indicates a villa, or a farmstead of sufficient status to have had a stone-built bath-house (like the recently excavated site at Great Holts Farm, Boreham: *Essex Archaeology* 1995, 12). Though it cannot be proven that the Dawes Heath site itself was subsequently wooded, the present pattern of field boundaries in the vicinity clearly suggests a woodland assart from Pound Wood to the south and east, and Tile Wood to the west (Fig 22). The assart is called 'Haggatt Lande alias Brett Lande' in 1613 (WAM Lease Book XI, f. 117b) and may equate with the land held in Thundersley by Stephen le Bret in the 13th century (WD temp. Hen. III, f. 609; temp. Edw. I, f. 609). In 1717, 'Brets alias Haggetts' amounted to 28 acres of land and 'a messuage with barns outhouses and several fields of customary land' (WAM 8039). All trace of this farmstead has now disappeared, and it is not shown on the map of 1777 (Chapman & André), although post-medieval building debris can be found in the field alongside Roman *tegulae*.

By the late Saxon period the Rayleigh Hills appear to have been relatively well wooded, indicated by the almost complete predominance of *-leah* names in Domesday (Fig 19: Hockley, Leigh, Rayleigh, Thundersley, Wheatley, Hadleigh). Most botanically ancient woodlands are not documented until the 13th century, though some, for instance Britcherley (now Potash Wood, Rochford), Fennley (now Pound Wood, Thundersley, Fig 22), Goldingsley (Leigh), Horseley (south of Barnes-juxta-Hadleigh, Fig 22), Kingley (Rayleigh) and Tilehurst Woods (Thundersley, Fig 22), may have pre-Conquest names (Rackham 1986b, 16).

Domesday records surprisingly little woodland in manors on the Rayleigh Hills (Rippon 1991, fig 3), though it is quite likely that woodland recorded on other manors in south-east Essex was actually located in enclaves on the Hills. In the same way these manors had grazing rights on distant coastal marshes (see below: Cracknell 1959, 10-11; Rackham 1986b, 16, fig 14; Rippon 1991; Round 1903, 369).

The well-wooded nature of the Rayleigh Hills may in fact be illustrated through analysing the acreage per population, plough and shilling of value in 1066 (Table 2). This date was chosen rather than 1086 to exclude the effects of any disruption to the landscape caused by the Norman Conquest (see below). The bounds of the numerous Domesday manors is not known, so for this analysis they have been grouped by medieval parishes. Most of the parishes whose centres lay on the Rayleigh Hills also extended onto the surrounding lowlands; only Leigh and Hadleigh were contained wholly on the Hills. Hart's (1957b) identification of *Lea(m)* as Hadleigh is accepted here. Rawreth is not named in Domesday and is assumed to have been included under Wickford. Table 2 shows that in Domesday the Rayleigh Hills had lower densities of ploughs, population and value per acre compared with areas both to the west (the London Clay) and especially the east (the brickearths).

Table 2 Comparison of agricultural conditions on the Rayleigh Hills and areas to the west and east in 1066 and 1334.

	western area (London Clay)	Rayleigh Hills	eastern area (brickearth/gravels)
acreage	**acres**	**acres**	**acres**
1066 per plough	398	491	294
1066 per tenant	92	171	159
1066 per shilling	21	26	17
1334 per shilling	64	47	33

By 1334, however, the situation had changed (Glasscock 1975), and though the acreage per shilling of value was still much lower than for the area to the east, the Hills were now more highly valued compared to the London Clays to the west. Assuming conditions on the Clay had not deteriorated in any significant way, this must mark a positive improvement in the value of land on the Rayleigh Hills. The very varied resources on the Rayleigh Hills, including the abundant woodland, thus supported a higher valuation than the wholly cleared areas to the west.

There is no firm evidence in Domesday for clearance between 1066 and 1086. A decrease in woodland between these two assessments has been noted throughout Essex, though this was not necessarily due to clearance for cultivation (Lennard 1945). For example, the change in Eastwood from woodland for 50 swine to that for 30 was matched by a decrease in ploughs from 10 to 7. This may in fact represent wasting after the Conquest (Lennard 1945, 36), and 30 acres of 'wasted wood' are indeed recorded in Fanton Hall, North Benfleet, which were probably located on the Rayleigh Hills (Rackham 1986b, 16).

An indication of active woodland clearance might be found in the region's social structure. Harvey (1979, 107-9) has suggested that the Domesday tenants called *bordarii* were 'a class of people, perhaps formerly servile, who dwell in cottages on the edge of the existing village and its fields, who had taken in a few acres of land from the waste, common and heathland, to form a small holding'. These holdings might amount to around 5 to 10 acres of land (Harvey 1987, 254). If this hypothesis is correct we might expect far larger numbers of *bordarii* on the Rayleigh Hills compared to the lower-lying surrounding areas. Table 3 gives the percentages of *bordarii* on the Rayleigh Hills and surrounding lowland areas in 1066 and 1086. The percentages of *bordarii* on the Hills in 1066 and 1086 are in fact lower than the regional average, and much lower compared to the areas further east, though higher than the London Clay areas to the west. In Essex as a whole *bordarii* were 36% of the villeins, bordars and slaves in 1066, and 53% in 1086 (Welldon-Finn 1972, 131). Thus, either Harvey's suggestion as to the nature of the *bordarii* is incorrect or there was not a particularly significant level of assarting on the Rayleigh Hills during the third quarter of the 11th century.

Table 3 Domesday bordarii *as a percentage of bordars, villeins and slaves, in 1066 and 1086, on the Rayleigh Hills and in neighbouring lower-lying areas.*

	west	**Rayleigh Hills**	**east**	**average south-east Essex**
	%	%	%	%
1066	41	48	54	50
1086	49	52	71	61

The extent of woodland on the Rayleigh Hills becomes more evident during the high medieval period. The existence of three royal deer parks suggests that in the late 11th to early 13th century, when the parks were created, there was a concentration of woodland in the area; in England as a whole, wherever licences to impark state former land use in over half the cases this was woodland (Rackham 1980, 191).

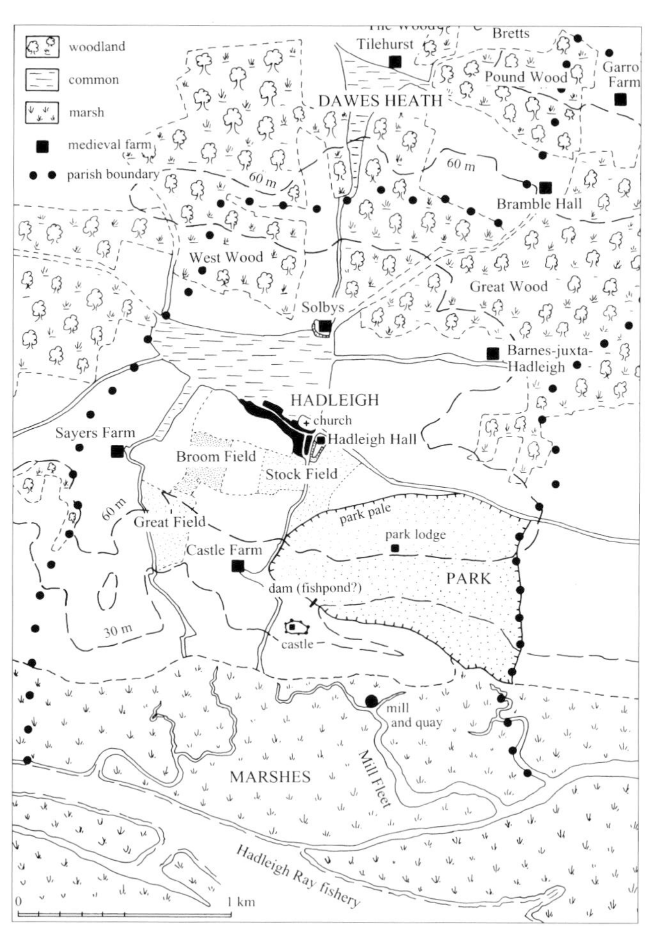

Fig 22 Hadleigh: reconstructed plan of the medieval landscape, including the village and outlying farmsteads. The extent of woodland in the late 18th century is shown: some at least of this may be post-medieval regeneration. (Cartographic sources: Hadleigh Park, (?) late 16th century (HRO M16/54); Hadleigh Marshes, 1670 (HRO M16/54); Barnes [Great] Wood, 1750 (ERO D/Dmq E7/1); Chapman and André (1777); Tithe Map, 1847 (ERO D/CT 154/A); Enclosure Map, 1852 (ERO TS/M 63/9).)

Other woods certainly existed around these parks, recorded for example in Hadleigh (CIPM vol I, Hen. III, 249; CPR Rich. II vol. II, 536-7), Thundersley (FF 1, 232; Burrows 1909, 28; Delderfield 1982, 14) and Dawes Heath (Delderfield & Rippon 1996). In fact, out of twelve Feet of Fines from 1254-5 to 1430 that describe holdings wholly in Hadleigh, six included small parcels of woodland, usually between 3 and 8 acres (see Table 4).

Large areas of woodland existed in the post-medieval period (Figs 20-22). Much of this is probably a direct descendent of the post-Roman regenerative woodland, though some was derived from medieval or later regeneration. For example, the Dean and Chapter of St Paul's had part of West Wood (Fig 22) on the Hadleigh-Thundersley parish boundary, which covered 81 acres in the 18th century (ERO D/DU 560/14/1; ERO D/DHt P51; Delderfield 1982, 14). Of this 64 acres were in Thundersley, which presumably represents the bulk of the 74 acres that St Paul's held in that parish during the late 1250s; of this just 22 acres were wooded (FF I, 226, 232; Delderfield 1982, 14).

The abundant post-Roman woodland on the Rayleigh Hills is in sharp contrast to the lower-lying areas in the rest of south-east Essex which lack *-leah* place-names. To the west of the Rayleigh Hills the potential survival of a rectilinear Roman field system south of Wickford (Fig 19) (Rippon 1991; Rodwell 1978) suggests that the landscape remained open throughout the Saxon period. To the east of the Rayleigh Hills the carefully planned road and field systems appear at least in part to be of later Saxon origin rather than a survival from Roman times (Fig 19) (Rippon 1991; Wymer & Brown 1995, 170-2). Though there is no evidence that they were created after woodland clearance, there are no *-leah* place-names nor is there abundant evidence for Early and Middle Saxon settlement (Crowe 1996; Jones 1980; Wymer & Brown 1995).

Table 4 Feet of Fines for Hadleigh 1254/5-1430 (source: FF I-IV).

	messuages	land acres	pasture acres	wood acres	marsh acres	heath
1254/5	1	8				
1254/5		5				
1261/2	1	20				
1268/9	1	12		5		
1275/6	1	15				
1288/9					80	
1305/6				30		
1320/1	1	3		3		
1323/4	1	23	1	8		
1324	1	10		3		
1324	1	14	1	3		4
1430	1	4½				

In the post-Roman period, therefore, large parts of the Rayleigh Hills appear to have been abandoned and saw the regeneration of woodland. However, the surrounding lowland areas continued to be occupied and settlements there held grazing rights up on the Hills. An analogy can be drawn with the extensive intercommoned pastures on Tiptree Heath between Chelmsford and Colchester, on which 16 parishes had rights of pasture in 'an unappropriated waste' (Britnell 1983, 52; Hunter 1995, 140; Round 1903, 370). This pattern of continuous occupation in certain lowland areas, and regeneration on the higher hills, is also mirrored in Norfolk where the central watershed appears to have been partly abandoned in the post-Roman period (Williamson 1993).

By the medieval period many lowland farms are recorded as having woodland on the Rayleigh Hills (Rackham 1986b, 16-17, fig 14). For example, in 1462 an estate is recorded as comprising 1 messuage, 240 acres of land, 3 acres of wood and 40 acres of marsh in Paglesham, Canewdon, Great Stambridge (all between the rivers Crouch and Roach) and Hadleigh, about 10 miles to the south-west (FF IV, 58). Presumably the woodland lay in Hadleigh since the other three parishes do not appear to have contained any ancient woodland: Rookery Wood in Canewdon, and Barton Hall Grove and Steward's Wood in Great Stambridge, are all of recent origin (Rackham 1986b, 103, 107). Some of the detached parcels of woodland on the Rayleigh Hills may date back to the period when the common wood-pastures were enclosed, such as 'Shoebury Grove' which later came into the hands of Prittlewell Priory (ERO D/DMq T3/1; Rackham 1986b, 18). Shoebury manor also retained 30 acres of woodland in Hadleigh (CIPM 1, 249; CIPM VII, 125; CIPM XVI, 179).

THE HIGH MEDIEVAL PERIOD

Clearance of the post-Roman woodland on the Rayleigh Hills appears to have started during the Middle to Late Saxon period: nationally, *-leah* names are rarely recorded before c. 730 (Cox 1976, 50; Gelling 1993, 198). By Domesday the Rayleigh Hills were clearly well settled, with numerous settlements and plough-teams suggesting extensive open areas. It was during this later Saxon period of clearance that the basic framework of the medieval and post-medieval landscape, including the broad pattern of settlements, roads, fields and commons, came into being (see Warner 1987 for the origins of green-side settlement in Suffolk). However, the subsequent centuries saw a series of major modifications, including the creation of three large deer parks, further erosion of the common land, and the resulting proliferation of dispersed settlements. Together, these amounted to an increased intensity with which the landscape was exploited.

The dispersed settlement pattern of the Rayleigh Hills has not left much in the way of documentation. Reaney (1935) collated the evidence for the date when many of the farmsteads are first documented, though in many cases it is actually a family name that is first recorded; for instance, Garrold's: Walter Gerold, 1324 (Fig 22) (Reaney 1935, 185). It is dangerous to assume that the earliest date when a farm is documented is close to that of its foundation; a farmstead may go undocumented for many centuries. What can be said, however, is that the dispersed settlement pattern on the Rayleigh Hills certainly existed by the early 14th century. Examples are, at South Benfleet, Jarvis Hall, 1254 (Reaney 1935, 143); at Kersey Marsh, Poynett's, 1308, and Reed's Hill, 1285 (Priestley 1984, 23); and at Thundersley, Haresland, 1319 (Reaney 1935, 172).

A number of other farms are not documented until the 15th and 16th centuries, and it is not clear whether they represent earlier farms that had escaped documentation or late medieval assarting of woodland and common land when the already weak manorial authority of this region was further eroded. Examples are, at Hadleigh, Bramble Hall, 1412, and Sayer's, 1491 (Reaney 1935, 185); at South Benfleet, Boyce Hill, (?)1412, 1563 (Reaney 1935, 143); and at Thundersley, Claydon's, 1554 (Reaney 1935, 143).

The estate of Westminster Abbey at Dawes Heath, in Hadleigh and Thundersley, is relatively well documented and has been studied by Bob Delderfield (whom I thank for allowing me to refer to his unpublished work). Westminster's main holding in south-east Essex was a large compact estate in South Benfleet acquired after the Norman Conquest (DB 6.1; Benton 1867-88, 55). In contrast, the Abbey's lands around Dawes Heath appear to have been obtained in a piecemeal fashion with a number of acquisitions in the 13th century, including lands, woods and tenements in Hadleigh (1222-46: WD f.497) and Thundersley (temp. Hen. III: WD 609, 610; 1222-46: WD f.614; temp. Edw. I: WD f.609; 1283-1307: WD f.616). There were also acquisitions in Wheatley (Fig 19) which give an impression of how the 13th-century landscape may have appeared. A grant in 1253-83 comprised 86 acres, of which 14 acres lay in 'the field called le Westfeld at Wateleye', along with 19 acres in 'le Estfeld', 20 acres in 'le Bernefeld', 33 acres in 'le Medefeld', and 21 acres in an unnamed location (WD f. 616). In c. 1300 Alice Watelege granted Westminster 18 acres of land in Thundersley, which was surrounded by a ditch and called 'Bernfeld', as well as the two roads leading from 'Bernfeld' to 'Pirifeld' and 'Almshale' (temp. Edw. I: WD f. 582). At about the same time Westminster was granted the tenement of 'Thielherst' (Tilehurst) (Fig 22), which was to become the centre of their estates at Dawes Heath (temp. Edw. I: WD f. 609; see Rackham 1986b, 17, for a survey of 1315). The overall impression given by these and other references (and see the discussion of Hadleigh below) is that during the medieval period the Rayleigh Hills were still relatively well wooded with a pattern of dispersed settlement scattered around numerous commons and heaths.

HADLEIGH: LANDSCAPE AND LORDSHIP

The early history of Hadleigh is somewhat obscure as it does not appear to be mentioned in Domesday. Benton (1867-88, 228) and Morant (1766-8, 279) suggest that it was included under Rayleigh, whereas Priestley (1984, 64-7) suggests that Hadleigh is in fact the otherwise unidentified *Atelia.* Hart (1957b) argues more plausibly that Hadleigh was in fact St Paul's manor of *Lea(m),* although Reaney (1935, 163) and Round (1903, 422) had assumed this was Lee Chapel near Basildon.

The earliest reference to Hadleigh *(Haeþlege)* is in a list of the estates of St Paul's dated c. 995-8 (Hart 1957a, 19). It is recorded as *Hadleg* in 1121 (Reaney 1935, 185) and *Hadlea* in 1182, when the church is first referred to (Pipe Rolls vol. XXXI, 103). Unfortunately very little is known of the St Paul's estate. The description in a lease of 1695-6 (ERO D/DU 560/14/1) matches a map of 1750 (ERO D/DMq E7/1) by showing the estate in two almost wholly wooded blocks: West Wood and Barnes (now Great) Wood. However, the estate was formerly more extensive and included several messuages and parcels of land in and around Hadleigh village (FF I, 240; HMC 29, 34, 37).

Sometime before 1217 Hubert de Burgh was granted the honour of Rayleigh, which included Hadleigh and a large number of other manors (Burrows 1909, 253; Helliwell & Macleod 1980, 6). In 1227 this grant was confirmed (CChR vol I Hen. III, 12), and in 1230 a licence was obtained to build a castle at Hadleigh on a hill overlooking the Thames Estuary (Figs 16 and 22) (CPR Hen. III, vol II, 417). In 1239, however, de Burgh was disgraced and his estates reverted to the crown. In 1250 the royal manor comprised 140 acres of arable, 2 acres of meadow, a curtilage, pasture around the castle and the barns of the castle for supporting a plough, pasture on the marsh for 160 sheep, a water mill, toll of the fair and a park (Sparvel-Bayly 1878, 92). In 1274-5 there is even reference to a vineyard (Colvin 1963, 662).

The earliest reference to a park at Hadleigh is in 1235 (CCR Hen. III, vol III, 57). In addition to sport and recreational use (CPR Hen. III, vol VI, 551), the park was a valuable source of timber (CCR Edw. I vol I, 200), underwood (CPR Rich. II, vol I, 482), and fresh meat both for the king (CLR vol VI, 291) and as gifts to others (CCR Hen. III, vol VII, 325). Horses were reared in a stud there (CPR Edw. II, vol I, 392). Various enclosures and assarts are recorded that would have compartmentalised the park (CFR Edw. I, vol I, 325; Min Acc II, 102), allowing for more intensive management, for example by coppicing woodland (CPR Rich. II, vol I, 482, 487). The earthworks of a dam across the valley north of the castle may indicate a fishpond in the park (Fig 22), and a stank (or fishpond) is recorded in the late 14th century (CPR Edw. III, vol XVI, 63; CPR Rich. II, vol IV, 406). The park also served an important social function as the object of patronage and gift; its keepership was clearly a prized possession with rights of grazing, cutting timber and a quota of deer (CPR Edw. III, vol XI, 96). The royal estate also contained a coastal fishery in Hadleigh Ray (Fig 22) (CPR Rich. II, vol II, 531).

The creation of the deer park represents an important statement about the authority of a major landholder. Just as rising population placed increased pressure on rural resources, a large area of land was devoted to non-agricultural production. It is not known whether arable land was used, although the location of the park, just to the south-east of the village, must make this likely. Much of the land to the west, north and east of the village was either common or part of the St Paul's Cathedral estate, suggesting that most of the arable must have lain to the area south of the village, out of which the park was carved.

A mill (first documented in 1250: CLR Hen. III, vol III, 11), and a small landing-stage lay on the edge of the marshes below the castle, adjacent to a tidal creek later called 'Mill Fleet' (shown on a map of the marsh dated 1670: HRO 1716/54) (Fig 22). During the construction of the railway across these marshes timber planks were recovered at a depth of 12 feet, from a vessel laden with Kentish ragstone (Burrows 1909, 255). This boat may have been delivering stone for the construction of the castle or mill, or subsequent modifications. In 1372 there is even reference to barges being made at Hadleigh, underlining the importance of the maritime role of the royal estate (CPR Edw. III, vol XV, 219).

The largest programme of work on the castle and other elements of the estate was carried out during the 1360s and 70s, when vast amounts of material must have been shipped in (Colvin 1963; Sparvel-Bayly 1878). In 1366, for example, 111 tons of stone were brought by boat from Kent, and 10 cartloads of stone, lime, sand, chalk and 'other necessaries' were carried from the mill to the castle (Min Acc II, 103). At the same time extensive repairs were also carried out on the mill, park lodge and pale (CPR Edw. III, vol XV, 224-6; CPR Edw. III, vol XVI, 340-1, 445, 473; Min Acc I, 78; Min Acc II, 102-7). Clearly this estate was a valued resource thought worthy of considerable investment.

The royal estate included part of the marshes below the castle, such as a marsh called 'Rousande' (CCR Edw. III vol XIV, 38). Other areas of marshland had been granted to two Essex monasteries. 'Russells Marsh' (or 'Rushe Hulles alias Priors Marsh') was held by Prittlewell Priory (CPR Edw. VI, vol IV, 87; ERO T/P 83/2; D/DU 514/29/28), while 'Clerkenwick alias Abbott's Marsh' was formerly held by Stratford Langthorne Abbey (CPR Edw. VI, vol IV, 87). Other marshes were held by smallholders; for example, a grant of 1412 included 'all the lands, marshes, rents and services in Hadleigh called Passages, Mascales and Johns atte Mersshe, and the whole marsh called Wodehammescotte' (CCR Hen IV, vol IV, 395). In common with most of the Essex coastal marshes, the Hadleigh marshes were left unreclaimed and used for grazing sheep (Cracknell 1959, 10; Hart 1957b, 40).

It is curious that there appears to be no evidence for the production of salt on the marshes, since this valuable commodity was certainly used for preserving meat from the deer park (CLR Hen. III, vol IV, 319; CLR Hen. III, vol IV, 350; CLR Hen. III, vol IV, 256). Medieval salterns, quite distinct from their Roman predecessors in having more prominent mounds and larger tanks, and lacking distinctive burnt red earth, are known from around both the Blackwater and Crouch estuaries (Barford 1988a; Christy 1907, 445; Christy & Dalton 1928; Fawn *et al* 1990, 49; Wilkinson & Murphy 1995, 197), though there is no evidence at all for such sites on the Hadleigh marshes.

The location of the original manor house is unclear, although it probably lay at the moated Hadleigh Hall close to the church (Fig 22). After the royal estate was sold in 1551 (CPR Edw. VI, vol III, 158-9) the manor passed through the Riche, Warwick, St John and Sparrow families (Benton 1867-88, 233-4). By the 19th century the manor and its court was located at Castle Farm (Benton 1867-88, 234). Hadleigh Hall had been owned by the Heber family since the 18th century, though in 1712 the 'manor of Hadleigh Hall' was held by the St John family whose estate also included Castle and Park Farms (HRO DDm 61/19). Thus it would seem that the medieval royal estate was divided into three farms, corresponding to the lands of the castle, manor and park, and when the Heber family acquired Hall Farm in the 18th century the manorial rights were retained by the St John family and so transferred to Castle Farm.

Hadleigh Castle was, therefore, not simply a fortress and occasional royal residence. It lay at the centre of an estate that exploited the varied resources of this rural landscape to the full; there was a demesne farm, a vineyard, a deer park serving a wide range of functions, a fishpond, a coastal fishery, coppiced woodland, a watermill and a quay. Several features that might have been expected are missing; there is no mention of rabbit warrens (although they are recorded in Rayleigh and Thundersley parks: CChR vol II, 27), and meadow was scarce, explained by the decision not to reclaim the marshes as they were already so highly valued for their sheep grazing. The possibility of salt production cannot be ruled out although evidence is lacking.

HADLEIGH: SMALLHOLDERS AND THE LANDSCAPE

The rest of Hadleigh's medieval landscape represents a sharp contrast to the intensively used royal estate. Much of the settlement appears to have been spread along the southern edge of the common, close to the church and moated manor house. Excavations to the south of the church revealed a long sequence of occupation, with the earliest pottery dated to the 12th century (Helliwell & Macleod 1969). In addition there were a number of farmsteads outside the main village that probably existed from the medieval period (Fig 22). Sayer's Farm may date back to at least 1491, when one William Sayer is recorded in Hadleigh (Reaney 1935, 185). Solby's (formerly 'Pollington's alias Strangeman's place'), on the northern side of the common, may be at least 14th-century (Benton 1867-88, 237). It farmed an assart from West Wood and may have been moated (Heygate 1859, cited in Hancock & Harvey 1986, 52). Two farms in the far north of the parish represent other woodland assarts: Bramble Hall is documented in 1412 (CCR Hen. IV, vol IV, 395), while Garrold's may be related to Walter Gerold recorded at Hadleigh in 1324; 'Geroldes heth' (heath) is documented from 1450 (Reaney 1935, 185).

Rackham (1986a, 172, 178) suggests that 'some regions, such as the south-east half of Essex, seem never to have had open fields at all'. However, nomenclature such as 'le Westfeld', 'le Estfeld', 'le Bernefeld', 'le Medefeld' and 'Pirifeld' in Wheatley, and the fact these fields contained at least 20-30 acres (see above; WD f.616), suggest that there may in fact have been a multiplicity of small common fields. Very little is known about the fields that surrounded Hadleigh. Early references are few, although a pattern of small enclosed fields is certainly apparent as early as *c.* 1700 (1696: ERO D/Ds 128/29; 1732 ERO D/Ds 128/31). The Tithe Map (ERO D/CT 154) shows a wholly enclosed landscape, though the field boundary pattern to the south of the village is rather different from that of the rest of the parish: fields are slightly larger, more rectilinear and there are several examples of two or more adjacent fields having the same name (for example, Broom Field, Great Field and Stock Field; the three 'Stock' names occur on either side of Castle Lane and in total cover a sizeable area south of the village: Fig 22). It is possible that these are the remnants of 'small areas of subdivided arable, often subject to joint or communal regulation' similar to those at Wheatley, which were characteristic of the 'woodland landscape' of south-east England (Hunter 1995; Newton 1970; Williamson 1988, 5).

The average size of landholdings in Hadleigh appears to have been small. In the early 14th century a survey describes 22 1/2 'terre' and 6 'moneday londs' in Hadleigh (Gray 1915, 392). The Feet of Fines for Essex have been published for 1182-1547 (FF I-IV). There are twelve holdings whose lands were wholly within Hadleigh, dating from 1254/5 to 1430 (Table 4). Each typically consisted of a messuage, between 3 and 23 acres of land, and 3 to 30 acres of woodland. Several holdings also had small parcels of pasture, while there were single examples of marsh and heath. No meadow is listed, which supports the impression that none of the coastal marshes was reclaimed.

In the landscape of Hadleigh a clear division can therefore be drawn between the estate of a single powerful landowner, in this case the Crown, and the remaining areas where the landscape was created through gradual and piecemeal assarting of woodland and heath by smallholders. The same two-fold division between seigneurial and peasant landscapes can be detected also in Cressing (Hunter 1995) and Writtle (Newton 1970), with the areas controlled by the great lords having a markedly more regular morphology and, in certain cases, open fields (Hunter 1995, fig 4; Newton 1970, 31).

DISCUSSION: THE ROLE OF LORDSHIP IN THE LANDSCAPE

The exploitation of the Rayleigh Hills during the post-Roman period demonstrates a number of points with regard to the role of lordship in landscape exploitation and management. The creation of Hadleigh Park clearly demonstrates that during the medieval period major landowners could transform their estates. The resulting landscapes tend to have certain characteristics in common; they were 'grand designs', intended to intensify the exploitation of rural resources for the maximum economic, recreational and sometimes social gain.

Major landlords did not always manage their estates in this way, however. For example, Westminster Abbey and St Paul's Cathedral were both major landowners on the Rayleigh Hills, although the exploitation of their estates was based upon woodland management and the grazing or cultivation of small assarts. The reason why these estates were not simply converted to large arable fields illustrates the value placed by contemporary society on the varied resources of a woodland region, rather than its being in any way a marginal landscape. Woodland itself was a valued resource, as were the coastal Thames-side saltmarshes which, unlike those in the rest of southern and eastern England, were left unreclaimed (Rippon forthcoming). Clearly, in certain cases, these natural resources were more highly valued than the increased agricultural production achievable through assarting and drainage.

Another reason why the Westminster estates were exploited in this fashion concerns the distribution of their land. The Abbey's estates were acquired piecemeal during the 12th and 13th centuries. Though their original extent is not known, the holdings appear to have been scattered rather than nucleated in one large block, which would clearly limit the scope for large-scale landscape reorganisation (see Rippon forthcoming for similar considerations applying to marshland reclamation).

CONCLUSIONS

In 1915 Gray wrote that 'the early field system of few English counties is so difficult to describe as that of Essex' (1915, 387). The early planned landscapes of Essex have attracted much attention, yet there is a much greater diversity in the Essex countryside: notably, large areas with more irregular patterns derived from woodland assarting. In south-east Essex the Rayleigh Hills, the London Clay region to the west and the brickearths and gravels to the east had markedly different medieval landscapes. Physical factors such as soil quality may have been a factor in the greater woodland regeneration seen on the Hills, for example through podsolisation due to over-exploitation. At a time of rising population, however, the variations in soil quality and resulting arable potential cannot explain why the area remained so wooded; the explanation must in part have been a conscious decision, taken by the numerous landowners, large and small, to leave them that way.

The pattern of landholding and the diversity of rural resources were major factors in determining how this landscape was shaped. The extensive royal estates saw the creation of three deer parks, reserved for hunting and pleasure. In contrast, the remaining areas had a weak and fragmented manorial structure and landscapes were created in a piecemeal fashion by numerous smallholders.

The way in which a landscape was exploited depended therefore upon a range of natural factors, such as soils, and cultural variables, such as population and landholding. Powerful estate owners could radically reshape the landscape, though it was not always possible or desirable for them to do so because of the scattered nature of their holdings. In sharp contrast, large areas of this landscape were created by smallholders who gradually cleared the woodland and heath, taking advantage of the rich natural resources that this landscape offered.

ACKNOWLEDGEMENTS

I would like to thank Ken Crowe and Bob Delderfield for their assistance with this research and for access to unpublished material.

4

Woods, parks and forests: the Cressing Temple story

by Oliver Rackham

Essex is one of Europe's classic areas for the history of trees and woodland as part of the cultural landscape. The primeval wildwood of Mesolithic times was destroyed and converted into farmland and heath in the Neolithic, Bronze and perhaps Iron Ages. By the Middle Ages Essex was not a very wooded county. There was no memory or tradition of wildwood; instead there were hundreds of woods, large and small, scattered as islands in a farmed landscape. There were also hedges and hedgerow trees, and trees isolated among grassland or heath in various kinds of wood-pasture. The original wood-pastures are now represented by wooded commons such as Burnham Beeches, Buckinghamshire. The husbandry of deer, devised by the Normans, gave rise to two other branches of wood-pasture, namely parks and wooded Forests (Rackham 1990).

I am concerned with natural, though managed, woods and wood-pastures, not with plantations. Plantations of trees are a much later feature, less prominent in Essex than in most counties.

Figures in Domesday Book, although unsatisfactory, suggest that woodland and wood-pasture in Essex amounted to little more than the average for England of 15% of the land area (Rackham 1980, 119(24). Some of this had been derived from wildwood; some had grown up on abandoned Roman and Iron Age farmland–for example, in what was then the second biggest concentration of woodland, around what is now Stansted Airport (Rackham 1989, 20(37).

Most of the Domesday Book woodland was to be turned into farmland and heath by the 14th century. Much of what escaped this destruction was still woodland in 1940. Since then there have been heavy depredations from wartime air-fields, agriculture and modern forestry (Rackham 1994, 48(9).

Essex woods are well represented in documents and early maps. Ancient woods tend to form islands of stability in an otherwise changing landscape; in Essex, where the landscape at large has changed relatively little, the woods tend to be more stable still.

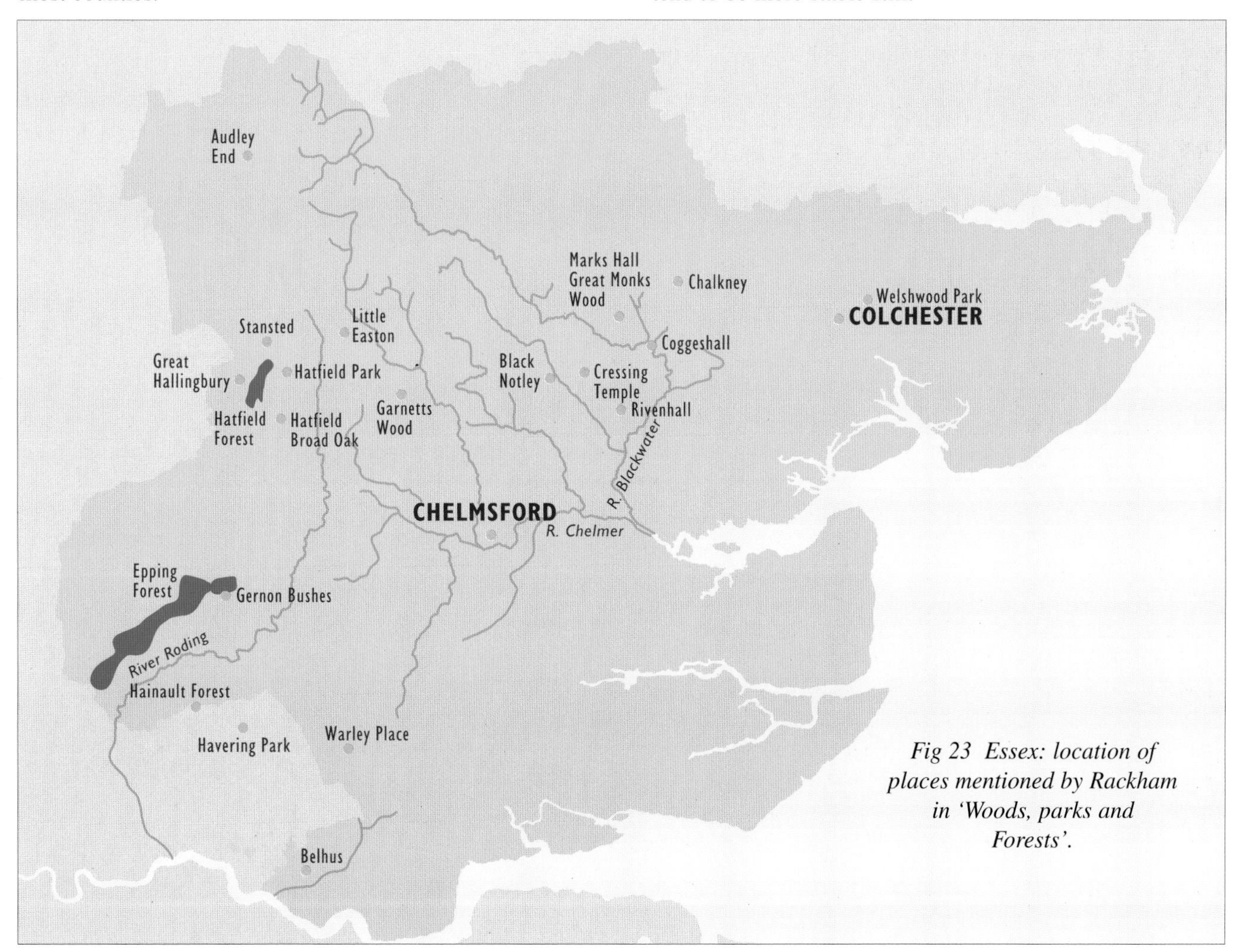

Fig 23 Essex: location of places mentioned by Rackham in 'Woods, parks and Forests'.

CRESSING TEMPLE AND THE ESSEX LIMEWOODS

Essex woods can be divided into four geographical regions based on the trees in them. The limewood region (Fig 24), though not the most extensive, is one of the most important historically and is an example for Essex woodland generally.

In the mid-north of Essex, extending into Suffolk, the commonest woodland tree is the small-leaved lime or pry, *Tilia cordata,* found in almost every ancient wood. In the rest of Essex it hardly occurs at all. It does not form the whole of each wood, but occurs in a mosaic with other types of woodland, such as ash-hazel, elm and hornbeam. (Each medieval wood is unique.) It is very gregarious: a wood that is 60% lime may consist of 60 acres of pure limewood and 40 acres of other trees. Lime most often occurs on loess soils, but is not choosy about soil. It has very little power to colonise and seldom gets into newly-formed woodland; nor does it normally occur outside woods; nor, until very recently, have people planted it (Rackham 1980).

Among classic Essex limewoods–indeed, among the finest in England–are Great and Little Monk Wood and Grange Wood, the woods of Coggeshall Abbey. King's Wood, the wood of the Knights Templars at Cressing (its name recalling the original royal gift in the 12th century)was destroyed in the 18th century (Hunter 1993b). It was probably a limewood; lime is in the surviving fragment, Lanham's Wood, which projects into Rivenhall. Chalkney Wood, the wood of the earls of Oxford at Earl's Colne, haunted by the ghosts of wild swine, is perhaps the best-known limewood in England.

Pry, like most trees, has traditionally been coppiced. It is not killed by cutting it down, but sprouts and yields a perpetual succession of crops of underwood. Until the 1970s Great Monk Wood was cut every 15 years or so in the ancient manner with edge tools by an old woodman who, I am told, used to supply loads of pry logs (under that name) to Diana Dors. Coppicing of pry can be seen by the public in Chalkney Wood and in Garnett's Wood. After chestnut, pry is the most reliable of coppicing trees. It rarely gets a chance to grow from seed; the coppice stools go on living virtually for ever, and in woods like the Monk Woods or Chalkney reach an immense size.

Limewoods, like most kinds of woodland, have a scatter of oak trees, grown for timber, among the stools. Pry is intensely competitive; it is a minor mystery how the succession of oaks was maintained, as somehow it was.

Essex limewoods have the usual characteristics of ancient woodland, such as ancient coppice stools (Rackham 1990). They are surrounded and sometimes subdivided by woodbanks. Often they preserve features of an earlier period of land use. The Rivenhall woods are fragments of a big wood in the 18th century, but this wood had a complex earlier history, perhaps connected with Rivenhall Roman villa, and numerous banks underlie the fragments. Chalkney Wood is bisected by a hollow-way, probably an Iron Age road, bordered by what may be the earliest woodbanks yet identified.

Plants characteristic of ancient limewoods include the pry-tree itself, service, anemones, herb paris and many others. (None of the Essex limewoods has oxlip, although a few

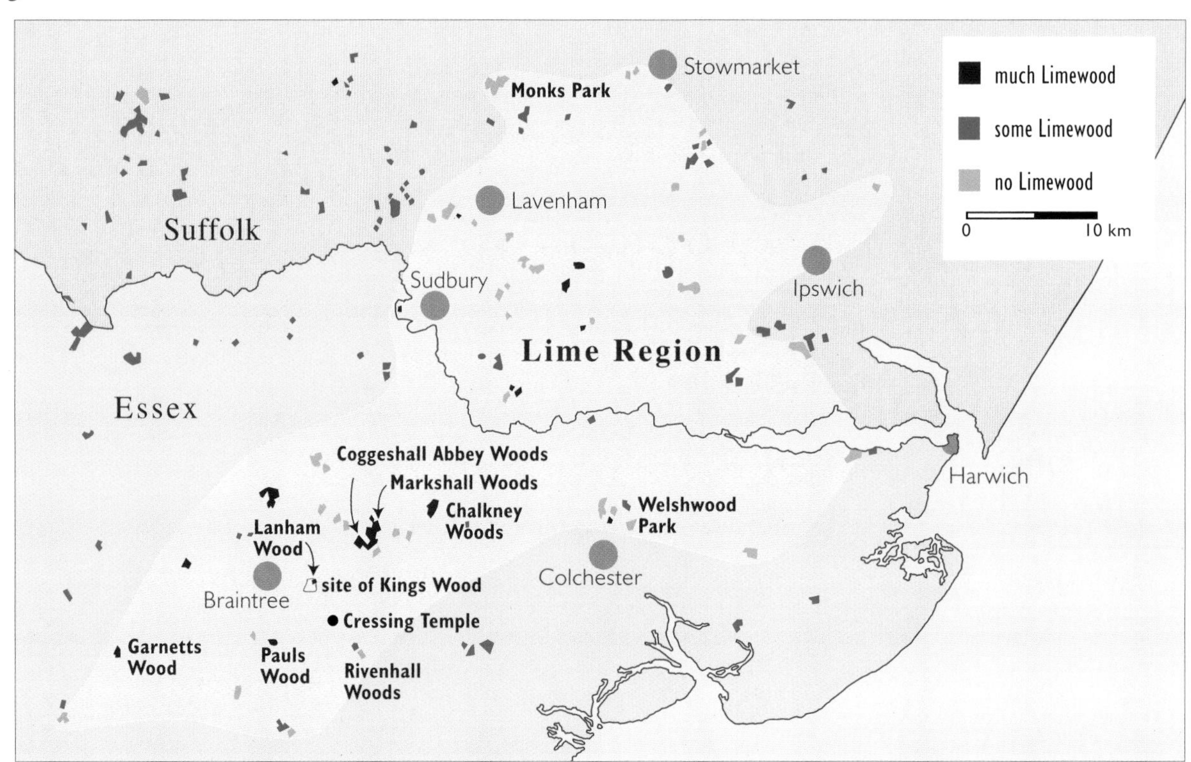

Fig 24 Extant ancient limewoods of Essex and Suffolk.

of the Suffolk outliers do.) Ancient woods develop a characteristic coppicing flora every time the wood is cut down. The coppicing floras of limewoods are distinctive, including red campion, wild raspberry, the creeping St John's wort *Hypericum humifusum,* and, in Chalkney Wood, the rare sedge *Carex strigosa.*

HISTORY OF LIMEWOODS

Limewoods go back to the wildwood of Mesolithic times. Pollen analysis shows that in the Atlantic Period, down to 4500 BC, lime was the commonest tree in lowland England, taking its low pollen production into account. This was so not only in the present limewood areas but also in regions such as south Essex from which lime is now absent. Wildwood was not dominated monotonously by lime but was a mosaic of woodland types, much as ancient woods are today (Rackham 1980).

Lime declined over a long period, beginning in the Neolithic or Bronze Age. It probably grew on fertile soils which were worth converting into farmland. In some way wood-pasture seems to have been unfavourable to it. Once exterminated, it does not recover lost ground. However, lime is extremely difficult to kill–even digging it up is not a certain method. It is a great mystery why its decline should have been so uneven. In most areas, such as five-sixths of Essex, it has disappeared completely. In some areas, for no apparent reason, it is still as abundant within ancient woods as it has ever been.

The rare, distinctive and romantic pry has attracted more than its fair share of attention. Paul's Wood, Black Notley, had an Anglo-Saxon name, Lindris, from *linde* 'pry-tree' and *hris* 'underwood'. A thousand years later it still has giant stools of pry. This is one of many Essex place-names alluding to the tree. In the 15th century Simon Benninck, an artist in Flanders, painted a wonderful landscape miniature of a countryside like Essex: a hilly land, with thick hedges full of trees, small fields, scattered farmsteads and, in the foreground, a wood of pry, in which areas of one, two, and about twenty years' growth are discernible. He even has coppicing plants like broom and brambles in the one-year panel.

Essex limewoods come into book-learning, in Turner's *Herball* in 1568. He says:

> 'It growth very plenteously in Essekes in a parke within two miles of Coltchestir in the possession of one Maister Bogges.'

The place is probably Welshwood Park, where lime grew until recently.

The agricultural poetaster Thomas Tusser in 1573 exhorts his readers to:

> 'Lop poplar and sallow, elme, maple, and prie,
> well saued from cattle, till Sommer to lie.'

As a Rivenhall man, Tusser would probably have encountered pry in Lanham's Wood.

Soon after, Roger Harlackenden, squire of Earl's Colne in succession to the earls of Oxford, was selling loads of 'prye wood' out of Chalkney. Some areas of this wood then consisted wholly of pry, some were partly pry and partly hornbeam and other trees, and part had no pry–much as the wood is now. Pry was valuable because its bast, the inner bark, was used for cordage and string (Rackham 1980, 250).

Fig 25 The Barley Barn, Cressing Temple: (a) south-west corner post, and (b) a reconstruction of the non-woodland oak that it would have come from.

John Ray, earliest and greatest of English botanical scientists, also came from pry country, at Black Notley. He invented the name 'small-leaved Lime', and says it was 'frequent in woods and hedges in Essex and Sussex, also in the county of Lincoln and elsewhere' (Ray 1690). It is now uncommon in hedges and rare in Sussex.

THE BARNS AND WOOD OF THE KNIGHTS TEMPLARS

The three great and ancient barns, Cressing Temple Barley Barn and Wheat Barn and Coggeshall Grange Barn, are all probably connected with limewoods. Lime itself, not being a timber tree, now forms no part of them. As underwood it may have contributed to wattle-and-daub in the walls, as it does in Lavenham in the Suffolk limewood area, but none of this survives. It will, however, by its competition have shaped the growth of the oaks from which the barns are built.

The Barley Barn is a complex structure which has passed through several phases of alteration. Enough of the original timbers of c. 1200 remain, either in situ or reused, to enable us to reconstruct the original timber content. As in later medieval buildings, every post, tie-beam, rafter and so on represents the whole of a log hewn to shape out of the smallest tree that would serve the purpose. This is clearly seen in the small part of the original high-roof that remains in place (Rackham 1993).

The Barley Barn, according to my analysis, originally contained some 480 oaks. Twelve of these, the great posts, are from a different source from the others. Each post, 16 inches square and 21 feet long, is hewn from a fast-grown, crooked, branchy and tapering oak, which grew up without competition from neighbours (Fig 25); it seems to be a hedgerow tree from the 12th-century countryside. Although not particularly big by modern standards, these trees were barely big enough for the job. The carpenter tried to create one sharp straight corner on the angle of each post facing the middle of the barn, but the less conspicuous angles are waney, irregular and rounded, where they intersect the curved surface of the tree.

Fig 26 A woodland oak, growing among lime underwood, of the kind that might have provided one of the lesser timbers of the Barley barn, Cressing Temple.

All the other timbers appear to come from woodland. They represent smallish trees, typically some 10 inches in diameter, not very straight, though less crooked than the posts. They imply a wood in which the oaks had a moderate degree of competition from lime or other underwood between them (Fig 26). Above about 18 feet many of the oaks taper markedly; evidently the underwood ceased at this height, allowing the oaks to branch out. A small number of trees, forming tie-beams and arcade plates, are bigger or longer than this, but probably represent the natural variation among oaks growing in the same wood.

The Wheat Barn, some 70 years younger than the Barley Barn, is similar in general construction, but differs in the carpentry details and has been less altered. It represents about 470 oaks. Here, too, the great posts form a separate category of fast-grown, branchy trees. Although the posts are somewhat smaller, 14 inches square, it was evidently difficult to find twelve matching trees. They are placed so that the best corners face the middle of the barn. The most crooked posts are in the darkest corners, and one of these, at the south-east corner, was apparently rotten before the tree was cut down. The smaller timbers are less crooked than in the Barley Barn. If they are from the same site they imply a change in woodland structure between the building of the two barns: the underwood (for example, lime) had become more vigorous and was competing more strongly with the oaks. More competition still is implied by the oaks used in the later medieval rebuildings of the high-roof of the Coggeshall Barn and of most of the high-roof of the Barley Barn.

A great barn was an awesome architectural achievement and not just a workaday store. What does it represent in terms of timber supply and consumption? These barns are the grandest buildings that could be built, with difficulty, from the ordinary oaks of woods and hedges. Anything bigger, such as cathedral roofs or the works of the Tower of London, called for outsize trees from special sources such as the Forest of Dean.

I have estimated that the Barley Barn represents 50 years' growth of timber oaks on 11 acres of woodland, at a reasonable balance between timber and underwood. The Wheat Barn represents about three-quarters of this. The barns would thus have been well within the capacity of the Knights Templars' woodland. Having 110 acres of wood, they could (had they nothing else to do) have built one Barley Barn every five years, or one Wheat Barn every four years, for ever. In the 18th century the Honeywells, owners of the Markshall limewoods, were embarrassed by having to do almost this. They had to find enough uses on the estate to keep up with the growth of oaks in their woods, since an eccentric forebear had made a will forbidding them to sell any timber (ERO).

WOODED FORESTS

Wood-pasture involves an inherent contradiction: the shade of the trees suppresses the pasture plants and the grazing animals eat the young shoots that would grow into future trees. Wood-pastures were traditionally different from woodland, usually less dense and with a savanna-like appearance; this can still be seen on an immense scale in the *montados* of Portugal and the *dehesas* of Spain. The trees are usually pollarded, so that the young shoots shall be out of reach of livestock.

Wood-pasture commons, abundant in Anglo-Saxon times, tended to lose ground to coppice-woods (Rackham 1990). One of the few surviving in Essex which was not part of a Forest is Gernon Bushes in Theydon Garnon, now reverted to woodland but with pollarded (rather than coppiced) hornbeams betraying its savanna-like origin.

The wood-pasture scene was transformed by the Normans' interest in deer as semi-domesticated animals. The Norman kings set up the Forest of Essex in the early 12th century. They introduced fallow deer, as new to England then as ostriches are now. They gave themselves the right to kill and eat the deer, to set up Forest Law, to create jobs in the bureaucracy that administered it, and to pocket the fines (Rackham 1990).

Forest Law was supposed to protect both deer and their habitat. In theory a man could be fined for felling his own wood anywhere in Essex. In reality (alas for the historian!) it was tacitly agreed that ordinary woodcutting (for use or sale) and timber-felling did not breach Forest Law. The Knights Templars were not fined for building their barns, nor was the tilemaker fined for cutting the wood needed to fire the roof tiles. In practice Forest Law operated mainly around the five physical Forests where the deer actually lived–those of Waltham, Hainault, Hatfield, Writtle and Colchester. Each of these was a large common, and each had its own Forestal bureaucracy.

Waltham and Hainault Forests survived almost unaltered into the 19th century. Waltham still exists today as Epping Forest; its shape and extent are little changed, but its character has been much altered for lack of browsing and woodcutting (Rackham 1978). Hainault was reduced to a fragment in the 1850s. Colchester Forest consisted of heaths and woods north of the town; the heaths have long vanished and the woods, though notable, are not much different from other ancient woodland.

Hatfield Forest displays wood-pasture at its greatest elaboration in Europe. It is divided into coppices and plains. The coppices are demarcated woods, each with its name and boundary bank; they were felled on a cycle theoretically of 18 years, and then fenced to keep out deer and other livestock until the wood had grown again. The plains are areas of grassland accessible to animals at all times, in which the trees are pollarded. New trees arise in the plains in the protection of thorny scrub. Other aspects include a medieval Forest lodge, a 17th-century rabbit warren with its keeper's cottage, and Roman and Iron Age sites from long before the Forest was heard of. Details reflect the fortunes and interrelations of the parties involved: the king as owner of the deer; the landowners; the lord of the manor; the various kinds of commoners; and the hereditary woodwards. The deer are now probably as numerous as they have ever been. Hatfield Forest has belonged to the National Trust since 1924, and its story includes the varying fortunes of a site under seventy years of conservationist ownership (Rackham 1989). The Trust has recently made a determined effort to recover all the working aspects of the Forest, including returning sheep to the plains and starting new pollards.

Writtle Forest, although much less well known, is a compartmented wood-pasture in the hornbeam region of Essex. It still belongs to the family to whom Edward VI granted it. It was organised similarly to Hatfield, and is nearly as well preserved. It too is a survival of European-wide importance.

PARKS

The Normans not only scattered deer around the landscape in Forests; they kept them in parks, confined by a deer-proof fence called a pale. A park was a private deer-farm. It had a social rather than economic significance; venison was a special meat, eaten at feasts, which mere money could not buy (Rackham 1990).

Essex had what may have been the prototype deer park, mentioned in a will in 1045, at Ongar. The perimeter of this vast park, which would have been created for the native red deer, and much of its interior woodland remained until the Age of Destruction in the 1950s. With this exception, parks date from Norman times and were mostly for fallow deer. By 1300 there were at least 160 parks in Essex, more per square mile than in any county except Hertfordshire.

Parks could be uncompartmented with pollard trees on the Epping Forest model, or compartmented on the Hatfield Forest model. The classic examples of both are in Suffolk: Staverton Park near Orford, with several thousand ancient pollard oaks, and Monks' Park, part of the Bradfield Woods near Bury St Edmund's, with internal banks dividing the coppices. Essex parks are rather fragmentary, often only an outline (a rectangle with rounded corners) on the map, perhaps with the place-name Park Farm. Hatfield Park, to the east of Hatfield Forest, is an example. It was a royal park, probably used to hold stocks of deer out of the Forest for ready consumption. Havering Park, similarly attached to Hainault Forest, was a major source of deer for the table royal.

A rarity was the swine-park formed from Chalkney Wood, in which the de Veres, earls of Oxford, 'bredd and mayntayned wylde Swyne', as a 16th-century map relates (Rackham 1990, frontispiece). The wild boar, long extinct as a free-living animal, was kept as an honorary deer in a few, very grand parks. The de Veres were attached to him, and liked to be thought of as swine (Vere being misread as the Latin *verres*, a boar).

There were three later periods of park-making: Tudor, Georgian, and Victorian. The Tudor park fashion was started by Henry VIII. 'Queen Elizabeth's Hunting Lodge', the last survivor of Henry's courtly timber-framed buildings, was built by his carpenter in 1543. It was the 'standing', or observation tower, in a park which Henry made (briefly and illegally) out of part of Epping Forest, whose landowning rights he had confiscated from Waltham Abbey. Parks, which had been mainly deer-farms in the Middle Ages, now took on a new function as the scene of ceremonial hunts, culminating in a gory kill enacted in view of the standing (Rackham 1990, 158–9).

Tudor and Stuart parks are well represented in Essex, although not well studied. The 20th century has been unkind to them, with the destruction of the parks of Markshall (now being rehabilitated by the Markshall Trust), Little Easton, and Belhus. Parks by now often had a third function as the picturesque environment of mansions and villas. In places one can trace deliberate design, anticipating the designer landscapes of the 18th century. An example are the giant pollard oaks regularly spaced round the edge of the park of the Barringtons at Hatfield Priory, in Hatfield Broad Oak.

Designer parks of the classic period, *c.* 1690–1810, are dealt with in another paper in this volume (Cowell). Of course they were not normally created out of nothing; they incorporated trees and woods already on the site. They might grow out of an existing medieval park, as at Great Hallingbury, or a random sample of 17th-century countryside with a multitude of pollard trees. Often there seems to have been a definite attempt to imitate a medieval park; the result today is that an 18th-century park, such as Ickworth, Suffolk, may contain many trees older than the park.

Of Victorian parks the full story has yet to be told. Only two in Essex, Warley Place and Ham House, are well known. However, most 18th-century parks have a 19th-century phase. The Victorians loved bizarre and exotic trees like horsechestnut and wellingtonia. Being tidy-minded, they often destroyed earlier work; at Audley End little even of the 18th century remains. They could, however, preserve much of the ecology and archaeology of the previous landscape. Hatfield Forest, the subject of an Enclosure Act in 1857, was not destroyed as Hainault Forest had been: John VII Archer Houblon, on acquiring the freehold, incorporated the entire Forest, little altered, into Great Hallingbury Park. Parks are of value not only as conscious works of art but for what they unintentionally preserved.

ON THE WORD 'PRY'

The derivation is unknown; the tree is known in most European languages by some variant either of *lind* or *tilia.* The term is still current. I was once lecturing in south-west England and uttered this word, whereupon a lady came to me afterwards and said, 'Yes, I know about pry trees; where I was brought up there was a whole wood of them at the bottom of the garden'. 'And where might that be, madam?' 'At Pattiswick in Essex.' She was referring to Great Monk Wood.

5

Medieval and later rural settlement in Essex: a new survey from a national perspective

by Stuart Wrathmell

Between the late 1940s and the early 1980s students of medieval rural settlement focused their attention largely on the sites of nucleated settlements–on deserted medieval villages (Roberts & Wrathmell 1998, 110-111). True, there was from 1971 a separate research group devoted to the study of moated sites that, in some counties like Essex, though by no means all, frequently marked the location of isolated medieval homesteads (Aberg 1978, fig 1), and there had been localised studies of single medieval farmsteads and small hamlets in parts of upland England, notably in the south-west and the north (Linehan 1966; Addyman *et al* 1963; Faull & Moorhouse 1981, 601-606). By and large, however, dispersed hamlets and farmsteads had been ignored by archaeologists, despite the fact that a significant number of English counties in both north and south, and east and west, had been dominated by such forms of settlement in the Middle Ages and in later centuries, and had contained relatively few nucleations.

The division of England into regions of nucleated and dispersed settlement was recognised in print as early as the 16th century. In 1577 William Harrison noted that some parts of England were characterised by 'champaine ground', areas of classic open-field agriculture, where dwellings were grouped into villages, while other regions were 'woodland countries' characterised by dwellings which were 'scattered abroad' (quoted in Homans 1941, 25). Almost sixty years ago George C Homans explored this contrast in more detail, listing the counties which were dominated by dispersed settlement with enclosed fields in a woodland context, and those dominated by villages with open-field systems (Homans, 12-21). His mapping of 'champion' England relied partly on Slater's map of open fields enclosed by act of parliament, showing that they were 'concentrated in a band running diagonally across England from the North Sea coast through the Midlands to the Channel' (Homans, 19). This distribution finds support in the plotting of deserted medieval villages recorded up to 1968 (Beresford & Hurst 1971, fig 13), which, with a few very interesting exceptions, is largely confined to the same area. In 1986 Oliver Rackham gave greater definition to this band by filling in the blank areas on either side of it: recording place-names with Old English elements indicative of woodland settings (Rackham 1986, fig 8.7). He identified these as 'ancient countrysides' of winding, deeply hollowed lanes, thick hedges and scattered farmsteads, to be contrasted with the 'planned countrysides' of large villages and enclosed, former open-field landscapes (Rackham, 4-5).

The subject of this paper is a further stage in the national mapping of regional variation. It began some five years ago, at the request of English Heritage's Monuments Protection Programme, and has been carried out by the writer and by Brian Roberts. By the late 1980s deserted medieval villages formed the bulk of medieval settlement sites which had been given statutory protection as Scheduled Ancient Monuments; yet the work of Harold Fox (1983), Peter Warner (1987), Christopher Dyer (1990a) and others had begun to shift the balance of academic interest towards the large areas of England where such nucleated forms had always been uncommon, and where the protection of hamlet sites, the remains of isolated farms and the like was vital if the regional character of medieval rural settlement was to be preserved.

Two criteria were established at the beginning of the mapping project. The first was that in order to provide a comprehensive and reliable picture of rural settlement, the base line would have to be the first edition, one-inch Ordnance Survey maps of the mid-19th century. Though a number of medieval sources listed rural communities more or less systematically, for example the 13th and early 14th-century Lay Subsidies (see for instance Glasscock 1975), they did not record the forms of settlement occupied by these communities: some nucleated forms may be inferred from later cartographic evidence and settlement remains; some dispersed elements may be inferred from the place surnames of taxpayers (e.g. Fraser 1968, 3), but none of this is either sufficiently comprehensive and reliable or rapidly accessible. The difficulties attached particularly to the recording of dispersed sites, and the role of early 19th-century maps in such recording, has been discussed in a much more detailed and thorough regional study of medieval rural settlements in Warwickshire (Dyer 1996, 121).

The second criterion concerned the method of mapping data from the Ordnance Survey maps. Nucleated settlements could be marked individually, with dots of sizes graded to represent the varying sizes of nucleations shown on the maps, but it was decided to represent dispersed settlement, both in terms of the size of dispersed elements (a single farmstead, or two, three or four farmsteads clustered together) and in terms of the distances between these elements, through conventional shading. The methodology adopted is being published elsewhere (Roberts & Wrathmell forthcoming); suffice it to say that the more dense the shading, the more intense the dispersion; and across England as a whole there is, reassuringly, an inverse relationship between the density of dispersed settlement and the density of nucleated settlement. Our settlement map, constructed according to a methodology which owes nothing to Harrison, Slater, Homans or Rackham, is clearly in accord with their find-

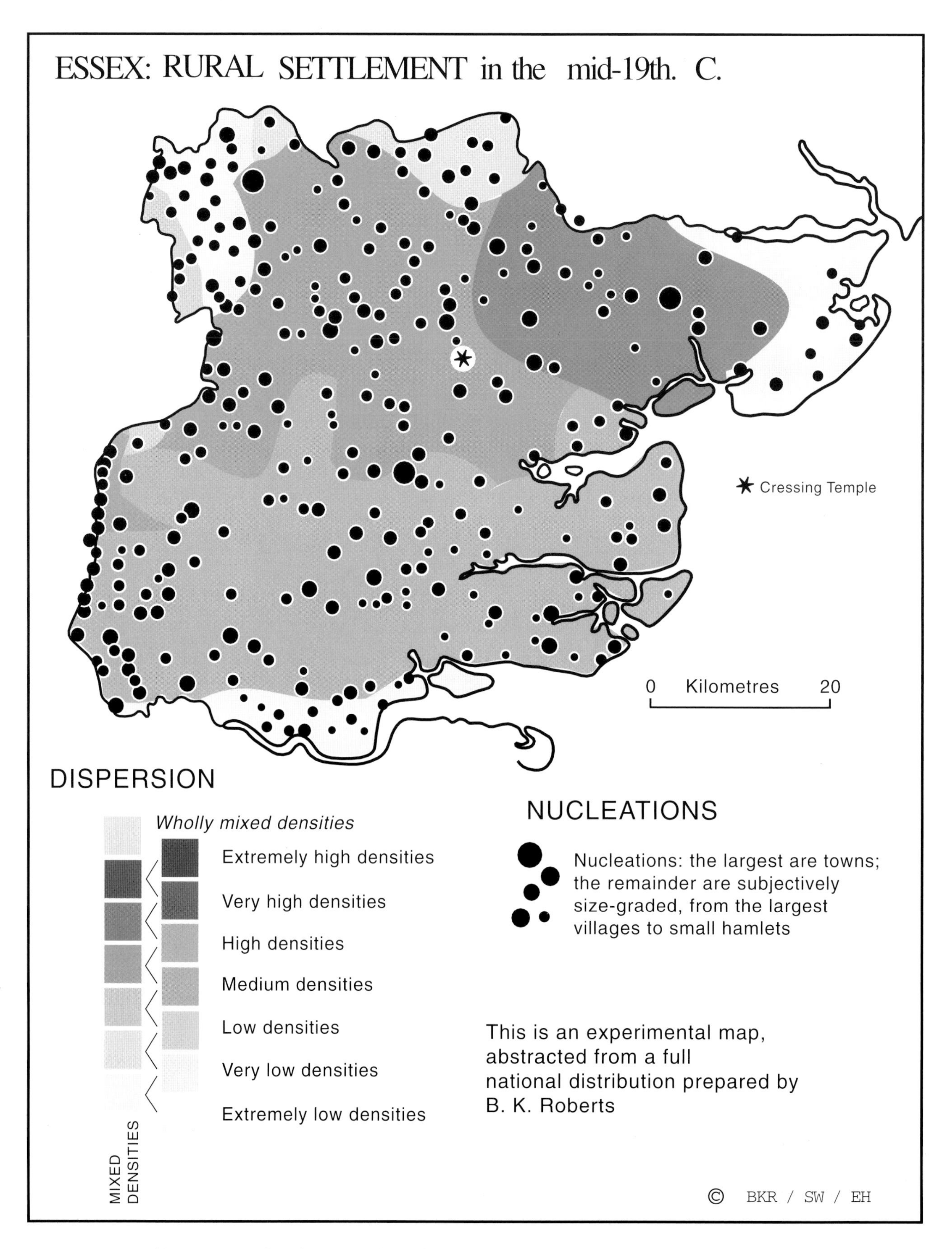

Fig 27 Essex: rural settlement in the mid 19th century (from Roberts & Wrathmell forthcoming).

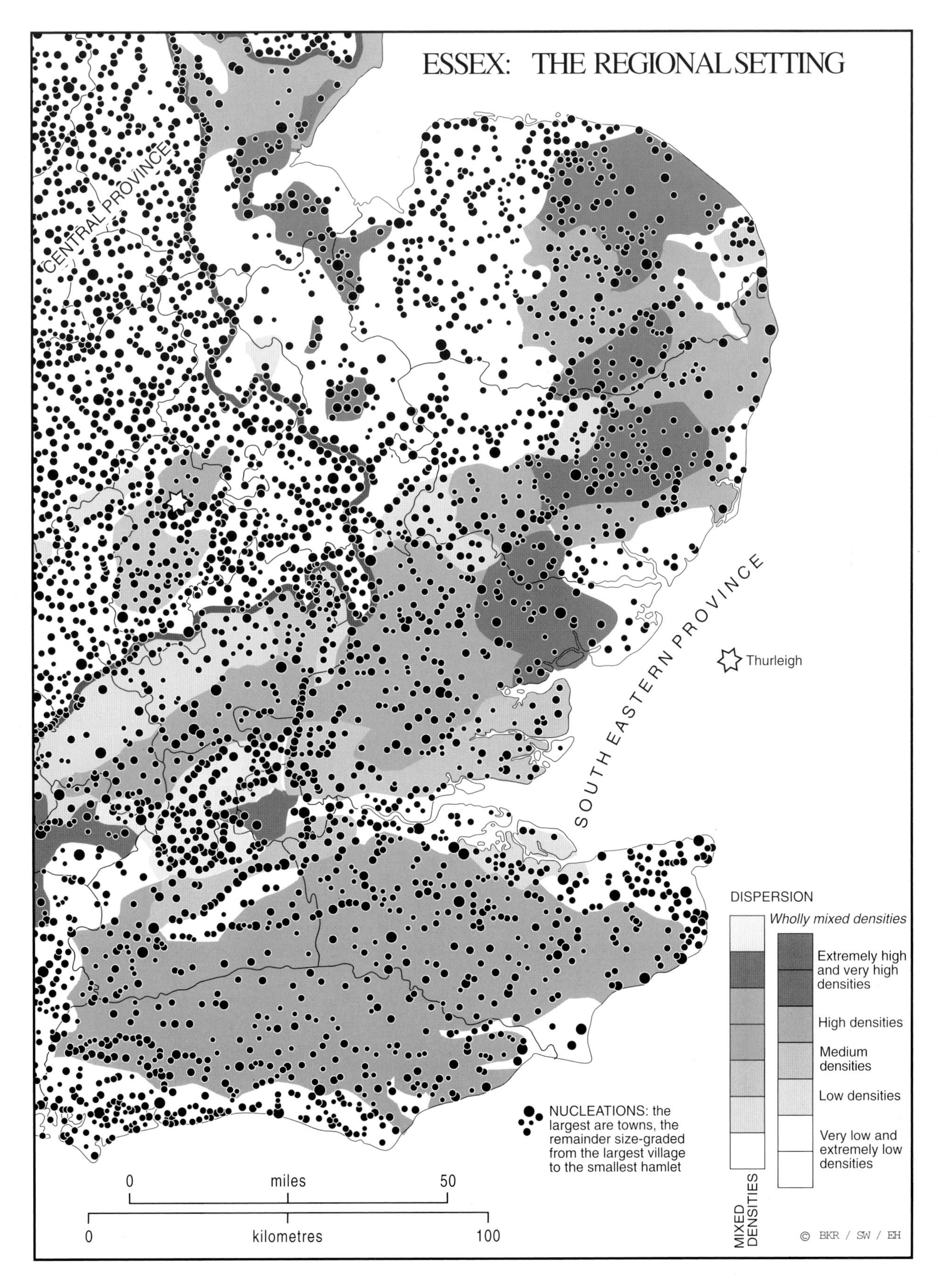

Fig 28 Essex: the regional setting of its settlement patterns (from Roberts & Wrathmell forthcoming).

ings. We have distinguished a Central Province dominated by nucleated settlement, which reflects Homans' 'champion' England, and two other provinces, a South-eastern Province and a Northern and Western Province, dominated by dispersed settlement and corresponding to Rackham's 'ancient' countrysides.

The mapping project has, however, gone much deeper into regional settlement variation, identifying sub-provincial areas and regions on the basis of their detailed mixes of settlement characteristics. Focusing in on such regions provides a vital link between the national picture and regional and local studies which have been, are being or will be carried out by others. In this way, it is hoped that the project will provide an overall framework for regional and local studies. Before it can be accepted in such a role, however, two issues have first to be clarified. The first is whether mid-19th-century settlement data have any real value for researching medieval settlement; and even if they do, the second is whether the patterns which can be observed at a national scale have visibility and meaning at a local level.

Both these questions have been addressed in detail elsewhere (Roberts & Wrathmell 1998, and forthcoming). For present purposes, we can say with regard to the first question that the settlement mixes of some regions in the mid-19th century were then recently acquired characteristics; a remarkable intensity of dispersed settlement in Lancashire, for example, was undoubtedly due to industrial development during the preceding hundred years, and the relatively dense concentrations of nucleations in parts of Nottinghamshire and Derbyshire were the result of coalfield exploitation. On the other hand, some boundaries, including stretches of the western edge of the Central Province, can be traced with confidence back to Anglo-Saxon times and possibly earlier still. In general terms the regions defined on the basis of 19th-century data seem to have had considerable longevity despite changing characteristics: their attributes in remote times, which distinguished them from adjacent regions, caused them to follow distinct trajectories through time, as Harold Fox has argued in relation to the Wolds (1989, 96-101).

With regard to the visibility of these regions at the local level, relevant published studies have been examined for detail which might either support or contradict the variations identified at the national scale. One of the most interesting discoveries was a study of medieval settlement in northern Bedfordshire, published by Tony Brown and Chris Taylor (1989). The area in question is firmly within the Central Province of open-field countryside and nucleated villages. Yet our map of 19th-century settlement shows that it contained several patches with abnormally high levels of dispersed settlement. The investigations of Brown and Taylor had been centred, quite fortuitously, upon one of these patches, and they had identified Thurleigh and adjacent areas as a landscape of dispersed settlement with ancient enclosed fields and relatively small cores of open-field land. This group of medieval settlements had found an echo in the mid-19th-century settlement map.

One of the principal research topics in rural settlement studies in the past twenty years has been the origins of nucleated settlements and associated 'regular' two- and three-field open-field systems: what circumstances may have led to the emergence of such structures during the period between the 9th and 12th centuries? Or to put the question another way, why did such structures fail to dominate the regions outside what we have termed the Central Province? The origin of open-field systems is a matter on which there has been considerable disagreement. We can take, from a single volume of papers, Fox's suggestion 'that in the Midland heartlands a decline in the availability of pasture was the stimulus which had led to the adoption of the two- and three-field system' (Fox 1981, 94), and compare this with Campbell's statement that 'the physical development of these alternative [i.e. non-Midland] field systems often matched, and sometimes even exceeded, that of their Midland counterparts: waste [permanent common pasture] was virtually eliminated...' (Campbell 1981, 112-113). It would be difficult to reconcile such contradictory statements, were it not for the fact that Fox used Devon for his comparanda, while Campbell used Norfolk: the differences between the Central Province and the Northern and Western Province on the one hand, and the Central Province and the South-eastern Province on the other, need not have been due to the same set of factors in each case.

One of the most significant differences between the core East Midlands area of the Central Province and the rest of England is, our mapping suggests, the relatively small amounts of woodland which remained there in the later pre-Conquest period. A replotting of Domesday woodland from Darby (1977, fig 64) and of Anglo-Saxon place-names indicative of settlement in a woodland context from Rackham (1986, fig 8.7) suggests that much of that area was devoid of significant areas of woodland in the 9th to 11th centuries, whereas Norfolk, Suffolk, Essex and other parts of the South-eastern Province retained much greater amounts of woodland (Roberts & Wrathmell forthcoming).

As we therefore focus on Essex we find a county which is firmly within the pattern attributed to the South-eastern Province: a county which seems to have had relatively large areas of woodland remaining in the later Anglo-Saxon period, contained relatively few examples of the classic open-field systems of the 'Midland' type, and was dominated by dispersed rather than nucleated settlement. Figure 27 shows the densities of dispersion and points of nucleation as they were recorded in the mid-19th century. There are several zones marked by low intensities of dispersed settlement as measured on a national scale: in the north-east of the county, in the south and in the north-west corner. This last area is a good example of the value of taking a national perspective on county distributions, for it can be seen in Figure 28 that this is not merely some small isolated group of nucleated settlements; it is a tongue of the Central Province stretching southwards along the valley of the Cam between Great

Chesterford and Saffron Walden. Its distinctive character, with nucleated settlements and former open fields, has been observed in local documentary and field studies by Tom Williamson. He has contrasted it with the pattern elsewhere in north-west Essex, where farmsteads and hamlets were more evenly dispersed and had more consolidated landholdings (Williamson 1986, 120-21; see also Hunter 1995, 138).

The dispersed settlement of one part of Essex has been studied in considerable detail by John Hunter (1993b; 1995), and it seems appropriate in the context of this volume to conclude with some thoughts on the landscape of Cressing itself. His research suggests that medieval Cressing can be divided into two parts. There was a northern zone of dispersed settlement, characterised by small farms with shared fields, woodlands, greens and moated sites. To the south was an area of open field associated with the demesne of the Templars, centred on Cressing Temple itself (Hunter 1993b, 32-4 and fig 9; 1995, 133). Furthermore, the northern 'peasant' zone is regarded as an earlier element, having been in existence in late Saxon times at a period when the Templars' demesne was unenclosed common pasture (Hunter 1995, 138).

A comparison of Figures 27 and 28 will enable the reader to locate Cressing within the more generalised shading of Figure 28, and to identify a small patch of similar shading to the north-west, isolated within the Central Province of dense nucleations and minimal dispersion. This patch is the zone centred on Thurleigh in north Bedfordshire, referred to above. A detailed study of Thurleigh's medieval settlement and land use has revealed a remarkably similar pattern to that identified at Cressing: a demesne centred on the 'Bury Farm' site at Thurleigh, with an associated area of open field, and around it a more wooded landscape of dispersed settlement in the form of isolated moats, small hamlets and irregular enclosed fields (Brown & Taylor 1989, 63-8). Thus the construction of a national framework for settlement diversity, albeit based upon mid-19th-century sources, can be used to explore local medieval variation in a more structured fashion, by providing a broader context for detailed landscape studies, and by providing a rationale for comparing regions within a county such as Essex with regions elsewhere in the country which had, *prima facie,* similar settlement characteristics.

6
The 16th and 17th centuries: manors, mansions, parks and fields

by David Andrews and Pat Ryan

INTRODUCTION

The 16th and 17th centuries were, as is well known and recognised, a period of transition from the Middle Ages to the modern age. It is not, however, a period normally associated with great changes in the landscape. In parts of the Midlands at this time wholesale enclosure took place and arable land was converted into pasture for sheep, but this was not so in the south-east. Nor were there alterations of the type wrought by the agricultural revolution and the parliamentary enclosures of the 18th century, whilst the advances in garden design have left less in the way of relict landscapes than those of later ages. Landscape evolution is a continuum, the changes effected by one age being erased by another, so that many changes can seem less notable than they were, and identifying and defining them can be difficult.

One significant change that did occur at this period was the construction of many 'great houses' in brick, and these will be the starting point of this paper, which is based to a large extent on research carried out over the last 13–25 years at many Essex manors and sites (see Ryan 1996). It draws in particular on work carried out at Cressing Temple, which has proved a most valuable laboratory for investigating Essex history and archaeology; on the in-depth study of the adjacent parish of Rivenhall by the Rodwells (1993); and on the well-known late 16th and early 17th-century maps made by the Walker family of Hanningfield (Edwards & Newton 1984).

BRICK MANSIONS

The 16th century saw a notable redistribution of wealth within society and the appearance of many 'new men' who amassed considerable fortunes. Factors in this process, which we need not examine in detail, were a generally prosperous economy and the rise of new industries, the rapid development of a more elaborate government machine and bureaucracy offering opportunities for advancement and enrichment, and the dissolution of the monasteries in 1536-

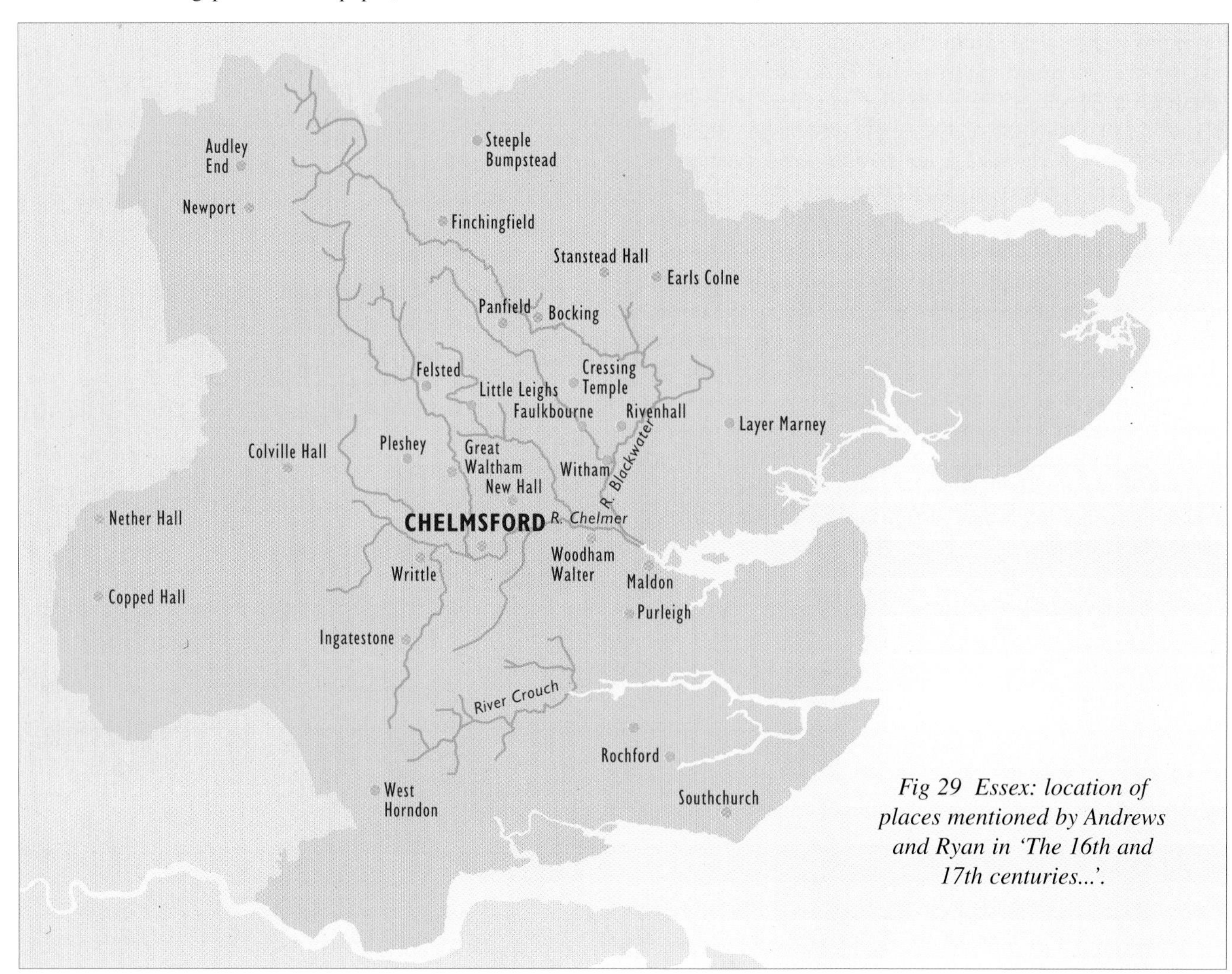

Fig 29 Essex: location of places mentioned by Andrews and Ryan in 'The 16th and 17th centuries...'.

40. Those who had profited in government or in trade and business in the City of London found Essex a convenient place for a country retreat. This had been true long before the 16th century and is still true today. Defoe was particularly impressed by this phenomenon as he journeyed out east from the City of London where he found that the villages were 'increased in buildings to a strange degree, within the compass of about 20 or 30 years past at the most.' He observed too that 'the increase is, generally speaking, of handsome large houses, from £20 a year to £60, very few under £20 a year; being chiefly for the habitations of the richest citizens, such as either are able to keep two houses, one in the country and one in the city', and observed that 'there are as many gentlemen of good fortune and families as I believe can be met in so narrow a compass' (Defoe 1724).

Great houses built entirely in brick began to appear in the 15th century. Earlier in that century Lewis John, a London vintner and goldsmith, originally from Wales, who benefited from the patronage of members of the royal family, imparked 300 acres at West Horndon and built a new brick house there. His compatriot John Montgomery, who was at Agincourt with Henry V, purchased the manor of Faulkbourn and enlarged the old house in brick.

Another striking example is Nether Hall, Roydon, built by Thomas Colt, whose family came from Carlisle. He prospered as a London lawyer during the complicated politics of the Wars of the Roses, being allied to Warwick the Kingmaker and serving Edward IV. It was probably in the 1450s that Colt acquired his sub-manor in a low-lying area of the valley of the River Lea, where we find a classic medieval manorial layout of the more highly planned type, comprising two rectangular enclosures, one with house and outbuildings and the other being the farmyard. The farmhouse may have preceded Colt by a little, or may have been built when he first acquired the manor. Whatever the case it did not satisfy his aspirations for long. In the 1460s he built himself a miniature castle on a new axis, just to the north of the old enclosure, and surrounded it with a moat. Traces of narrow ridge and furrow indicate that it was laid out in former open fields (Fig 30).

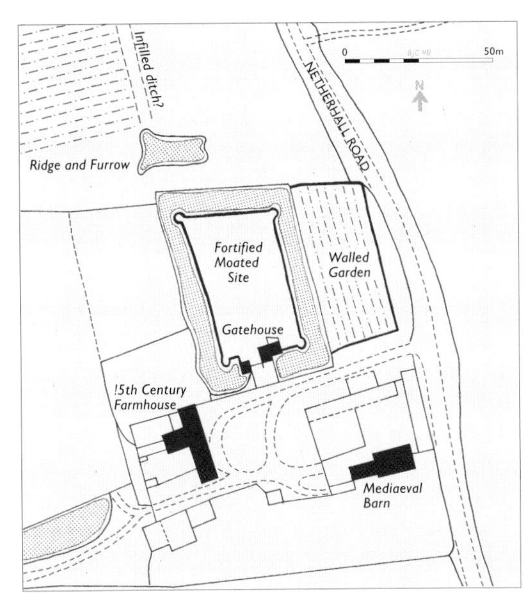

Fig 30 Nether Hall, Roydon: the brick-built moated castle was laid out in the open fields at right angles to the axis of the older manorial buildings, represented by the timber-framed house and barn.

Few medieval manorial sites in Essex are well preserved, but we know that they could be architecturally pretentious. Southchurch Hall, for example (now in Southend-on-Sea), had a chapel and other buildings in stone, a moat with a palisade and stone abutments for a trestle bridge with a drawbridge. The layout of the buildings is not well understood, but the constraints of the moated site would have imposed a degree of regularity upon it. Typically a manorial site consisted of a predictable suite of buildings–hall, kitchen, brewhouse, dairy and so on–which were disposed in a not necessarily predictable fashion round the manorial enclosure. This can be seen in our reconstruction of Cressing Temple *c.*1300 (Fig 31), which contrasts with the regularity of the 15th-century farmhouse and farmyard at Nether Hall. What surprises about Thomas Colt's buildings of the 1460s is not just their regularity or their architectural ambition but their overtly castle-like character, the large-scale use of brick, a new building material, the radical reorganisation of the site and its environs, and the social level at which this was happening–in the sense that he was not a great noble or a holder of one of the great offices of state. In Colt's toy castle we see the fusion of the regularly-planned castle with the grander courtyard houses of the early 16th century at a time when, of course, the castle was in decline, particularly in a country where castle-building had always been restrained by a centralised monarchy. Theoretically a licence to crenellate was needed to erect a fortification; no such licence is known for Nether Hall.

A Fleming was probably in charge of the building work at Nether Hall (a conclusion based on the use of tying rods

Fig 31 Cressing Temple: reconstruction of the Templar manor as it is likely to have appeared c.1300 (by Frank Gardiner).

and lacing timbers, techniques comparable to the use of tying rods in late medieval and early modern brick buildings in what is now Belgium). Dutch and Flemish brickmakers and bricklayers were employed at several sites in Essex in the 15th century, including Rochford Hall, Pleshey Castle, Earl's Colne Priory, Writtle and probably the D'Arcy tower in Maldon (Ryan 1996, 57, 67). Low Countries influence is suspected at a number of other early brick buildings dating from the 1430s to the 1480s. By 1500, however, the expertise to cope with the new building material was well established amongst English craftsmen, and this enabled the proliferation of brick buildings in large quantities, funded by the affluence of a parvenu class of 'new men'.

As the 15th century drew to a close and Henry VII's measures to curb the more military activities of his principal subjects took effect, many of the defensive aspects of the castle-like establishments of men of wealth and position became redundant. The educated men of the 16th century required more privacy; large windows; space for both indoor and outdoor leisure-time pursuits in galleries, gardens, bowling alleys and so forth; and these requirements found expression in the courtyard house. These houses often incorporated individual lodgings for the officers and senior servants of the household. However, history and custom are powerful influences and more than half a century was to pass before the popularity of gatehouses, moats and crenellations, all badges of the medieval ruling class, was to decline and houses with symmetrical fronts which looked outward over the gardens became fashionable.

Essex is particularly well endowed with brick buildings (Ryan 1996). By the end of the 16th century their construction had become a deeply competitive process. Many of these buildings impress because of their enormous size, often having sides of 200 feet or more in length, enclosing a courtyard, and sometimes as many as four courtyards. They were generally taller than previous manorial buildings, and their red brickwork would have made them a conspicuous landscape feature. The impression that these houses would have made on contemporaries is difficult to appreciate today as most are now a fragment of their original size.

By the middle of the 17th century the building of brick houses had filtered well down the social scale to the level of the minor gentry. On the basis of the 1671 hearth tax it is possible to calculate that almost 50% of the 400-odd medieval parishes of Essex had acquired a newly-built or rebuilt manor house with 15 hearths or more, and that at least 33% of these houses were of brick. The size of a house with over 15 hearths is difficult to give with great accuracy for a variety of reasons, but some impression can be obtained from Spains Hall, Finchingfield, today incomplete but still substantial and originally with 20 hearths. The scale and expense of such building works was considerable. John Petre spent 20 years remodelling and enlarging the old house which belonged to Lewis John at West Horndon (or Thorndon as it was later known), at an annual cost of £300-£800 (Ward & Marshall 1972, 2).

Some idea of the exceptional nature of mansion building in Essex can be obtained by making comparisons with the hearth tax returns for Oxfordshire, Bedfordshire and Suffolk. In contrast with Essex's 162 houses with over 15 hearths, Oxfordshire and Bedfordshire could boast only 42 and 30 respectively, whilst Suffolk returned a more respectable total of 118. These totals include only a very modest number of brick buildings. In Bedfordshire there were 3, in Oxfordshire 6, and in Suffolk 40 (Kennett 1984, 8). It is probable that Essex's only rival for the largest number of houses with more than 15 hearths, and built in brick, is Hertfordshire.

Table 5 Hearth tax houses in Essex. Of 162 houses with 15 hearths or more, one-third were built of brick, or brick and stone. The other two-thirds were either timber-framed or it has not been possible to identify of what materials they were built.

Brick houses		**Timber-framed houses, and houses not identified as being of brick**	
Over 100 hearths	2		
50-99 hearths	5	50-99 hearths	1
40-49 hearths	5	40-49 hearths	0
30-39 hearths	9	30-39 hearths	9
20-29 hearths	18	20-29 hearths	18
15-19 hearths	18	16-19 hearths	43
		15 hearths	34
Total	**57**	**Total**	**105**

GARDENS

These buildings represent a reorganisation of the old manorial enclosure within the framework of a vast brick edifice, which constituted in effect a small nucleated settlement, containing a household of 50 or more servants as well as the owner's family. The Walker maps of the late 16th and early 17th centuries reveal the environs of these buildings as being reorganised in a series of rectilinear enclosures, which surprise by being rather haphazard and showing little sign of any concept of landscape design, whatever the pretensions of the main building. These enclosures were often of brick, too, giving them an unprecedented permanence in the landscape. They could be very extensive. One of the better preserved large complexes can be found at Lord Riche's mid-16th-century Rochford Hall where, with the house itself, the walled enclosures cover 6-7 acres (Fig 32). The larger houses might be fronted by an extensive grassed enclosure approached by a brick gatehouse. Sometimes these gatehouses were set in fences and survive today in isolation, as at Colville Hall, White Roding. Other enclosures comprised a hierarchy of pleasure gardens located adjacent to the house and, further away, orchards and farmyards.

Although gardens and gardening have been shown to have been more widespread and highly developed in the Middle Ages than was once thought, it is probably only in the 16th century that the pleasure garden began to permeate lower down the social scale, rather than being the preserve of royalty and the great ecclesiastical and secular lords. The

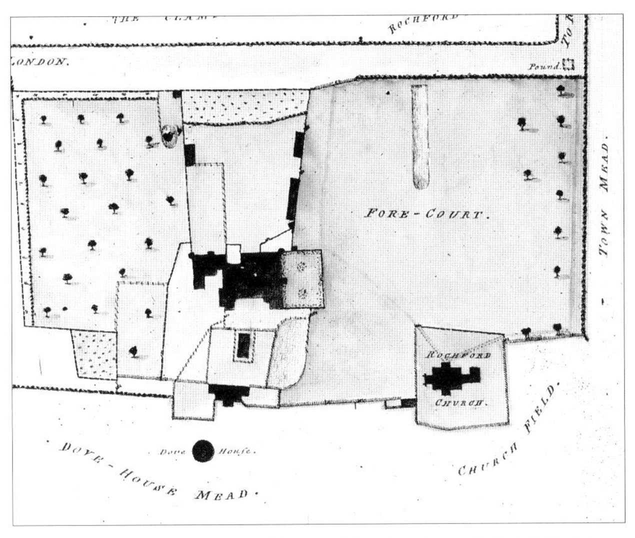

Fig 32 Rochford Hall, Rochford: plan, 1796 (ERO).

use of brick made the widespread diffusion of the walled garden possible, especially in south-east England. The earliest walled gardens seem only to date from the later 15th century. In Essex it is probable that very few surviving examples predate the Reformation. The Cressing walled garden was just such a pleasure garden, located on the north side of the great house, shoehorned in uncomfortably close to the 13th-century Wheat Barn (Fig 33). Excavation has failed to reveal much of its layout beyond a brick pavement round at least two sides and a raised terrace running along the west side, marked by a narrower 20th-century successor (Ryan & Andrews 1993, 115). The Walker maps also commonly show extensive orchards, which as well as being useful and productive look from their position as if they were perceived as an adjunct to the pleasure garden. At Ingatestone Hall the bowling alley was in the orchard (Emmison 1961, 35). Addison thought an orchard in flower looked 'infinitely more delightful, than all the little labyrinths of the most finished Parterre' (quoted in Hunt & Willis 1975). This contrasts with the practice of the 18th century, which was to distance the walled kitchen garden to a spot where it could not intrude into the landscaped vistas in which the house stood.

Fig 33 Cressing Temple: reconstruction of the great house as it might have been c. 1630 (by Frank Gardiner).

If Samuel Hartlib is to be believed, the kitchen garden and the proliferation of orchards was a new development. In 1652 he wrote:

> 'Market-gardening is but of few years standing in England ...About 50 years ago...this art of Gardening began to creep into England, into Sandwich and Surrey, Fulham and other places. Some old men in Surrey...report that they knew the first Gardiners that came into those parts to plant Cabages, Colleflowers, and sowe Turneps, Carrets and Parsnips, to sow Rape, Pease, all which at that time were great rarities, we having few, or none, in England, but what came from Holland and Flaunders... In Queen Elizabeth's time, we had not onely our Gardiner's ware from Holland, but also Cherries from Flaunders; Apples from France; Saffron, Licorish from Spain; Hopps from the Low-Countreys; ...whereas now...the Licorish, Saffron, Cherries, Apples, Peares, Hopps, Cabages of England are the best in the world' (Fisher 1934-5).

Towards the close of the 16th century great country houses became more outward looking. The Walker maps record these rather haphazard arrangements of enclosures before they were reorganised in the 17th century in more formal, geometric landscape designs, based on an aesthetic that considered high brick walls unsatisfactory in themselves and calling for the creation of formal vistas, which began to have an effect on the wider environs of the country house.

The innate conservatism of the 16th century can be seen in the contrast between the Walker plans of the Petre mansion at Ingatestone built from 1540 (Fig 34) (Emmison 1961, 27-40) and their later house at Old Thorndon (West Horndon) built 1575-95 (Ward & Marshall 1972). Old Thorndon differed in not being built round a courtyard and in presenting a long facade opening onto the countryside to the south. In front of the house was a large grass quadrangle, whereas at Ingatestone the approach was dominated by a base court with an untidy scatter of farm and service buildings. At Thorndon the outbuildings were neatly grouped to one side and to the rear of the great house (Figs 34 and 35). Thorndon had none of the semi-defensive character of Ingatestone, where parts of the house were embattled and the garden wall had what look like turrets on it; a retrospective licence to crenellate was granted in 1551. Thorndon had a larger and more elaborate formal garden behind the house rather than one awkwardly situated on a corner, as at Ingatestone. But there was little hint of what could be called true landscaping; that, it seems, had to wait until the projects undertaken by the 8th Lord Petre in the 1730s.

Two further instances of what seem to be Tudor walled garden enclosures overlaid with formal gardens can be found in representations of Copped Hall, Epping, and Bower Hall, Steeple Bumpstead. Copped Hall was built on a medieval site by Sir Thomas Heneage from 1564 and

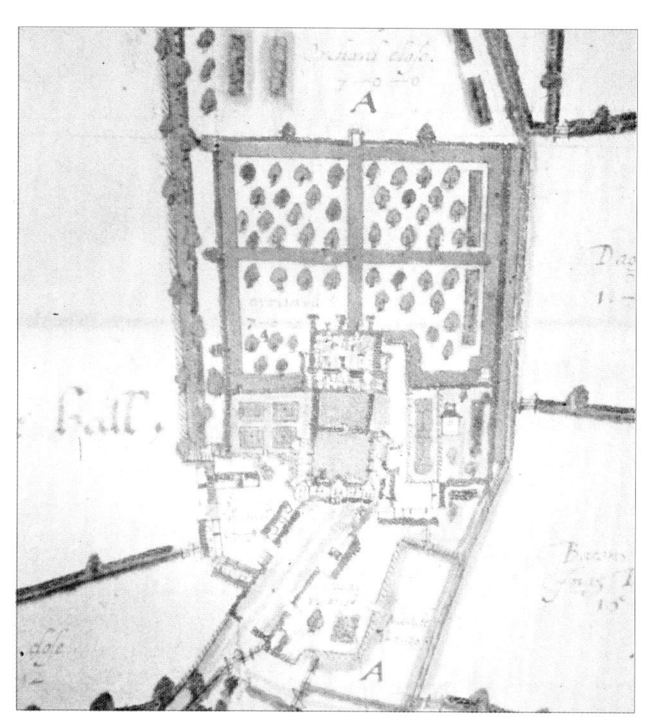

Fig 34 Ingatestone Hall, as represented in the Walker map of 1602 (ERO).

embellished by Lionel Cranfield, Earl of Middlesex, in the 1620s (Fig 36; *cf* Andrews 1986). The Palladian house which replaced it from *c*.1748 was burnt out in 1917 and is now a ruin. The Tudor mansion was a large courtyard house flanked by walled enclosures which seem to include kitchen gardens. To the south, however, is a long axial vista encompassing two formal gardens, the more distant on a slightly raised terrace. It is tempting to see these as part of Cranfield's improvements.

Bower Hall too was a sub-manor of medieval origin which has not survived, having been demolished in 1928. The house of *c*.1710 built for the Bendish family is illustrated in a painting by Knyff now in the Essex Record Office (Fig 37). The walled enclosures look as if they were inherited from an earlier brick house. The formal garden with its parterres is surrounded by a crenellated wall with turrets reminiscent of Ingatestone Hall.

Another lost mansion and garden is Woodham Walter Hall. Its site and environs survive in the form of what is, for a county not rich in such things, an astonishing series of earthworks which have been recorded by the Royal Commission for Historical Monuments (NMR TL 80 NW 15). The manor of Woodham Walter belonged to the Fitzwalters from the 12th to the 15th centuries, passing then to the Radcliffe family. In 1542, Robert Radcliffe was made 1st earl of Sussex, and it natural to assume that this ennoblement was accompanied by the aggrandisement of the mansion at Woodham Walter and improvements to its setting. By 1573, however, the family had moved to New Hall, Boreham, and the house at Woodham Walter was demolished *c*.1700. It stood in a flooded valley and must have been partially surrounded by extensive sheets of water. The

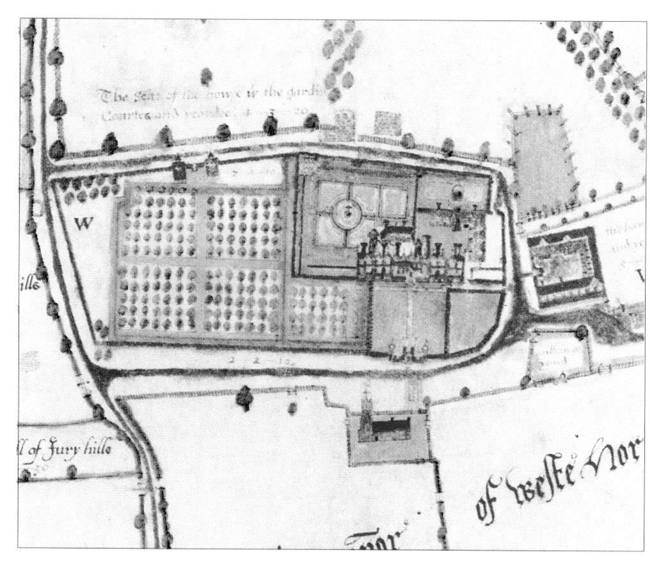

Fig 35 Old Thorndon Hall, from the Walker map of 1598 (ERO).

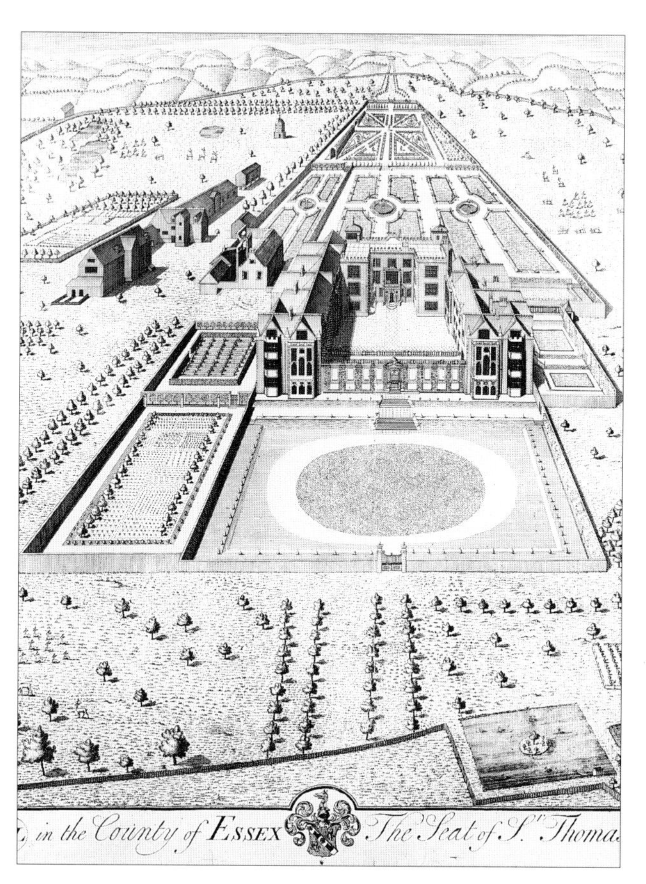

Fig 36 Old Copped Hall, Epping (from Farmer 1735).

garden flanked the south side of the mansion and its formal design is still apparent (Fig 38). It was sunken, about 20m square, with terraced walks around it. In the centre was an oval feature, on which converged paths laid out on the diagonals of the square. To the east was a moated mount or island. A complex pattern of earthworks and terraces lies on the east side of the stream valley. The admittedly circumstantial historical evidence suggests this garden dates to the

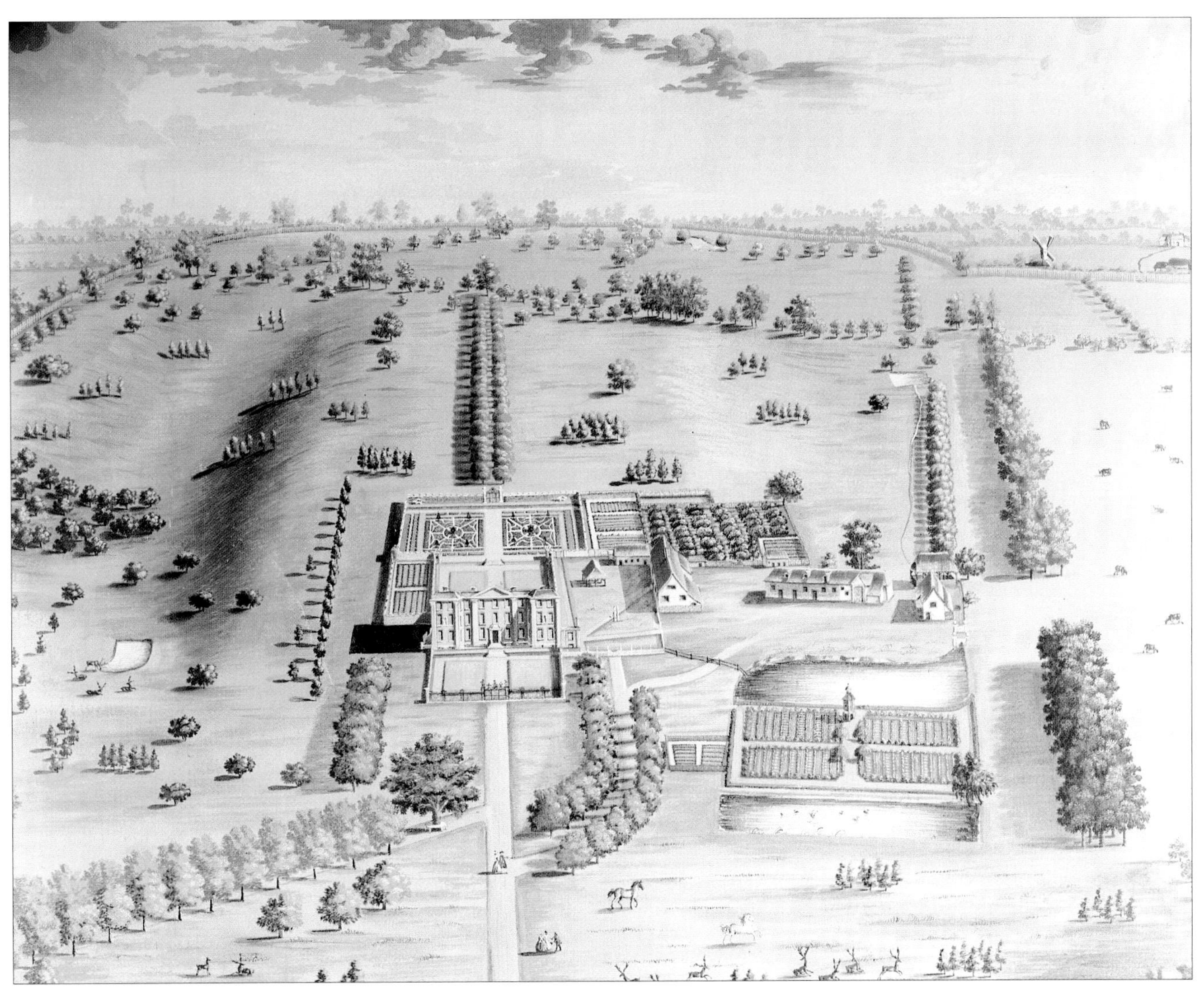

Fig 37 Bower Hall, Steeple Bumpstead, by Knyff c. 1720 (ERO).

middle or second half of the 16th century. Whether these are all contemporary features or a palimpsest of elements of varying date, some as old as the manorial site itself, is uncertain. If the former is true, it is an important early example of a designed landscape.

GREAT HOUSES, MANORS AND LOCAL TOPOGRAPHY

While some of the great country houses, such as Layer Marney, Panfield Hall and Stanstead Hall, were built by 'old families', the majority were built by the new men of the 16th century. Some obtained former monastic sites, like William Petre at Ingatestone and Richard Riche at Leighs Priory, but generally they found it easier to acquire a sub-manor than the traditional principal manor. Thus at Rivenhall the manor by the church remained a relatively modest late medieval H-plan house, whereas the gentry house is Rivenhall Place, originally the sub-manor of Archers, bought and enlarged by the Wiseman family in the 16th century (Rodwell & Rodwell 1993, 153).

Nevertheless, there is little evidence of anything approaching the large-scale reorganisation of the landscape associated with the 18th-century landscaping schemes of, for example, 'Capability' Brown and Repton, except at the highest social levels and with the further exception of parks, which will be discussed below. It seems, for instance, to be rare that roads and villages were moved at this period (a rare Essex example of a settlement being altered to fit in with the landscaping ambitions of a lord of the manor is Terling, where the Strutt family realigned the roads and probably cleared some houses when they built Terling Place at the end of the 18th century). At Audley End, a truly exceptional enterprise allegedly costing £200,000 (DoE 1977), it is possible that a new village was laid out down the street to St Mark's College at this time. Another exceptional instance is Woodham Walter Hall. In 1563 the church was removed from a position close to the mansion house (Fig 38) and rebuilt on a new site to the south of the village, where it was more convenient for the parishioners and did not disturb the views enjoyed by the earls of Sussex (Ryan 1989, 29;

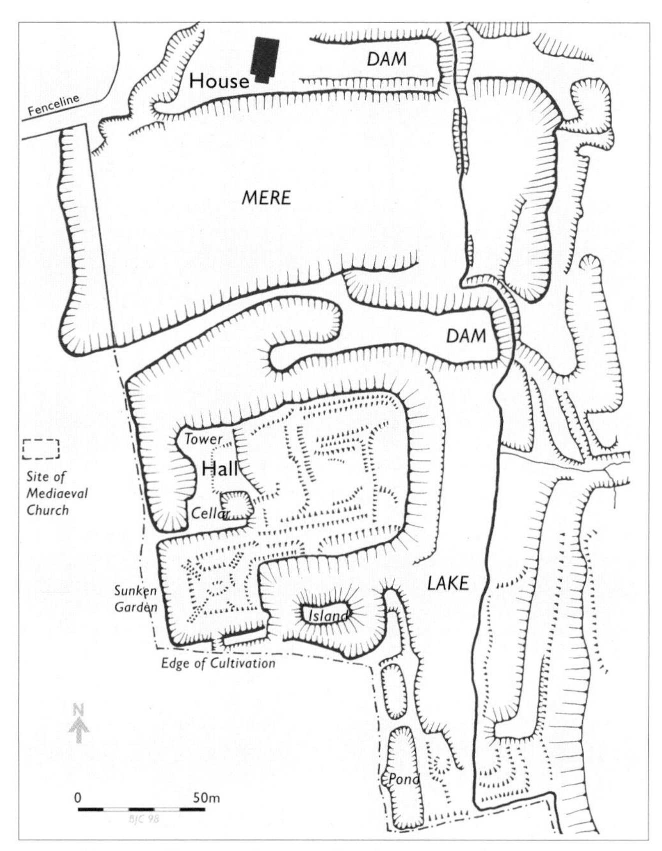

Fig 38 Woodham Walter Hall: plan of earthworks on the site of the hall and its surroundings (based on a survey by RCHME).

Ainsworth *et al* 1991). It was more usual, however, for churches to be rebuilt on the same site to complement the new house, as at Old Thorndon or Layer Marney.

Building operations themselves had an impact on the environs of the great houses. Clay had to be dug, and the clamps to fire the bricks must have created a smoky industrial image at odds with a rural setting. At this period brick and tile manufacture was invariably carried out locally. Clamps have disappeared leaving very little trace, apart perhaps from a field name. At Cressing it is thought that the clamps were on the other side of the Braintree to Witham road to the house. The site of a clamp was found at Rochford Hall at the time of the 1987 gale when trees were blown over exposing scorched brickwork. At Hill Hall, Theydon Mount, Sir Thomas Smith's widow directed in 1578 that for the finishing of the great house her husband's executors could dig 'within the soyle or ground of Hill Hall...or of Monthall earth or ure sufficient to make 150,000 brick...' and sufficient wood and straw for the burning of the same, and to allow them enough earth, wood and straw over two years to make and fire sufficient 'tyle and lime' to cover the new building (Drury 1983, 116).

Clay pits have sometimes left a more enduring impression as ponds or lakes. It may be that some of them are to be associated with the broad expanses of water that appear at some mansions. These are distinct from the relatively small fishponds of the medieval manor and the valley-bottom lakes of the 18th century. This difference can be illustrated by the small brick-lined fish tanks found on the golf course at Rochford Hall, which are quite different from the lake to the south-east of the Hall shown on a plan of 1796. A wide, shallow artificial lake or mere measuring 165m by 50m existed just to the north of Woodham Walter Hall (Fig 38). As well as clearly being a designed landscape feature, this is likely to have been the site where clay was extracted for bricks for the hall or the new church.

PARKS

In the Middle Ages a park was the most prestigious landscape feature of a manorial estate and the aspiration of any status-conscious lord. It was no less so in the 16th century and the majority of country houses were surrounded by parkland. Some of the new mansions were built in the old medieval deer parks. In other cases the demesne fields were converted into a park, and on occasions neighbouring farms were purchased and incorporated into the park.

Copped Hall, Epping, and Bower Hall, Steeple Bumpstead, are good examples of houses in a parkland setting (Figs 36 and 37). In both cases the park has probably come to occupy most of the nucleus of the relatively modest estates attached to these manors. At Copped Hall the park is broken up by long avenues of trees and a scattering of other features, such as a kitchen garden, small fenced enclosures, rectangular ponds and a mount, possibly a mill mound in origin. At Bower Hall the 'New Park' was being added to by Sir Thomas Bendish in the 1640s (Glover 1990, 719). As well as avenues of trees, there are what look like clumps of trees, some of which were the precursors of the thirteen plantations in the park which were recorded on the 1840 tithe map. As seen in these contemporary illustrations, there is a tension in these landscapes between their formal planting and less regular elements, so it is easy to understand the 18th century desire to achieve more natural solutions.

The size of individual parks and the overall extent of parkland in the county was capable of considerable variation from one time to another, despite the constant prestige and desirability of parks, and it is difficult to say without detailed research whether there was a net increase or diminution in the 16th and 17th centuries. The problem is that parkland was not only a status symbol but also an economic asset in terms of the trees it contained. On the other hand, the land it occupied might be put to more profitable use as arable, so that there could therefore be an economic benefit to disparking, particularly if the landlord did not live locally.

In the Middle Ages Rivenhall park, which was located to the north of the manor house, was remarkably elastic in shape, ranging in size between about 250 and 500 acres (Rodwell & Rodwell 1993, 108-120). In the 16th century a new manorial seat, Wiseman's Hall, now Rivenhall Place, was established in the south-west corner of the park, which once again had its boundaries altered. A formal geometric layout with tree-lined avenues was imposed upon the park in the following century, as a plan of 1716 shows. In the process a medieval farmstead was absorbed and abandoned. This layout seems incomplete, perhaps because the male line died out in 1692 and the estate was sold to the Western family. The design was of some sophistication. Rodwell compares it with the earl of Essex's park at Cassiobury, Hertfordshire, and speculates that George London, the royal gardener, may have been involved.

Similar cycles of enlarging and reducing parks can be seen elsewhere. At Stanstead Hall, Halstead, the park was partially broken up in the 16th century under a rapid succession of owners, some of whom were probably engaged in asset-stripping. A much smaller park was recreated *c.*1628 (ERO D/DHt T119 66, 73). At Woodham Walter the 1st earl of Sussex is known to have enlarged the park in the first half of the 16th century. The 3rd earl, however, moved to New Hall, Boreham, in 1573 and in the early 17th century most of the park was leased as farms (Ryan 1989, 18). The 300-acre Ingatestone Hall Park created by William Petre had been disparked by 1605 (Emmison 1961, 40).

In the area of Pleshey, Great Waltham, Felsted and Little Leighs, Richard Lord Riche created a series of extensive parks covering nearly 3000 acres (Hunter 1994a). Absol Park, Pleshey Great Park and Littley Park were medieval and had belonged to the manor of Walthambury. Riche extended Littley Park northwards (Hunter 1994b) and created Pond Park and Leez Park out what seems to have been farmland, thus completely surrounding his mansion, Leez Priory, with parkland. He also acquired the neighbouring park belonging to Little Leighs Hall. These parks were short-lived; they were progressively reduced in size during the 17th century and disappeared in the 18th, if not before, their boundaries being fossilised in the landscape.

Littley Park immediately to the south of Leez Priory was one of the more enduring parks, part of it surviving till the mid 18th century (Hunter 1994b). In the 17th century Henry, Earl of Holland planted an elm avenue along the Causeway, a main approach to the mansion from the south 1.5 miles in length. The trees were killed by elm disease and their boles survive today. This invites comparison with New Hall, Boreham, where in 1624 John Tradescant planted an avenue for the duke of Buckingham, thought by some to be the earliest avenue axial to a great house in England. This, however, may have been anticipated by 60 years by Sir Thomas Smith of Hill Hall, Theydon Mount. As ambassador to France in the 1560s Smith had absorbed Renaissance influences, and his mansion was precocious in its classicism, in particular the superimposed Doric and Ionic orders of the courtyard and the giant orders on the south and east fronts. Smith's interests included gardening, something in which he is said to have found recreation. The classical remodelling of Hill Hall was accompanied by the planting of an orchard in 1568 or 1572, whilst to the east of the house there was an avenue of double rows of elms. No direct proof connects the avenue with Smith, but tradition has it that he planted the elms and they were described as very large by 1698 (Drury 1983, 114).

ESTATES AND FIELDS

The great house at Cressing Temple was supported by an estate of about 1200 acres that had been kept intact since the 12th century by a powerful landowner. Many great houses were, however, underpinned by newly accumulated landholdings, many of which had formerly belonged to religious houses. William Petre at the time of his death in 1571 had 20,000 acres in Essex and lands elsewhere of similar extent. In Rivenhall Sir Ralph Wiseman systematically bought up much of the parish, acquiring at least 1,000 acres.

As has been observed by Rackham (1980), Essex is old countryside where the open fields had begun to be enclosed very early in the Middle Ages. In the Cressing and Witham area, and in much of the county, it is clear that the process of enclosure was substantially complete by the 13th century. A typical field pattern presented by many Essex parishes is a contrast between larger fields in the area of the manorial demesne or home farm and smaller ones belonging to the peasantry or originating as land reclaimed from woodland and waste. This is well illustrated in the case of Cressing which exhibits a contrast between the large fields of the Templars' manor in the southern and central part of the parish and the smaller holdings and woodland in the north (Fig 39).

If the Walker maps of *c.*1600 are contrasted with 18th and 19th-century maps, one of the most striking features of them is the similarity of the field pattern. This is hardly surprising; boundaries, once established, readily become fossilised, as archaeology repeatedly demonstrates. The principal changes that have taken place are the subdivision of very large fields and the amalgamation of very small ones, imposing a greater uniformity of field size on the landscape.

In Essex the process of land accumulation usually involved the buying up of smaller farms and rarely significant enclosure. In Rivenhall, Ralph Wiseman purchased at least nine farms, most of them of the order of 20-50 acres. For the most part, these farms seem not to have disappeared as entities, unless absorbed into the park; but their acquisition by a single landlord was the first step towards the possibility of further rationalisation in the following centuries.

The Essex landscape with its ancient enclosure gives rise to a complex picture of the amalgamation and disaggregation of small landholdings. This is not easy to unravel and it can be difficult to detect trends without in-depth study of the patterns of landholding, which in most cases remains to be carried out. One parish which has been analysed in detail is Purleigh to the south of Maldon, where Stephen Potter, a farmer, has brought a lifetime's experience to the problem. In 1984 a field was levelled and two post-medieval house sites were discovered. This field was at the edge of Howegreen Common, which probably had its origins in piecemeal woodland enclosure that had taken place by the 13th century. The house sites were identified as two of a total of five small farms ranging in size roughly from 2 to 50 acres which, with several other farmsteads, formed the hamlet of Howegreen. As landscape units these farms and their

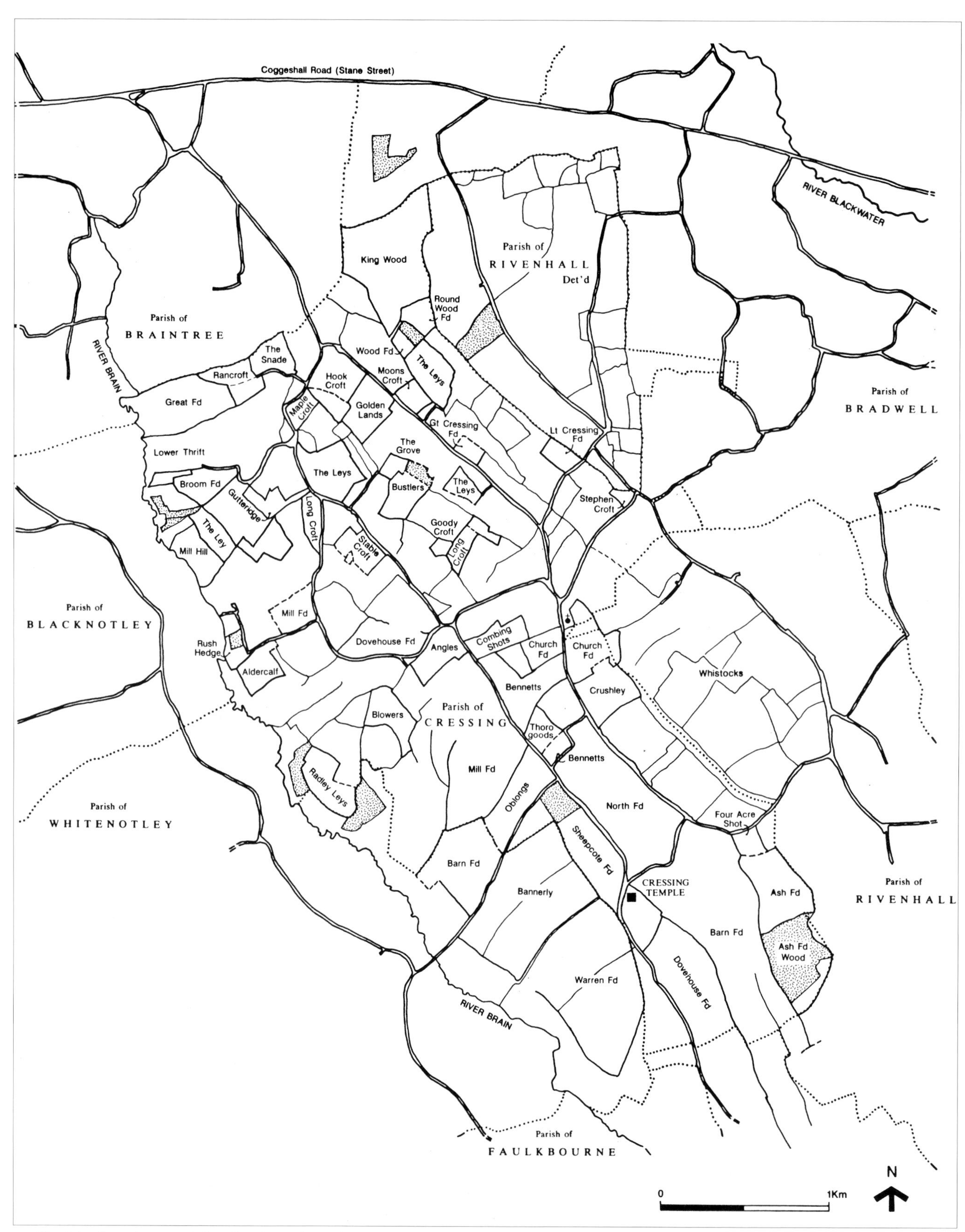

Fig 39 Cressing parish: plan based on the tithe map of c.1840. In the south of the parish it is possible to recognise the large fields of the former manorial home farm based on Cressing Temple (Bannerly, Warren, Sheepcote, Dovehouse, Barn Field, North Field, Ash Field, and Whistocks). These contrast with the pattern of smaller fields to the north which represent the crofts of the peasantry and clearance of the wood and waste, with a scatter of greens and moats.

fields seem not to have changed significantly from the 15th century to the 17th century. By 1653 four of the holdings were leased to a single tenant, and by 1722 all five were in one ownership and effectively formed what became known as Howegreen Farm (Potter *et al* 1986). Whilst it is true that in the long term the fields were enlarged and modified, the landscape features created directly by this process were ruined buildings, namely the two houses found in the levelling operations, and the barns and outbuildings that are known from documents to have accompanied them. This did not necessarily signify a net reduction in the local housing stock as a result of declining population; the other side of the common was at this time being nibbled away and cottages were being built on it.

By the time of the great parliamentary enclosures in the 18th century there was relatively little left to enclose in the greater part of Essex. However, in the open-field area of the county, typically the chalk lands of the north-west, it is probable that enclosure was accelerating at this period. At Newport, for example, the common on the site of the medieval fish pond known as Pond Common was partly enclosed by the lord of the manor by 1595, the process being completed not long after by the earl of Suffolk, builder of Audley End, when he acquired the manor. We also find another case at the end of the 16th century where the owner of Hospital Farm was accused of enclosing about 80 acres in the common fields (Nurse *et al* 1995, 38-9).

WOODS AND REBUILDING

Woodland is as difficult to quantify as parkland, but there had probably been a net reduction of this, too, by 1700. To documented contemporary concern about a shortage of timber can be added circumstantial evidence arising from the Essex Tree-ring Dating Programme, which has focused closely on the buildings at Cressing Temple to construct a county-wide master sequence of tree-rings. The great barns are built from timbers whose straightness and rapid growth, having obtained a diameter of 8-10 inches in about 60 years, manifestly reflect optimum growing conditions, a regime brought about by careful management of the woodlands whence they came. On the other hand the timbers of the Granary, which was built in 1623, are strikingly different (Andrews *et al* 1994). To begin with, about 50% of them are reused from medieval buildings on the site, which had been pulled down. Secondly, the new timbers came from trees of which had clearly not grown in such ideal conditions or well-managed woodland (Fig 40). Thirdly, a significant proportion of the larger timbers were of elm rather than oak. In surviving medieval buildings in Essex both reused timbers and elm are very exceptional. These facts, combined with the evidence of less intensive woodland management, imply a relative shortage of good quality timber and less extensive woodlands by the 17th century.

A factor in the consumption of timber was the great number of timber buildings erected in the late medieval and early modern period. These testify to the emergence of a prosperous yeoman class in the period after the Black Death,

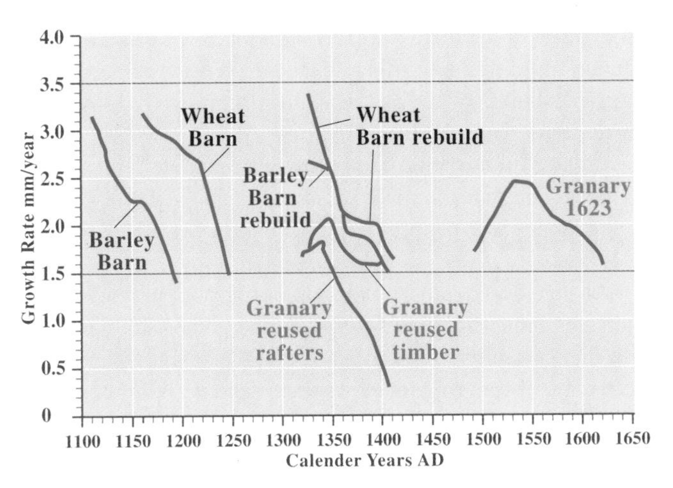

Fig 40 Diagram prepared by Ian Tyers from tree-ring analyses to illustrate average smoothed growth rates of dated timbers from Cressing Temple. They include timbers from the original 13th-century Barley and Wheat Barns and from the later phases of those barns dating to the early 15th century; reused early 15th-century timbers in the Granary; and timbers contemporary with the 1623 construction of the Granary. In contrast with those used in the older buildings, the trees from which the Granary was built display a growth pattern which slowed down markedly later in their lives (from Andrews et al 1994, fig 9).

to Essex's agricultural prosperity and the density of its population, all of which were underpinned by the growth of the London market. The pattern of dispersed settlement means that these buildings are one of the most distinctive features of the countryside and are not confined just to the villages and towns. A natural starting point in considering these buildings is W G Hoskins' notion of a 'Great Rebuilding' that occurred at the end of the 16th century and in the early 17th century (Hoskins 1977, 154). For William Harrison of Radwinter this rebuilding was a reality. He observed that 'in building, so well the hedge as the park go all one way, and never so much hath been spent in a hundred years before as in ten years of our time, for every man almost is a builder, and he that hath bought any small parcel of ground, be it never so little, will not be quiet till he have pulled down the old house (if any there were standing) and set up a new one after his own device' (Edelen 1994, 279). A chronological analysis of listed houses in the county also supports this picture (Table 6).

Table 6 Analysis of listed houses by century of construction, from the computerised database of Essex listed buildings held by Essex County Council Planning Division, April 1999.

13th century	27
14th century	166
15th century	624
16th century	1830
17th century	2462

These figures should only be regarded as indicative, and they underestimate the number of surviving 13th and 14th-century buildings. Nevertheless they do reflect the very considerable building activity in enduring materials that took place in the 16th and 17th centuries.

In their examination of the tiny but accurate representations on the Walker maps, Edwards and Newton (1984) found evidence to support the concept of a Great Rebuilding in Essex.

At Ingatestone an examination of the standing buildings indicates much building activity in the early 17th century, and this certainly seems to be true at Cressing. One of the potentials of tree-ring dating is that it should be possible to identify peaks and troughs in the building cycle. Dates obtained for Cressing suggest that there was such a peak in the first half of the 17th century, and perhaps also early in the 15th century. Thus the buildings which were amalgamated to form the Cressing Temple farmhouse have been tree-ring dated to 1607 and 1618. The 1618 part probably belonged to a remodelling of the Great House by the Smyth family, for which evidence has been found in excavations and with which the existing Granary dating from 1623 seems to have been associated. In Cressing parish New House Farm was built in 1633, whilst Hungry Hall is of two phases datable to 1594 and probably the 1630s.

However, without more complete evidence it is impossible to be certain whether this represents a significant increase in building activity. Evidence from Ingatestone (based on unpublished research by Pat Ryan) advises caution in drawing wider conclusions. Detailed comparison of a 1556 survey of the village with a Walker map of 1601 suggests that there was a continuum in house building, and what may be termed a 'housing revolution' at the time of the so-called Great Rebuilding. With its large numbers of surviving late medieval and early modern houses Essex does indeed seem to present a picture of continuous house building. The 'housing revolution' refers to the new amenities with which houses were provided, and the development of new architectural forms such as lobby-entry and long-wall jettied houses. William Harrison commented on the large numbers of brick chimney stacks which had been erected in his time (Edelen 1994, 201). By 1601 all the houses depicted in Ingatestone on the Walker map had a chimney, though a few were not in brick. An increasing number of houses had upper floors in the hall area and kitchens incorporated into the main building rather than detached in the yard. Many houses had cross-wings built on to them, either for the first time or to convert them into an H-plan house, and the addition of show gables at this period was to give many urban street scenes a distinctive character which endures today.

Research on Cressing parish also indicates the need for caution in interpreting the significance of new buildings. New House Farm and Hungry Hall, which have been referred to above, do not seem to represent an improvement in the housing stock in the sense of being a reconstruction of old and obsolete dwellings. Instead they seem to be associated with new farms established on the Cressing Temple estate and thus to reflect changes in estate management on the part of the Smyth family (Ryan *et al* 1997).

CONCLUSIONS

The later 17th century was a period of accelerated change, a prelude to the very different world of the 18th century. Many factors were at play in the way these changes found expression in the landscape. At Cressing Temple the fate of the site was decided by the Civil War. The Smyth and Nevill family backed the wrong side. They were royalists, and Henry Nevill was fined £6,000 for his sympathies in 1645. He paid the fine, but ten years later, faced with mounting debt, and doubtless influenced by the fact that the family's main interests were in Leicestershire, he sold Cressing Temple for £21,000. The purchasers were three business partners who asset-stripped the estate, felling the timber and dividing up the property. Having belonged to one family for over 100 years Cressing now passed through the hands of a series of owners until in 1703 it was acquired by the Olmius family. They held it for 180 years but lived elsewhere, notably at New Hall, Boreham, with the result that Cressing Temple became a tenanted farm. Probably early in the 18th century the great house was dismantled and its materials sold for reuse (Ryan 1993, 17).

What happened at Cressing was paralleled elsewhere. The owners of Stanstead Hall, Halstead, similarly backed the wrong side in the Civil War, and the house was drastically reduced in size. Changes in architectural taste, smaller households and, possibly, inadequate foundations, saw the partial dismantling, total demolition and replacement of a great many of these great houses. It required a very considerable income and landed property to maintain what had been equivalent, in effect, to a small village or hamlet. The Petre family by the end of the 16th century owned almost 60,000 acres and had an income which it has been estimated may have been as much as £10,000 a year (Edwards 1975, 19).

For the most part Essex was a county of smaller estates, in contrast, say, to Norfolk, and this must have been a factor in the decline of its great houses. Although not denying the changes brought about by the new ideas of men like Kent and 'Capability' Brown, which effectively swept away the geometric gardens and parks created in the 17th century, it was the fortunes of families and landholdings which probably had the greatest influence on the Essex landscape at this and, indeed, later periods.

7

The designed landscape

by Fiona Cowell

> 'The very name of Gardens has shifted its meaning...within these few years. It us'd to signify only Kitchen-Gardens, or at best Flower-Gardens; whereas its principal use now relates to the disposition of...Land, Water, Plantations and Views.'

These words of Joseph Spence, written in the 1750s, neatly sum up the subject of this paper: the brief period when the natural landscape and garden design joined hands, and the English landscape garden was created. This is not the place for a discussion of the complicated reasons which led to the emergence of the so-called English Garden; reasons which embrace politics, travel to Italy, social attitudes, economic developments and even literature. By the early 18th century there was a new spirit abroad respecting natural beauty and how it could be translated into a garden style, but it should be remembered that what was understood by 'natural' in the context of a garden changed dramatically in the course of the 18th century. Many of the layouts of the first third of the century, still relatively stiff and formal, were commended by contemporaries for their increased affinity with nature.

At what date can it be confidently stated that the naturalistic style of landscape garden, as we understand it now, was prevalent in England? Its most famous practitioner, Lancelot Brown, was already at work in the 1750s, and as a generalisation, the style was present in a recognisable form in a few seminal gardens by the 1740s or even earlier, as at Painshill, Surrey, which was started in 1738. However, the large-scale map of Essex produced by Chapman and André in 1777 shows that many gardens, even large and grand ones, were still 'unimproved' at that date, for instance Easton Lodge (Fig 42). The squire even more than the aristocrat was often resistant to the idea of a new garden until surprising late in the century, although most eventually followed the fashion. It was a relatively affordable luxury, providing no major earth moving was involved, as there was scope within a designed landscape for grazing, woodland

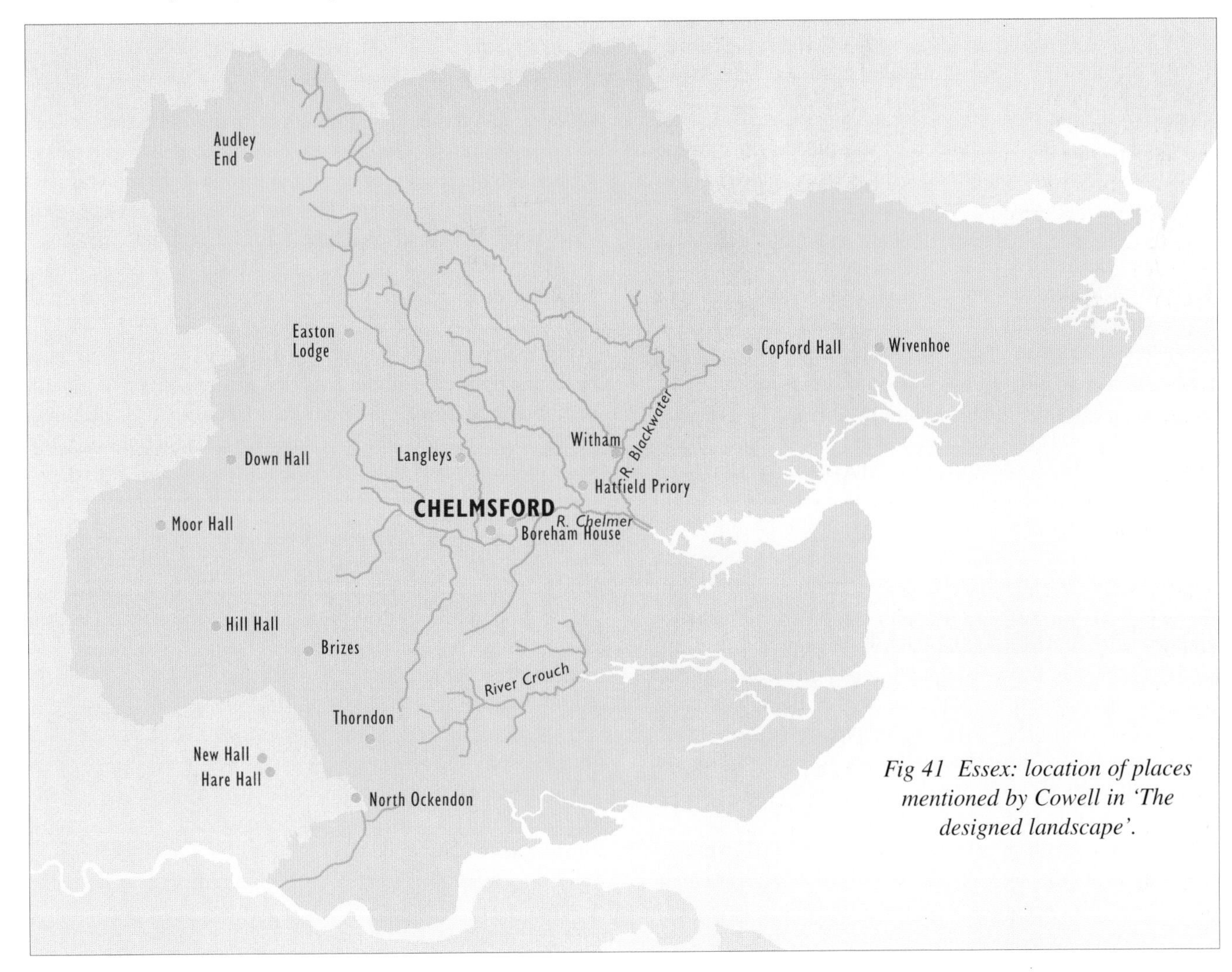

Fig 41 Essex: location of places mentioned by Cowell in 'The designed landscape'.

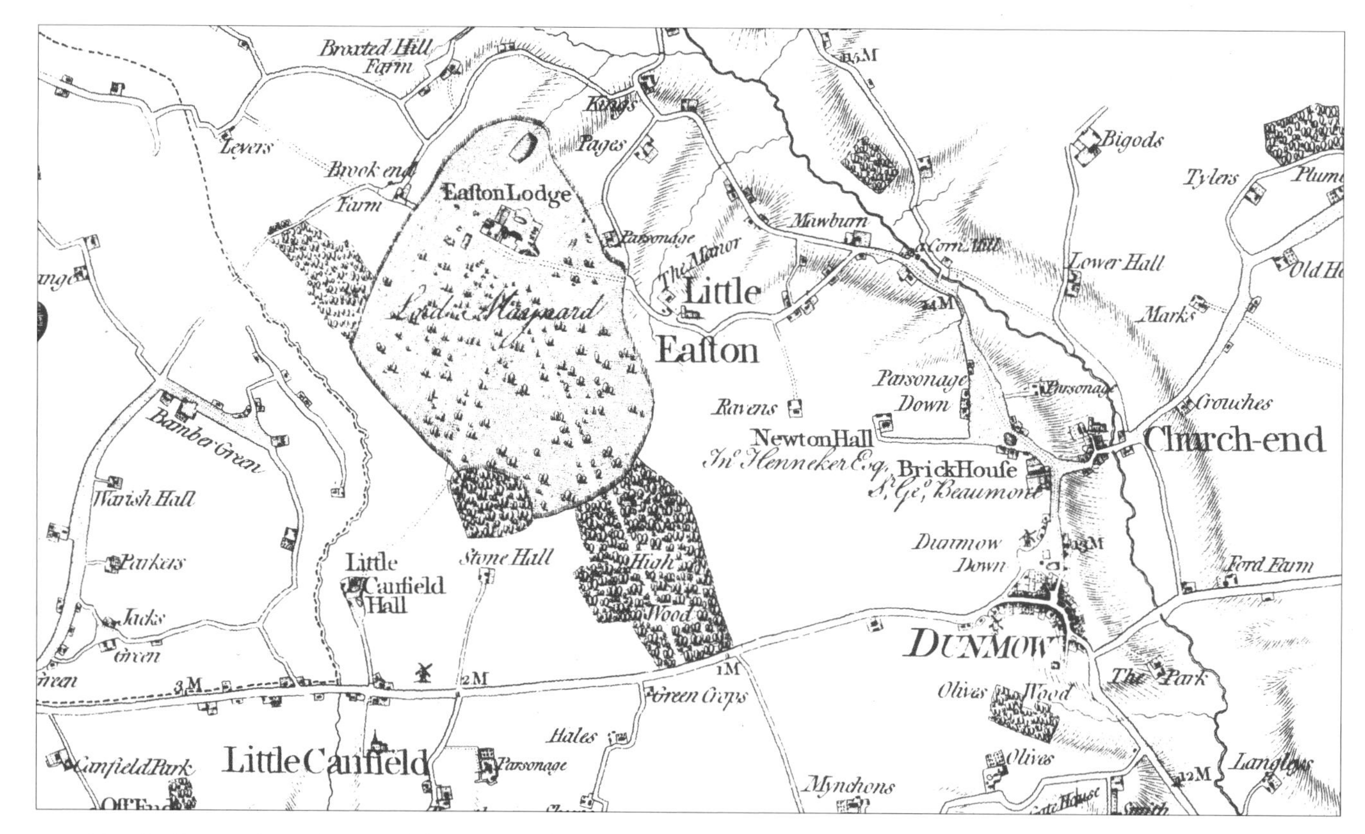

Fig 42 Extract from 'A map of the County of Essex' by Chapman & André 1777. Reproduced by kind permission of Phillimore & Co Ltd,. Shopwyke Manor Barn, Chichester, West Sussex.

management and haycutting. It can even be said that the designed landscape had come to be accepted as the one correct style only in the late years of the century, shortly before the return to a greater degree of formality.

It is obviously impossible to create a designed landscape without a consolidated land-holding, but in Essex in the 18th century enclosure was not a major issue. More important was a change in attitude towards the open country. Instead of enclosing a garden snugly within sheltering walls the idea grew, fostered by the virtuosi like Pope and Addison, that it was desirable to 'call in' the nature that lay beyond the garden boundary. Such 'nature' might be a deer park, in the case of a wealthy landowner, or chequered fields, the latter being preferably one's own but if necessary those of a neighbour. To achieve this a simple invention was needed, the sunken fence or ha-ha. This revolutionary device that enabled a garden and the landscape beyond it to be integrated in a single design was imported, ironically, from France and probably first used in England by Beaumont at Levens, Cumberland. The opening of views outwards from the garden into the country and the softening of lines within the garden were two developments that proceeded in parallel. They were finally amalgamated in the ultimate landscape garden, in Brown's style, where the house seems to be sitting in the middle of an open park.

A convenient place to start an overview of the history of the designed landscape in Essex is with Charles Bridgeman (*c.* 1680-1738), who was the most influential man of his time in garden design. Although virtually all his work was swept away as the fashion for the landscape park gained ground, he played a crucial role in the early years of softening the geometric garden. His work included features that have been described by Peter Willis as formal (parterres, avenues, rectilinear ponds); transitional (lawns, mounts, amphitheatres, cabinets); and progressive (ha-has, rides and walks to take in a view from a vantage point).

In Essex his achievements at Langleys (Great Waltham) have disappeared without trace or record, but in 1720 the poet Matthew Prior commissioned Bridgeman to design a garden for Down Hall (Theydon Mount) which he had just acquired. Prior was delighted by the setting of Down– 'It is impossible to tell you how beautiful a situation Down is, and how fine the wood may be made'–as he wrote to Edward Harley in July 1720 (Willis 1977), and the first design of Bridgeman's includes modern meanderings inside the spaces left by the more formal features. In another design, presumed to be later, the winding paths have been suppressed, so it may be that the poet preferred to stay with a purely geometric style, avoiding a daring innovation (Fig 43). By December 1720 he was writing 'We have laid out squares, rounds and diagonals, and planted quincunxes' but made no mention of anything sinuous. Unfortunately there is no painting to give us an idea of the result, which Bridgeman had said 'he would make...the finest and noblest thing in England' (Prior to Harley, March 1721, quoted in Willis 1997).

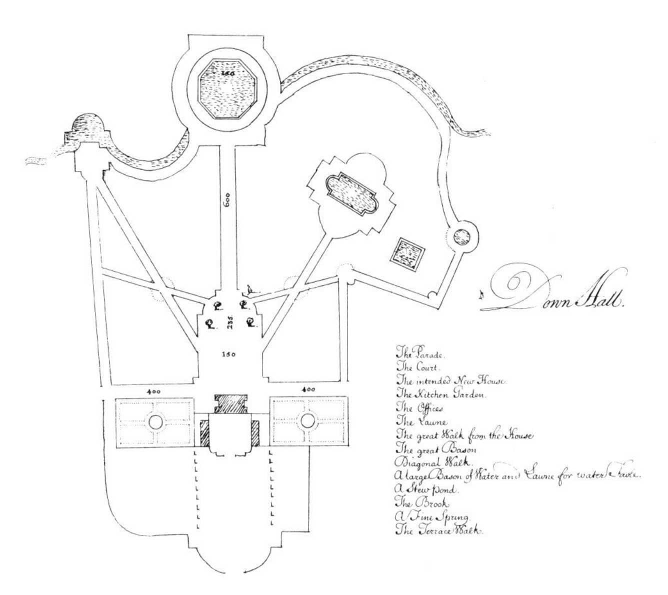

Fig 43 Down Hall: plan by Charles Bridgeman (Bodleian Library, Gough Maps 46 182R).

The 1730s bring us to a new strand in the development of the designed landscape, and to a famous man of the time who was truly of Essex. Robert James, 8th baron Petre, showed an interest in botany and gardening from childhood. By the time he moved at the age of 19 with his young wife from Ingatestone to Thorndon in 1732, he was already a skilled garden designer and associate of the leading horticulturists of the time. His own design for the grounds at Thorndon was drawn up by the surveyor Bourginion and is breathtaking in its detail and complexity (Fig 44).

The process by which such a design was arrived at can be seen through Petre's plans for Worksop, Nottinghamshire, where he suggested a similar kind of garden for his kinsman the Duke of Norfolk. When the working sketches are studied it becomes clear how much careful consideration went into its various aspects, particularly the planting schemes. The bold, almost surreal folds of the hillside were treated with the greatest detail. At one place, for instance, he specified 'Yews with Pinaster in clumps. Theas clumps must consist of 4 or 5 trees each and be plas'd from 30 to 80 feet apart', and so on for the whole plan (ERO D/DP P150). In spite of the formality round the house, this was a conscious attempt to 'call the country in' and make the surrounding landscape into a foil for the garden.

Petre was not just a designer of gardens but an accomplished botanist and plantsman. He corresponded with John Bartram and Peter Collinson, through whom he introduced as many of the new American plants as were available, by no means using them only behind sheltered walls. Ten years after Petre's death in 1742, Collinson wrote that he had 'coppy[ed] Beautifull Nature in his beautiful plantations...enrich'd with the Trees of America from the Lodge in the Great Avenue up to the Esplanade at the Head of the Park' (Linnean Society, Collinson MSS). Petre's nursery at Thorndon was prodigious, and his stoves or greenhouses were rivalled only by those at the Chelsea Physic Garden and Oxford Botanic Garden. His use of trees, both familiar species and the new exotics, heralded a great step forward in the idea of the designed landscape. Planting was no longer simply to delineate shapes–as the high walls of hornbeam hedge, for instance, had created compartments in earlier gardens–but was to become a subtle art in itself. Trees could be used in clumps and drifts to engage and lead the eye into the distance, and could be made into architectural formations of shape and colour to create 'painting with living Pencils', as Collinson described the planting at Thorndon. Joseph Spence wrote in his Anecdotes (1820) that Southcote considered 'Mr Pope and Mr Kent were the first that practised painting in gardening. But Lord Petre carried it further than either of them'.

Lord Petre naturally leads to William Kent, who cannot be omitted from a discussion of this subject even though none of his work was in Essex. In spite of Spence's comment, Kent is acknowledged to be the first designer of gardens to work in the landscape style, although a later generation found his planting ideas stiff and unnatural. With Kent, the garden based on a defined axis, which was still prevalent with Bridgeman and even Petre, gave way to serpentine paths with an axially framed vista suggested by symmetrical planting. It is of the greatest significance that Kent began as a painter, spending ten formative years in Italy collecting art and antiquities for his patrons. He never lost his passion for things Italian. Walpole, writing the *History of the Modern Taste in gardening* (1780), originally part of his *Anecdotes of painting in England,* of 1771, says of Kent that in his plantings 'he realised the compositions of the greatest masters in painting'. All Kent's garden designs were just that: compositions, not working plans or planting lists. Unlike Petre he was not a plantsman; his trees were architectural elements, not living organisms. But Kent is associated with a highly significant quotation in the study of the landscape garden: Sir Thomas Robinson wrote to the Earl of Carlisle in 1734 that 'There is a new taste in gardening just arisen...after Mr Kent's notion of gardening, viz to lay them out, and work without either line or level...And this method of gardening is the more agreeable, as...it has the appearance of beautiful nature...' (HMC: Castle Howard).

The closest we can get to Essex with Kent's work is Euston Hall in Suffolk, where he worked in the 1730s and 40s for the Duke of Grafton. Here his clumps were disposed less stiffly than in some of his designs, but Walpole was still scathing about 'Mr Kent...sticking a dozen trees here and there until a lawn looks like the ace of spades' (20 June 1743, in Toynbee 1903). Thomas Robinson, describing Euston to Lord Carlisle in 1731, liked the 'pretty rivulet cut in a winding and irregular manner', which may have been the beginning of Kent's work there (Hussey 1967, 155-6), and the temple or banqueting house, placed at the end of a long view, is still considered one of Kent's best surviving garden buildings.

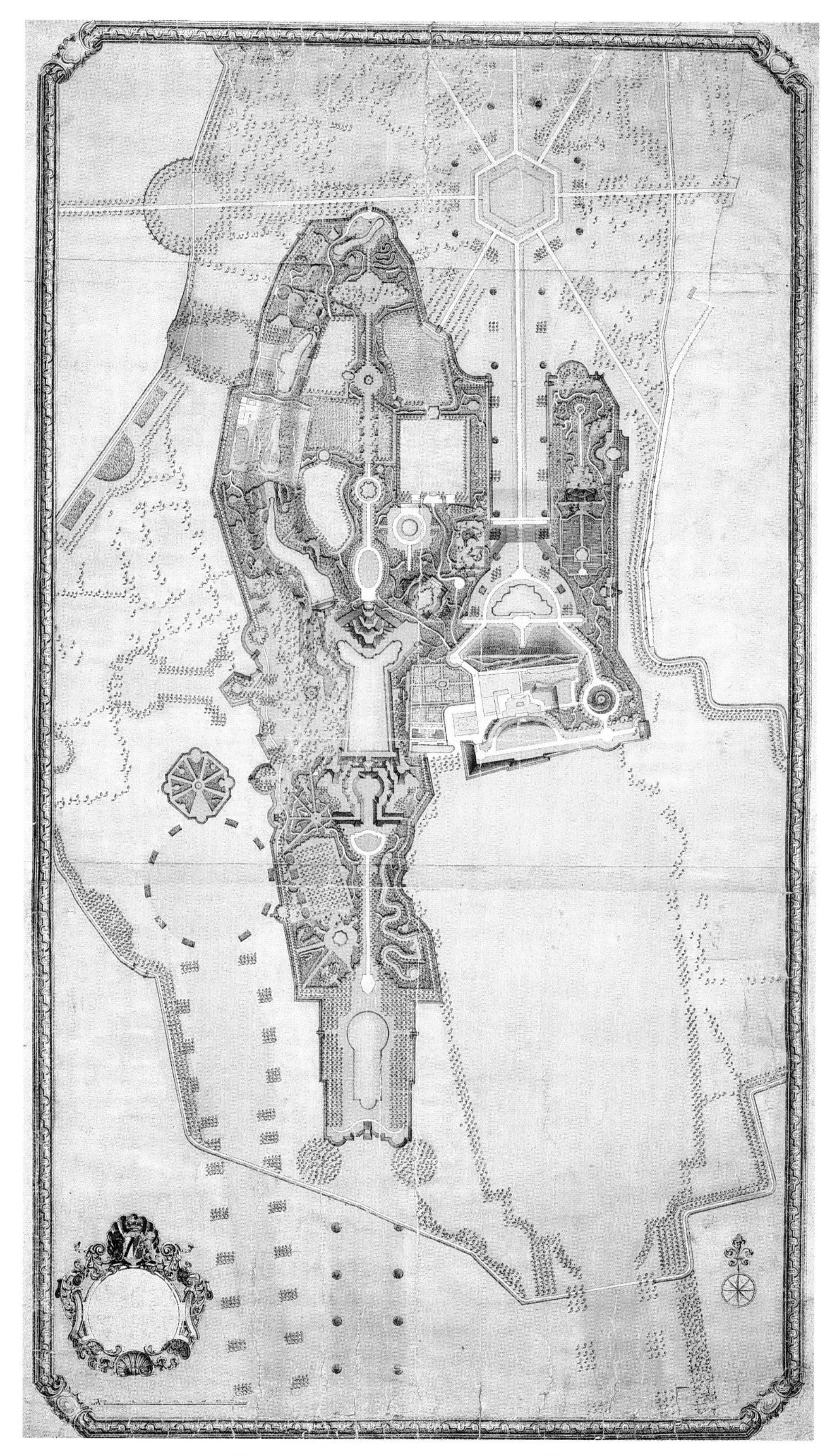

Fig 44 Thorndon Hall: design drawn by Bourginion, 1733 (ERO D/DP P23/2).

While Kent was experimenting with naturalism, another related development was the *ferme ornée*. The notion of combining the utility of a farm with the beauty of a garden had been voiced and to some extent practised by Switzer, but the first *ferme ornée* recognised and admired as such was made by Philip Southcote at Woburn Farm, Surrey. Here Southcote threw a walk round the working part of the estate, a walk bordered by flowers and scented shrubs. Southcote, a native of Witham in Essex, a friend of Pope's and related by marriage to Petre, first put his hand to garden design at Witham. Walpole in 1749 described the property: 'There are sweet meadows falling down a hill, and rising again on t'other side of the prettiest little winding stream you ever saw' (20 July 1749). The grounds contained a cold bath, a cascade, a statue in Home Field, and a piece of water behind the house (Fig 45).

By the time Kent died in 1748, 'Capability' Brown was promoting a further shift in attitude towards greater naturalism, but another of the 18th-century improvers must be discussed first. Richard Woods was an exact contemporary of Brown (they were both born in 1716), but stylistically he continued throughout his career to owe much to Kent. Tom Williamson makes the point (1995, 4) that 'the landscape gardens designed by Kent and others in the 1730s and 40s-relatively small areas of grass, shrubbery and ornamental buildings-were quite distinct from...the more extensive landscape parks created by Brown...in the second half of the century'. Woods was far better at designing parks on the scale of Kent's gardens, and with many of Kent's stratagems, than the more extensive acreage in which Brown saw 'capabilities'. In the 1760s it looked possible that Woods' career might be as successful as Brown's, and when he moved to Essex in 1768 he had the means to rent and furnish a most respectable property at North Ockendon. But he failed to move with the times, or perhaps did not see that the times were changing, and never made the jump to the large-scale landscape park that was Brown's hallmark and success.

Contrary to what is usually said of Woods, he was neither an imitator nor a follower of Brown and their styles are quite distinct. Although it is not proved, it seems very likely that Woods was in some way associated with Philip Southcote (they were both Catholic); it is also quite possible that Woods had a connection with the Petre household in his youth, as well as ending his career as surveyor to the 9th baron. Woods was at his most successful as a designer of properties of no more than roughly a hundred acres. Within such a space he could create, with considerable skill, a small landscape containing gardenesque features or a prominent pleasure garden or shrubbery.

Woods' commissions in Essex, which had started by 1764 before he moved to the county, follow a similar pattern: landscape features allied with flower-bordered walks or pleasure grounds, as at Boreham House, New Hall and Hare Hall in Romford. In the last example the spoil from excavating the lake was piled up to form a mount, to give the planting there extra height and importance. Wivenhoe was possibly his most important work in Essex. Unfortunately

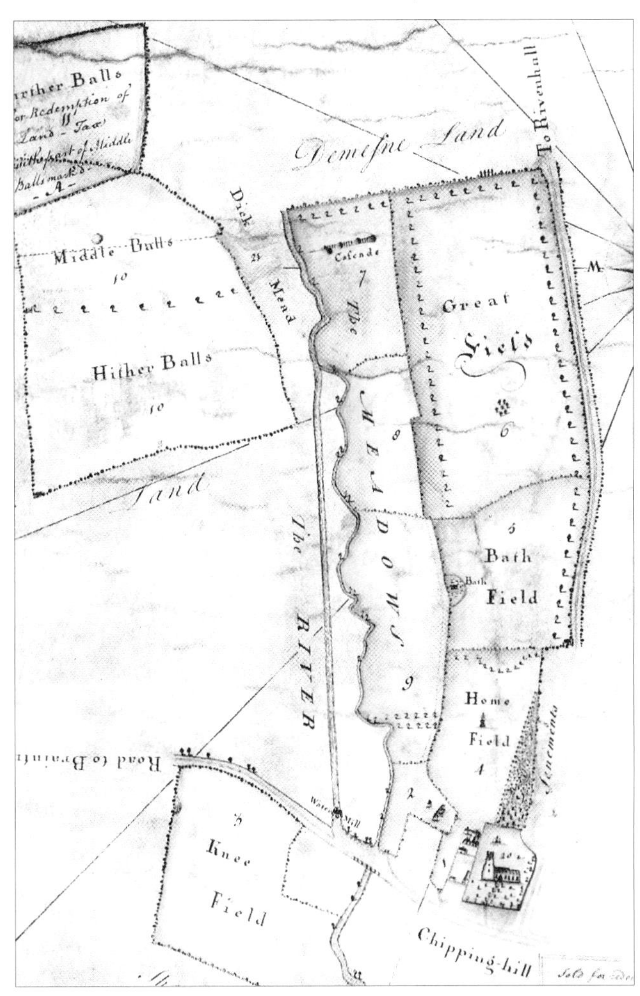

Fig 45 Witham vicarage garden: design by Philip Southcote, and a survey of glebe land by Timothy Skinner, 1762 (ERO D/P 30/3/5).

the plan is lost, but Constable painted a view of the piece of water, with its bridge-cum-dam and boathouse grotto. The plan for Copford of 1784 is particularly interesting, showing that at the social level of the gentry the layout mapped in 1766 needed only to be softened and altered slightly to make an acceptably modern garden (Fig 46). Woods' last full-size commission was for Brizes at Kelvedon Hatch (Fig 47), which lacks a piece of water but otherwise includes many features typical of his work: the 'Lady Walk inrich'd' (specified in the reference to the plan), with a bench looking over a flowerbed to the view beyond; a greenhouse for tender exotics; a temple to be seen at the bottom of the park where a position is marked for it, with views from the house delineated. The plan of 1765 for improvements at Hatfield Peverel Priory was one of Woods' simplest designs (Fig 48); it is being partly restored, partly new-created as it might have been. The ponds were made from the little stream running through the park, and the labour and expense of digging them out by hand means that they are very shallow. A temple was recently erected at the bottom of the park where it could be viewed from the house, in a position suggested by the plan for Brizes.

Two subsidiary elements of the designed landscape that were important during the working life of Richard Woods, *c.* 1758–90, were architectural features and the flower garden. The little temples that started to spring up in English landscape gardens were derived rather from those in the Italian countryside as depicted in paintings than from examples in the Italian Renaissance gardens studied by Kent. Designers high and low, from the most famous architects to the gentleman sketching on a piece of paper, whether following pattern books or their own imagination, produced thousands of ideas for the ornamentation of parks, in every conceivable style. The most popular were the classical in its various forms, but the Chinese, the Gothic and the rustic also appeared, and no fantasy was ruled out.

The second element, the flower garden, is a vexed topic. It is a myth that dies hard that during the middle years of the century, under the reign of 'King Brown', flowers were banished from the designed part of the grounds and were given room, if at all, behind or in front of the walls of a kitchen garden. Evidence to disprove the myth is continually coming to light, so it has to be asked why the misunderstanding ever took hold. It can partly be explained by the fact that the 18th-century improvers were commissioned to modernise grounds that had become old fashioned, but this did not necessarily mean that they were to sweep away pleasure grounds near the house. The work of the improvers generally stopped with the outline of the pleasure ground, and the choice and planting of the flowers within it lay with the lady of the house or the gardener. Woods on several occasions simply mentions that in the clumps or borders a wide margin should be left for flowers. In accordance with the hierarchy of heights typical of the period, these flowers stood in front of the shrubs, which in their turn were backed by small trees. The pleasure ground was seldom illustrated explicitly because artists were recording what was new, not what had always been there. Although its position in the grounds might remain the same, its form was naturally softened and opened up to come into line with fashion. Rutter and Carter (1767) write that 'the pleasure-garden is designed not only to delight the eye with its own products, but with the distant view of woods, waters, enclosed ground, and a pleasant country... The views of the country should be through vista's well disposed'. For the choicest, newest, most expensive flowers there might well be a separate walled flower garden, not from any sense of banishment but because, in the words of John Hill (1757), 'the shelter they require, and their

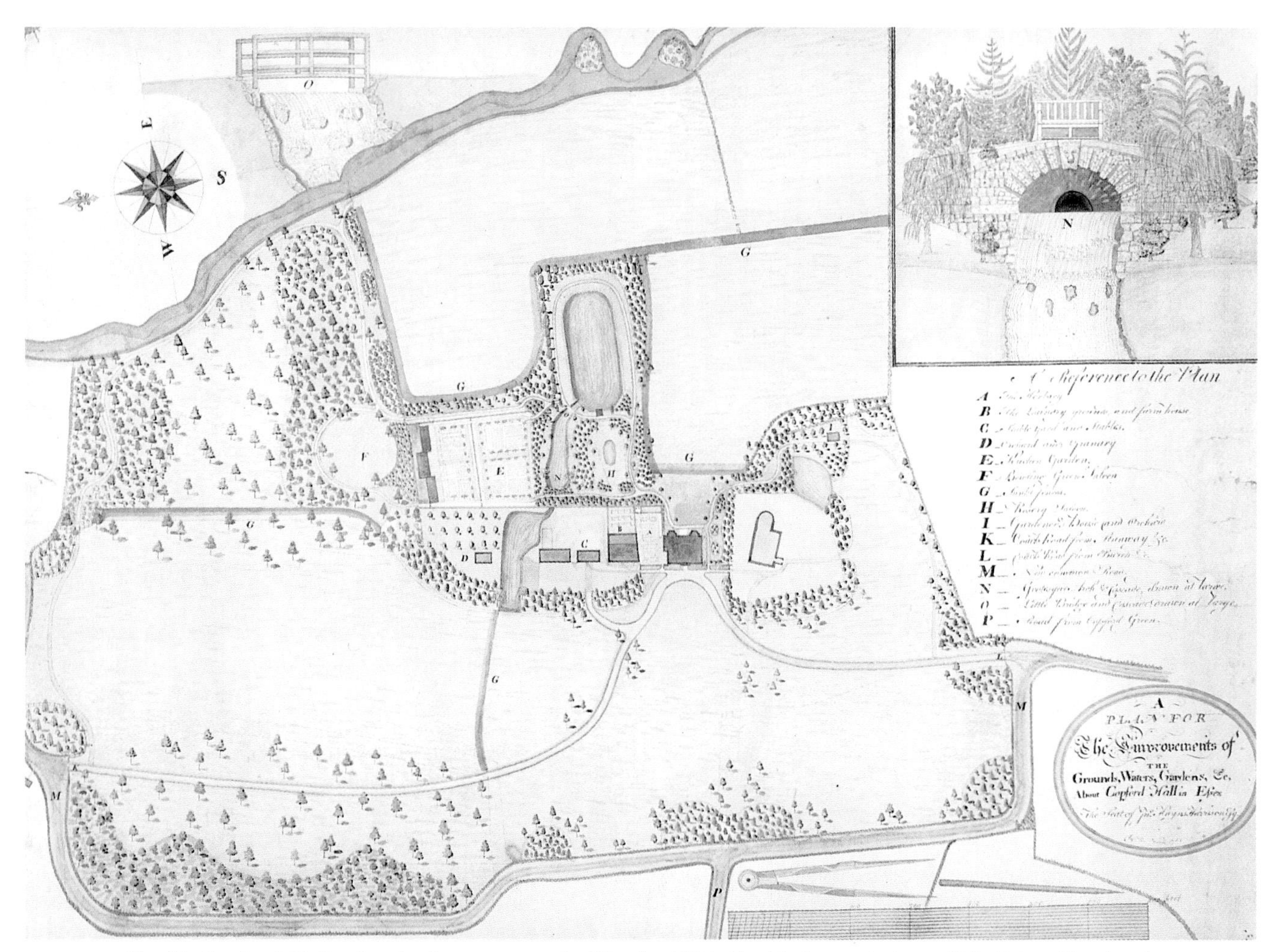

Fig 46 Copford Hall: plan for improvement by Woods, 1784, (by kind permission of Mr Brian Harrison).

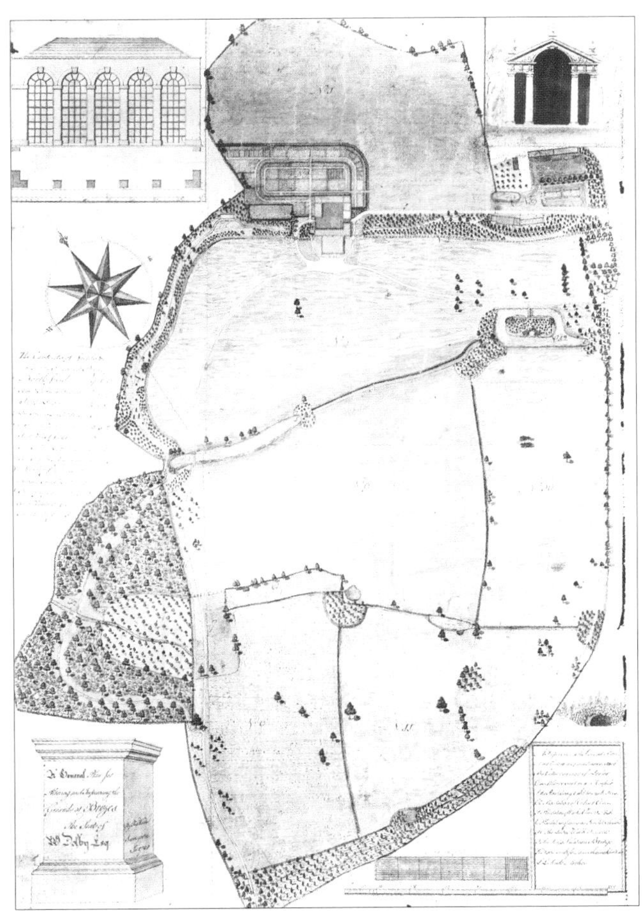

Fig 47 Brizes, Kelvedon Hatch: plan for improvement by Woods, 1788 (ERO D/DRO P1).

whole management, is ill-suited to the disposition, intent, and air of [the pleasure ground]'. There certainly were houses which stood in a sea of grass, and were criticised for it within decades of being laid out; but, as Samuel Fullmer wrote (1781), before Brown's death and before Repton had set up as a landscape designer, in general the pleasure ground should include 'different compartments consisting of ornamental tree plantations and shrubberies comprising beautiful flowering shrubs and evergreens and compartments of elegant flowers'.

Lancelot 'Capability' Brown is the first garden designer of whom almost everyone has heard, and of whom it was said that 'when he was the happiest man, he will be least remembered; so closely did he copy nature that his works will be mistaken' (anonymous obituary pasted by Walpole into his notebook at Brown's death). In fact art had a very considerable part in these ultimate designed landscapes, as is obvious as soon as one looks at any of his 'plans for improvement'. Brown is the most famous name in 18th-century garden history, and still the most controversial: criticised within ten years of his death for producing landscapes that were too smooth and too bland; yet reviled in the 19th century for quite a different reason, seen–often unjustly–as the destroyer of the formal grandeur of the 17th century.

Attitudes are still changing: just as flowers are being allowed to resume their rightful place in 18th-century garden history, so some of what Brown is supposed to have swept away is being revealed as having gone before he was called in–a recent surprising discovery is that Vanbrugh's renowned military garden at Blenheim, which Brown has been roundly condemned for destroying, was no longer in

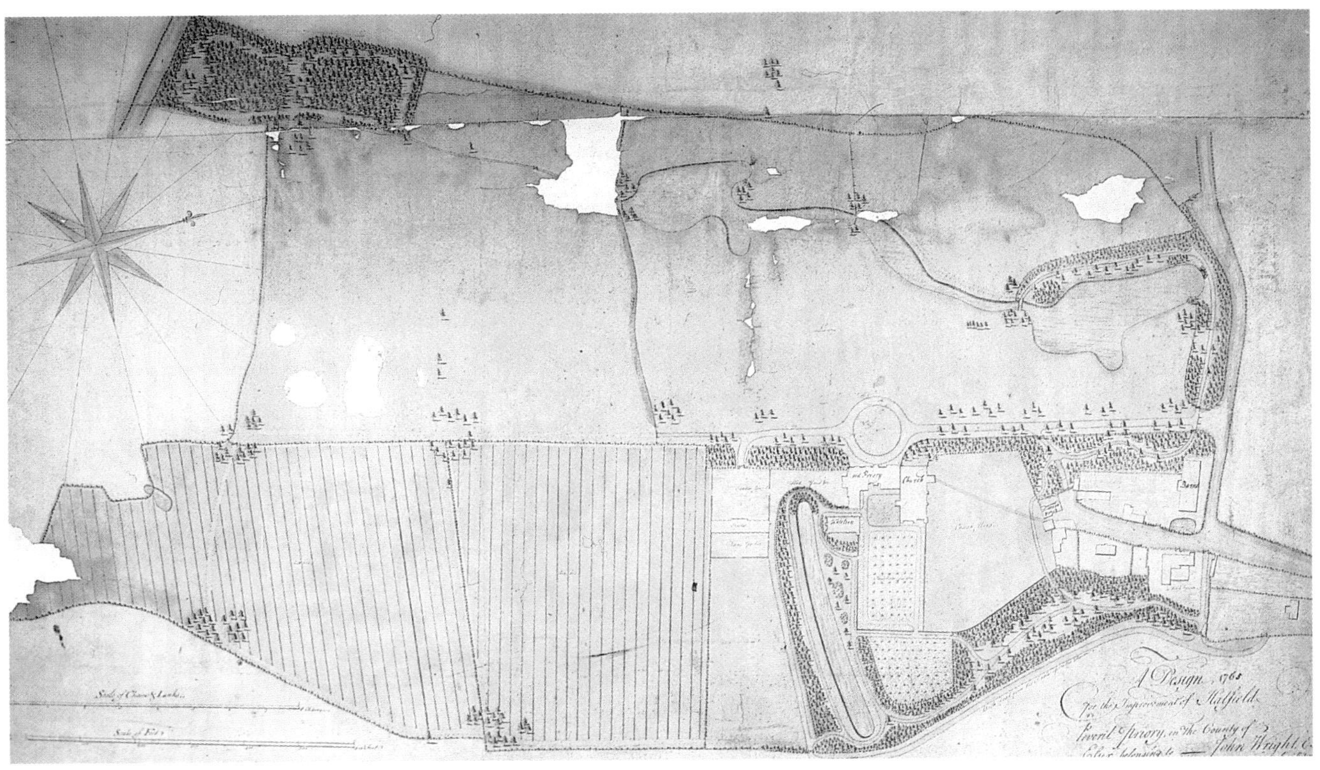

Fig 48 Hatfield Priory: plan for improvement by Woods, 1765 (ERO D/DBr P2).

existence when Brown began his improvements, according to a survey drawn up just beforehand (Booth 1995). On the other hand, it has been suggested that Brown's genius has perhaps been overstated, and that his true skill lay in promoting his business, which was to impose a rather static and unvarying design on his patrons' properties. This argument will doubtless ebb and flow, but whatever position one takes in this regard it is difficult to make an informed judgement from Brown's work in Essex, as it did not include any of his most important commissions. At Audley End, however, where he improved the west side of the park (Fig 49), his talent for realising the potential of a piece of ground cannot be denied.

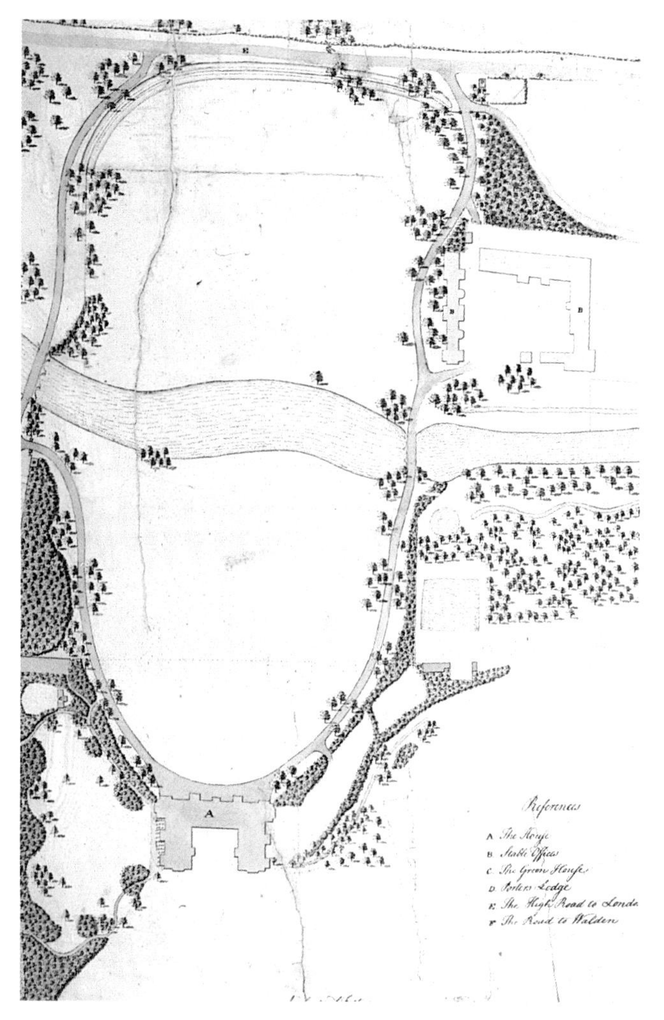

Fig 49 Audley End: design for partial improvement by Brown (English Heritage Data Library DoE Folder 24, appendix II).

Audley End is extremely well documented, and the development of the gardens and landscape is easy to follow. A plan of *c*.1726 attributed to Bridgeman shows the enormous Jacobean mansion still intact, and the River Cam channelled into a formal pond, symmetrically divided in front of it. By the time Sir John Griffin Griffin inherited the property in 1762, the gardens had lost the crispness of that layout, and it is hardly surprising that a visitor in that year found that 'the grounds are not remarkable, and will be improved by the changes which the owner is now busy making' (Kielmansegge 1902).

Brown signed a contract with Sir John in 1763, the most important clause of which concerned the widening of the Cam and softening its outlines as it ran in front of the house. A survey by Thomas Warren in 1783 (ERO: D/DQy 8) gives the result of the landscaping in cartographic form (Fig 50). Achieving the effects designed by Brown entailed far more than altering the course of the river, establishing new paths and planting trees. Accounts itemise the cost and labour of levelling, draining, grubbing out hedges and trees in the wrong place, planting elsewhere, and seeding, rolling and watering lawns. A small army of labourers was at work with wheelbarrows, at a halfpenny per barrowful of earth. New carriageways involved digging for gravel, excavating the roadbed and building the road up painstakingly. Between 1762 and 1786 Sir John spent a total of £61,072 in 'ornamenting, building–plantations, gardens and other out of doors improvements' (ERO: Audley End building accounts 1762-86, D/DBy). A quarrel with Sir John cut short Brown's work at Audley End, and the bridges and temples to finish the scheme were designed by other architects.

Thorndon was also given the Brown treatment between 1766 and 1772, having lain virtually dormant during the minority of the 9th baron. In the absence of estate accounts for this period, the extent of Brown's alterations have to be divined from a comparison of Petre's plan of 1733 and a survey of 1778 by John Spyers, a surveyor who worked for Brown (ERO: D/DP P30). It is still possible to see on the later plan much of Lord Petre's design: the menagerie remained with little change; the fish-tail pond to the east of the old house was reshaped by lengthening one tail and shortening the other; some of the block plantings flanking the subsidiary avenue were retained, surprisingly, and the remnants of the D-shaped pond and its associated planting behind the old house are still discernible (Fig 51) Most important, much of the previous Lord Petre's planting was obviously incorporated, even to the extent of using some of the grove with serpentine paths round the new house. Nevertheless, the overall effect, achieved at a cost of £5,000, is dramatically different, and brought Thorndon from an incomplete and overgrown layout of the 1730s to an elegant modern setting for Paine's new mansion.

Brown died in 1783 at the height of his fame. One of the few written accounts left by him, in mid-career in 1775, advised that the essentials for good landscape design were 'a perfect knowledge of the country and the objects in it, whether natural or artificial, and infinite delicacy in the planting etc. So much Beauty depending on the size of the trees and the colour of their leaves to produce the effect of light and shade'. This would make the 'English garden exactly fit for the owner, the Poet and the Painter' (letter of 2 June 1775 to Rev. Thomas Dyer, quoted by Stroud 1975, 157).

Fig 50 Audley End: survey by Thomas Warren, 1783 (ERO D/DQy 8).

In 1788, five years after Brown's death, Humphry Repton, by then 36 years old and with an unsuccessful business career behind him, living in relatively straitened circumstances in a cottage in Romford, announced his decision to become a landscape gardener; the first of the improvers, incidentally, to describe himself thus. His almost immediate success can be put down to two factors: the important social contacts he had made, and the fact that Brown had died only a few years previously and his style had not yet lost its appeal. Repton, indeed, set up initially as Brown's successor, and was seldom employed to rework a Brown improvement. More often he was consulted to bring still unimproved grounds, partly or wholly in a style by now lamentably unfashionable, into line with modern taste.

Without denying Repton's landscaping talents, it has been suggested that his popularity owed much to his skill with the paintbrush and his ability to present a prospective client with a most attractive package of suggestions, contained in one of his celebrated Red Books of 'before and after' views. Unlike Brown he was not a contractor, was a very indifferent cartographer, and did not provide planting lists. He frequently makes the comment in his Red Books

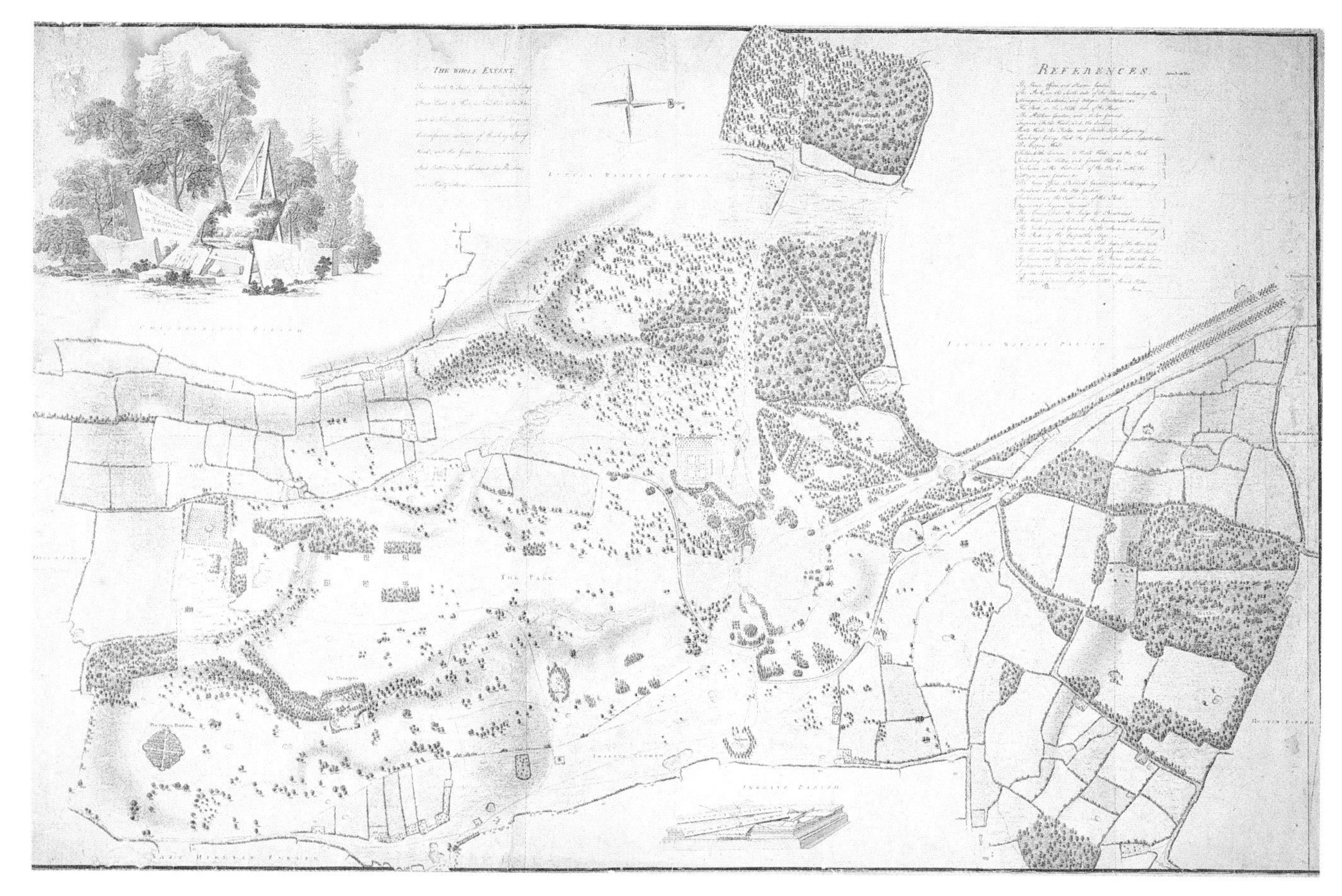

Fig 51 Thorndon Hall: detail of survey by John Spyers, 1778, showing avenue retained (ERO D/DP P30).

that his drawings show what potentially could be done, not what necessarily should be done. Unlike either Woods or Brown, whose styles remained fairly constant throughout their careers, Repton lived at a time when both political upheavals and public reactions to them, and the new, extreme aesthetic of the picturesque movement, forced him to adapt his ideas to suit the moment. His early designs are similar to Brown's in many ways, reflecting a period when the political notions of liberty and freedom were still felt to be expressed in naturalistic landscape, but by the time the French Revolution had passed through its worst excesses, Repton's improvements were reassuringly emphasising the values of property and the gentleness of nature.

Repton is associated with over twenty properties in Essex, although some of his work is known only from entries in account books or single watercolour sketches, and others were in that part of Essex now incorporated in Greater London. His *Red Book for Hill Hall* (ERO: D/DU 640/1), delivered in 1791, shows him steering a middle course between what he found already there and a full-scale reworking of the grounds. As so often, he was content to devise alterations to existing layouts (Fig 52), backed by new planting and possibly a road diversion, and so achieve a modern landscape without the upheaval that Brown's designs usually entailed. The illustration of the effect of the kitchen garden wall seen from the house evoked this comment: 'Who can see a glimpse of the distant country without wishing away that comfortless red wall to the right?' He spared the wall to the left, however, and in this he was probably unlike Brown, because its south aspect was of great value for sheltered winter walks. His very pragmatic solution was to remove the kitchen garden to a slightly more distant spot, and adorn the remaining wall in such a way as to make a useful and decorative feature of it. Similarly, the small building north of the house was to be made 'a little like the temple of the Sybills', but not only to improve its appearance; Repton felt that it needed 'shade against the western sun' which could be provided by 'a broad flat roof supported by collums'. Such an emphasis on practicality and comfort recurs continually. Repton stated unequivocally, 'However enthusiastically fond I may be of Landscape, yet I am fully aware... that... comfort and convenience... should take the lead of picturesque beauty' (*Red Book for Hill Hall*). He also remarks, however, that an insistence on utility can be taken too far and if, for example, the sweep of a carriage drive will be made less 'disgusting' by lengthening it into a more harmonious curve, then that is considered an acceptable sacrifice to practicality.

Privacy was of great importance to Repton, and to this end he frequently advised the diversion of a road or footpath to put a greater distance between a house and the public. The claim was invariably made, as legally it had to be, that the diversion was to the public benefit and sometimes this was even true. At Moor Hall, Harlow, Repton's suggested improvements of 1808 consisted mainly of diverting the road. He criticised 'the narowness of the skreen and shrubbery between the Garden and the high road' which would be remedied 'by removing the road to a better distance' (ERO: D/DEs T6). In this case the route for the public really was made shorter, but when two years later the nearby footpath was also diverted, the same excuse-although used-was no longer valid. The attitude to the passing public, and perhaps the character of the passing public itself, was disclosed by Repton in his *Red Book for Tewin Water* (Hertfordshire Record Office: D/Z 42 Z 1) where he notes that 'a foot path... passing close to the windows' laid the house open to 'carts, waggons, gypsies, poachers etc etc who feel they have a right of intrusion'.

Repton is perhaps best remembered for the enchantingly pretty designs he produced for the grounds near the house. Hilary Taylor has pointed out that these formal and ornate suggestions were features of his late designs, produced in direct response to a social and political situation in which liberty had led–specifically in France–to very undesirable excesses, and art was brought to the fore again in gardens, pushing nature gently into the background. This may be seen as the last stage in the designed landscape as garden, a style which passed from geometric stiffness and tortuous paths in the early part of the 18th century, to an emphasis on complete naturalness towards the mid-century, and culminating in Repton's synthesis of flower garden near the house with the park beyond. The way was now open for Loudon and a revival of interest in garden formality.

Essex is an interesting county in which to study the designed landscape: with few grand estates even in the 18th century, and even fewer remaining now, the majority of examples consisted of villa landscapes, relatively small properties bought by men of rising wealth and social ambition. Even Repton's work in Essex was largely confined to the south-west of the county, conveniently near to London for the successful entrepreneur, who could still feel that he had bought a country estate. Nevertheless, these acres of artificial naturalness made a considerable contribution to the wider landscape of Essex, which can still be glimpsed in the few estates, great or small, which have not been swept away by the pressure of housing development and the cost of maintenance.

Fig 52 Hill Hall: kitchen garden wall before and after improvement, as drawn by Repton in his Red Book, 1791 (ERO D/DU 640/1).

Essex in the 21st century

by Robert Tregay

I am a landscape architect and so I come to the landscape with a very different background from that of many of the other contributors. History and archaeology of the landscape are one part, and a very important part, of an approach to design and to larger scale environmental planning. My interest is in landscape history and its use in planning and designing for the future. How can we take historical knowledge and expertise, and use it in the planning and design of future landscapes, whether on a small scale–a park or a garden, or on a much larger scale–the whole county, a new settlement, a major housing development or a business park?

Twenty years ago the planning of the environment was dominated by engineers, architects and planners; landscape architects had a very minor role. There was something called SLOAP ('space left over after planning') and landscape architects, with few exceptions, were really relegated to filling in those bits of left-over space. Things have changed enormously and now landscape is seen as a prime consideration in major development projects. Unfortunately, most of the people involved in planning new environments have very little perception of the things that have been talked about today, with the exception perhaps of historic gardens. Historic parks and gardens are well-established assets of recognised importance. They are a field of specialist knowledge and are relatively well resourced. Historic landscapes, by contrast, are not widely recognised at all, although there is a core of academic knowledge amongst a small number of experts. There is much that we take for granted in the present forum that is completely unknown in the wider planning world. Because historic landscapes are rarely designated as such, the planning and development world takes not a jot of interest in them.

We are fortunate that the Essex landscape has been studied in depth; these studies have influenced planning policies and much can be learned nationally from this example. Given this background, how relevant are historic landscapes to the planning of future landscapes, as distinct from just being of interest in their own right as history? How do we get historic landscapes valued in the planning system? What about the concept of layers of history and how might the past influence new designs? When we are talking about the landscapes of the future, to what degree should the patterns and features of the past form part of them? When we have options to restore, to what period of history do we restore? When we have options to retain only parts of the past, which features do we preserve?

One of the interesting processes that helps to answer these questions is landscape assessment. This is a relatively new process of looking at landscapes on a large scale–very often a whole district, a county, or even a region. Such an assessment seeks to understand and categorise landscape in terms of its visual and historic character. The influence of landscape history and culture on the visual appearance and the ecological diversity of landscape is as great as the influence of geology, soils and landforms.

There is a strong link between the history and the ecology of the landscape. Not only have many historic features been lost in the landscape but so too has ecological diversity. Within Essex, 75% of coastal grazing marsh has been lost since the mid 1930s; 95% of flower-rich hay meadows have gone; between 1940 and 1973, 33% of ancient woodland was lost; and of the heathland which covered substantial areas of Essex, only 5 hectares of the true habitat are left. We can think of historic landscapes, therefore, also as habitats and as part of the pattern, detail and depth of the landscape. History is not just an academic matter–the study of the past; it helps to explain much of what we value so much in the landscape today.

How can we conserve the best of the past and ensure that it enriches the landscapes of the future? The first requirement is to understand and record the patterns and features of the landscape as an historic resource, and be able to put some value on this resource. A specialist historian might say categorically that all things from the past are important, but in making difficult, real–life decisions about development, conservation and design, one is necessarily making value judgements about what is important for the future. To do that, we need expert advice concerning the historic resource itself.

Many fascinating features, ancient parish boundaries, ditches and hedgerows remain unrecorded and unrecognised, except by a small number of specialists. In landscape planning rarely is any distinction drawn between one hedgerow and another. Even more rarely is an historic landscape pattern recognised, although there are exceptions, such as the shaws of south Essex, which have been brought to a wider audience. These special and irreplaceable features may be well known to the specialists but are completely unrecognised by the great majority of people actually involved in farming, owning or walking the land, and unrecognised even within the landscape planning professions. There are historic patterns going back a thousand years or more sometimes still extant in the present landscape. It is essential that these are recognised, appraised and, as far as possible, valued for their inherent importance, just as historic buildings and parks are, for example.

Once historic landscapes are researched, mapped and assessed, the next requirement is to incorporate historic features and patterns into plans for the future. This may mean simply recognising that such historic features exist and ensuring that no harm results to them. It may mean a far more conscious process that actually uses the past for inspiration in planning for the future, ensuring that historic features are not only conserved but are also interpreted and incorporated into a new landscape pattern, the character and richness of which stems from the many layers of history that can be discovered within it. This process needs to be a conscious, creative part of planning and design methodology, built into the system by which we plan for the future. It will not happen by accident.

Specifically, historic landscape assessment should form part of a broader landscape assessment, which in turn should be incorporated into masterplanning, design of new developments, countryside management, landscape guidelines for the countryside and so on. Therefore, we need to think of history in as broad a sense as possible. History is not just the property of historians; it is an integral part of our national culture, part of the landscape we value today, and often the key to understanding ecological diversity.

There are major processes of change going on in the countryside. Arguably some, such as hedgerow removal, are slowing down now, but many of the pressures are still there: 4.4 million new houses are to be built in the UK, according to government statistics, in the 20 years to 2016, of which 30% are planned to be in East Anglia. With the constraints of the Green Belt, there are substantial areas of the middle and northern part of Essex where there are enormous pressures for housing developments. Some of us may hope that those pressures will not result in major new developments, but they surely will. On the edge of Chelmsford and many other places, we can see them already going on. We need, therefore, to have our historic landscape information available now, and make sure that it informs the decisions that have to be made as part of the planning process.

An example from Essex of the use of historic information is the landscape assessment of Thames Chase. Thames Chase is a 'community forest', where Landscape Design Associates carried out a landscape assessment in order to prepare guidelines on how the landscape should develop in the future. We suggested that development of the community forest should be influenced by, and take place within, the context of the character and history of the present landscape. We used a methodology that we and the Cornwall Archaeological Unit had developed in Cornwall. When we applied it here in Essex some very interesting results emerged, illustrating how different parts of the Thames Chase area owed their origin to different periods of history, land clearance and agricultural processes (Fig 53). This work was of great value in determining the boundaries of the different character areas and forest action areas.

If a farmer now comes to the Community Forest Team and says, 'I want to do something to contribute towards the community forest, how do I do it?', these landscape design guidelines will provide a basis for advising on how the existing landscape might be developed in the future in a way which is consistent with the historic character of the area and its sense of place. Design guidelines are of value in helping to retain the differences, the sense of place and the special identity of each landscape character area and place. They prevent landscape change being driven either by available grants or ill-advised, ad hoc (but often well-meaning) improvements, which can lead to the destruction of assets of historic interest.

At West Horndon we were asked to look at a site in a typically denuded, 'arable-ised' landscape: one of large fields, clipped hedges and few trees. To the north of the village are two shaws, ancient linear woods following the characteristic north–south alignment of three parish boundaries and the field pattern in this area. There is an interesting question as to whether new shaws should have a place in the planning of the community forest in this area, rather than some other form of landscape pattern or feature. We believe that there was great scope for improving the visual character and the ecological richness of this landscape through planting. But how to design that planting? We suggested that in this particular area it should be by the creation of new shaws, in a pattern that stemmed from the historic examples. If we were in a different part of the country new shaws like this would probably have been inappropriate. In, say, the Forest of Arden in Warwickshire, the priority might be hedgerow conservation and the re-establishment of hedgerow oaks. In another part of the country it might be to plant up large blocks of woodland or plant peripheral woodlands by natural regeneration, or whatever was appropriate. The design recommendations, therefore, are informed by what we know about the history of the area. In the case of Thames Chase, the design guidelines provide practical advice about how shaws and other features might be formed, and how recreational use might be made of them. The guidelines visualise and make recommendations on the different forms and patterns which can be developed in each of the landscape character areas. The visualisation can be in the form of eye-level sketches, block diagrams, cross-sections or computer-generated photomontages.

A proposed housing development at Heybridge in Maldon District by Beazer Homes serves as an example of how new housing development can be planned to reflect the historic landscape. From the 1777 Chapman and André map it can be seen that the heathland around Great Totham, Tiptree Heath and Great Braxted has arms coming down through the site. Although the heath has been lost, the boundaries of these 'linear greens' remain–hence the name Broad Street Green Lane. This is an important historic feature, part of a former economy and land use of historic interest, which we needed to take into account in our masterplanning for a major new housing development. Interestingly, Heybridge Wood is recorded as ancient woodland (pre-1600), and is shown on earlier plans and on later plans, but is not shown on the Chapman and André map of 1777. This is perhaps not because it did not exist in 1777, but possibly it had been felled or coppiced at that time and was therefore not recorded. Many maps of this period were

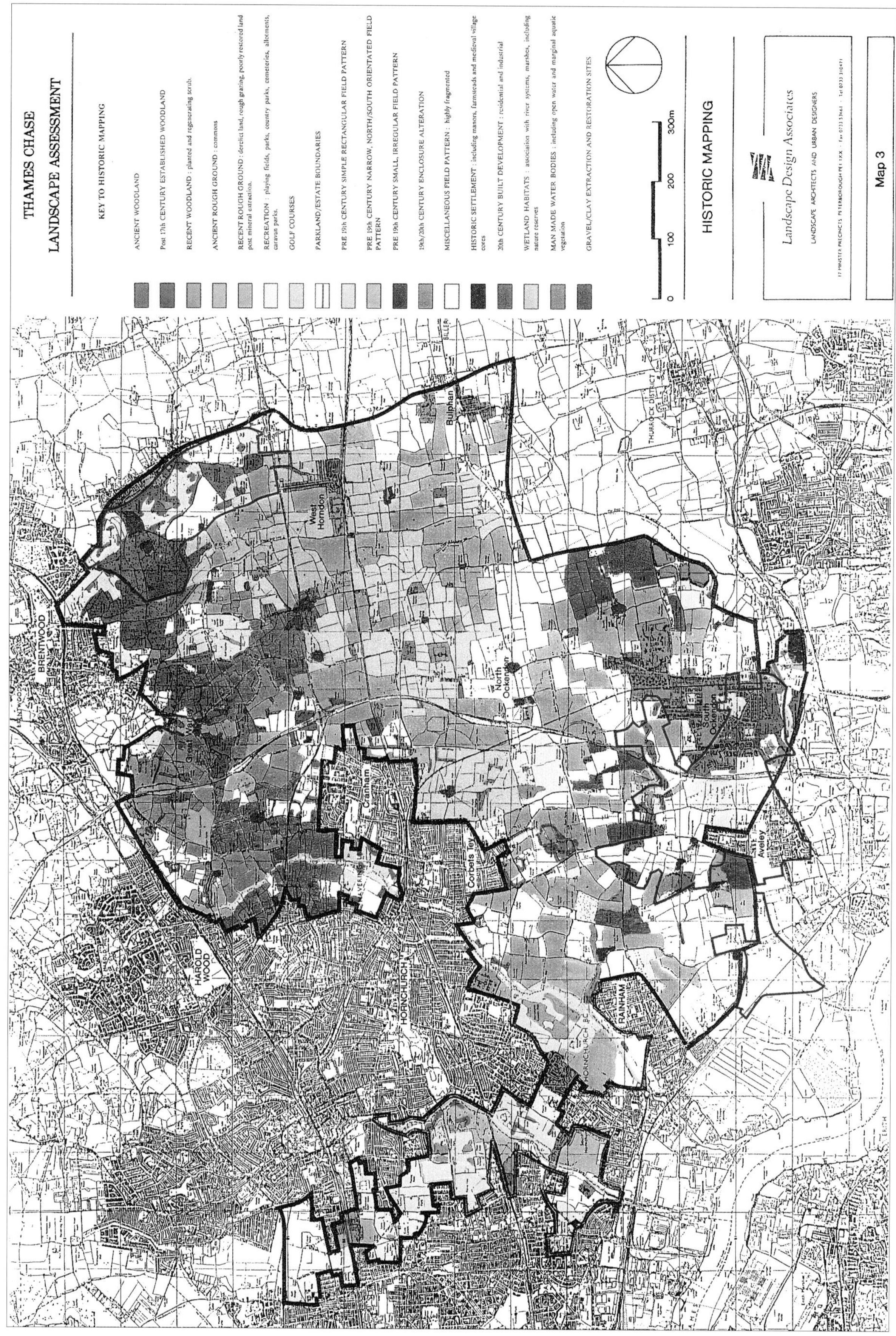

Fig 53 Thames Chase landscape assessment: historic mapping.

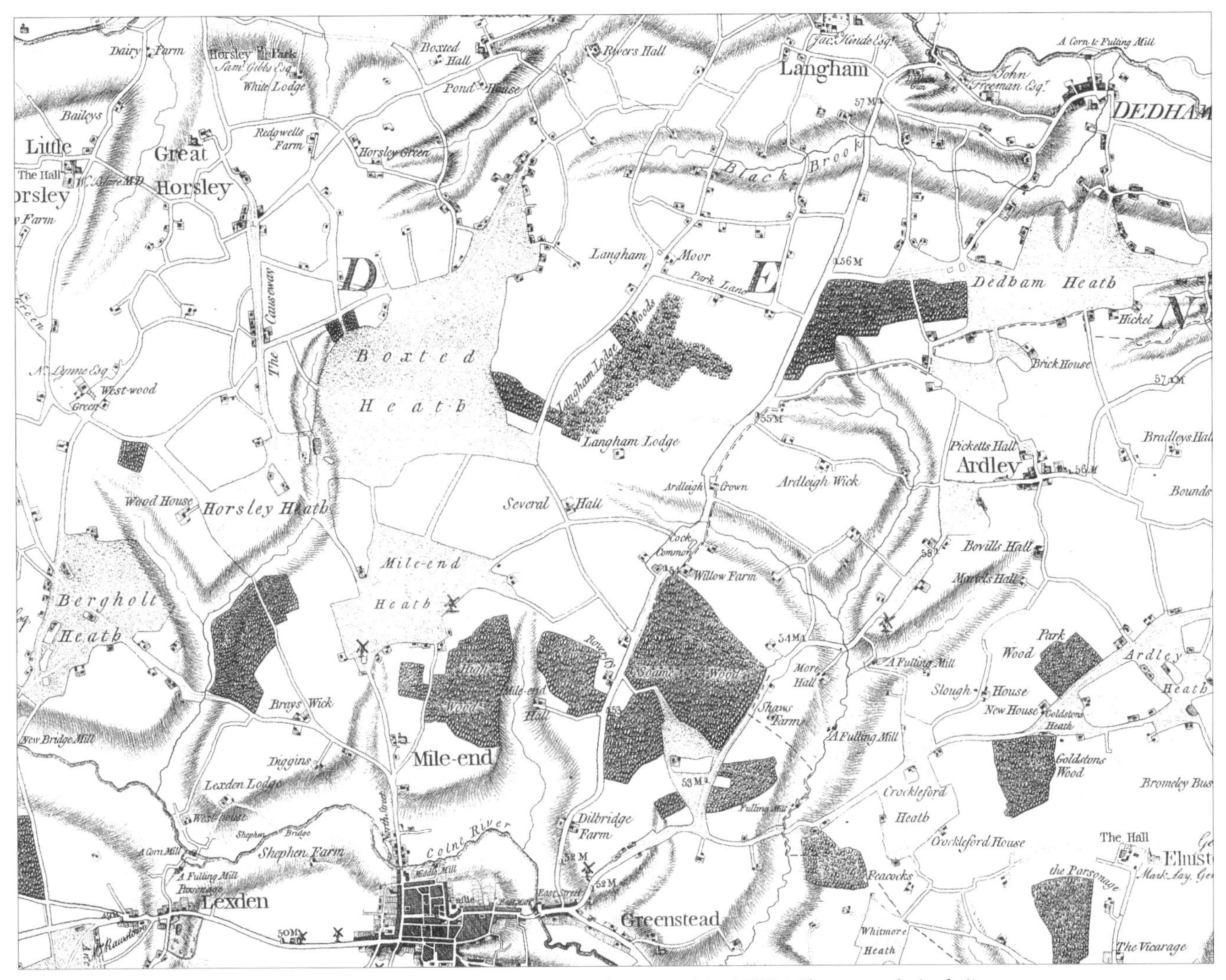

Fig 54 Dedham Vale: heaths to south mapped in 1777 (Chapman & André).

mapped from roads and not all were accurate. Heybridge Wood was only one of the historical features we found on early maps. A linear green, the former hedgerow system, other former woodlands, and a small manor house or grand farmhouse with ornamental gardens around it (of which no sign exists at the present time) are aspects which informed the masterplanning process, along with agricultural land quality, services, landform, landholdings and other factors which go into the design melting pot.

Another potential development site in Essex was at Andrews Airfield, which covered parts of the parishes of Great Saling, Stebbing and Rayne. Again, the 1777 map helps us understand the historical process. We took the historic name of Levells Green for our proposed new settlement from these early maps. Interesting interlinked linear greens shown on the 1777 map were swept away when Andrews Airfield was built in the Second World War, but the masterplan incorporated ideas for their recreation. Views from the site to the historic church spire at Stebbing was another one of the design influences. We reintroduced the lanes and the links between Saling and Stebbing as part of our plan. High priority was placed on the need to protect ancient woodlands. We proposed a major landscape restoration concept linked to the new development, together with the establishment of a Trust to run the farming landscape. The historic landscape pattern would be restored, and new features established, thus ensuring an environmentally-friendly landscape setting for the new settlement, complete with enhanced access to further enrich 'Living in the Countryside'.

A further case study is Dedham Vale, or 'Constable Country', as it is known. Partly in Essex and partly in Suffolk, it was designated in 1970 as an AONB ('area of outstanding natural beauty'), a designation that can be traced directly to mounting pressures for development in the mid-1960s and its cultural associations with the 19th-century landscape painter, John Constable. The historic landscape assessment once again formed part of the preliminary assessment work. The important features in the historic development of the landscape included ancient woodland or replanted ancient woodland, medieval settlements with possible Saxon origins, medieval churches with possible Saxon origins, 17th-century parkland that possibly originated in medieval deer parks, existing ancient small-scale field patterns, areas of former common and heathland, and 20th-century orchards, now disappearing but, in fact, very interesting features, and potentially restorable through the Countryside Stewardship programme (Fig 54). In this case, as elsewhere, culture, history, archaeology and ecology all come together and help us understand the landscape. As a result of the study Dedham Vale was divided into landscape character areas, each with its own special character, which can be understood as much by historic as natural factors. For each landscape character area, different design and management guidelines for its future development have been proposed, some reflecting a restoration of past character, some suggesting a completely new landscape character (Fig 55).

In Constable Country, the threat in the 1960s was housing and other development attracted by the improved A12 which runs through the area; if that has to be widened, it may be a threat again. The AONB designation has effectively prevented large-scale housing development. The latest threat comes from mobile telephone masts. There are three or four applications around Dedham at the moment which could affect the character of this 'rural idyll'. Even though it has changed since Constable's time, the landscape still retains the essence which Constable expressed for us in his paintings. That is what is being conserved for us now, and even a single intrusion like a mast, which breaks the skyline where Constable painted only trees and church spires, is a threat to such a landscape. If it comes to appeal at a public inquiry, to be able to justify the importance of those landscapes we need to understand them, to categorise them, and to have more accessible information about how we use history in the planning of landscapes for the future.

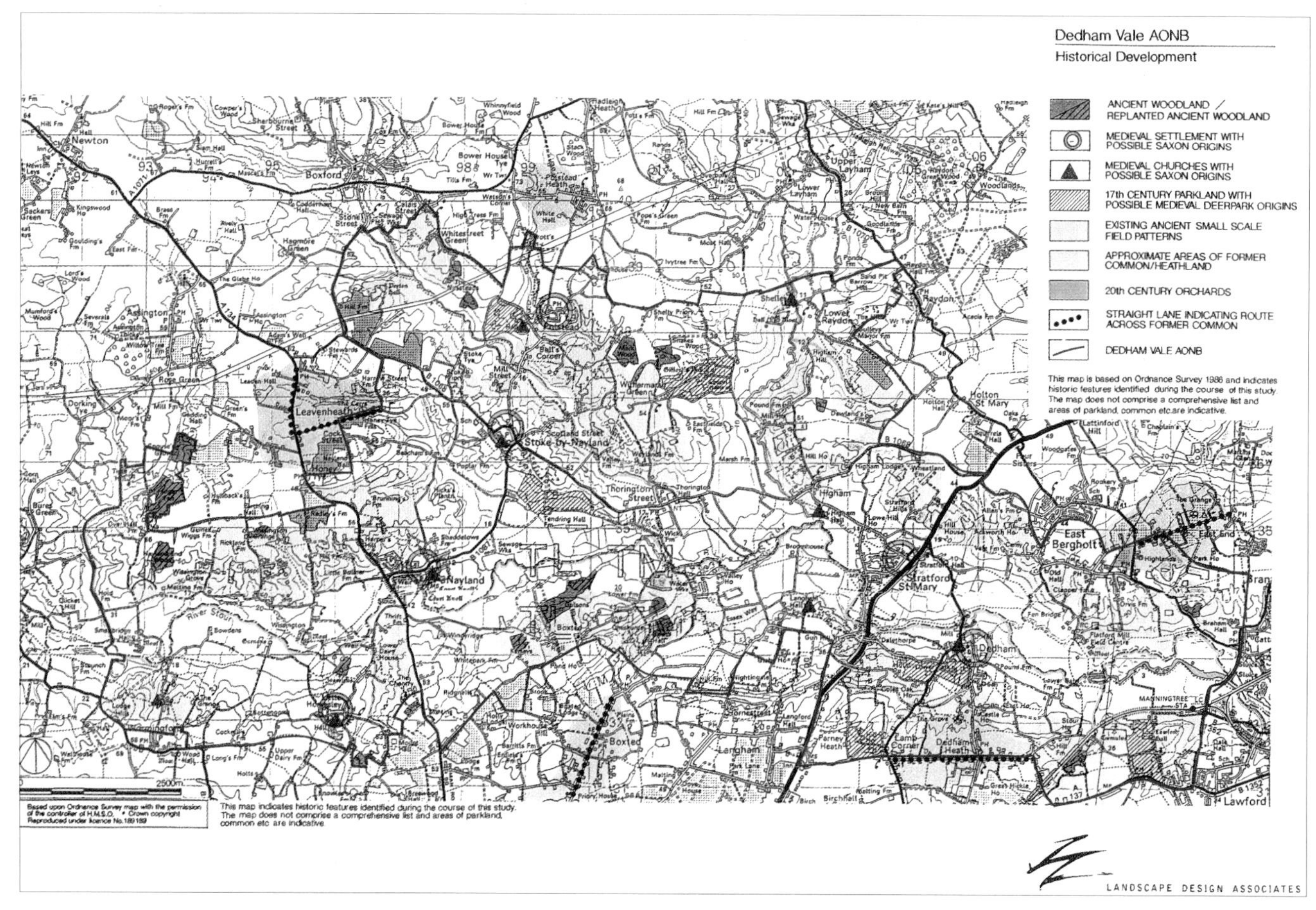

Fig 55 Dedham Vale: landscape assessment.

9

Change in the Essex landscape: a postscript

by Martin Wakelin

Individuals and small groups have limited influence on the landscape although the marks they make can be clearly evident. Ambition, power and planning enable larger-scale changes to be made. With the development of larger and more efficient machinery, through the 19th and 20th centuries, man's desire to shape the land whether for profit, improvement or pleasure has had increasing opportunity. The physical effect that can be wrought by modern tools in a short period of time is of quite a different order of magnitude and scale than the human hand alone could ever achieve. An increase in the rate and scale of change in the landscape, through history, is quite evident. As the pace of that change increased and became more noticeable, a reaction to that change began to be evident, commentators invariably looking back nostalgically to a previous golden age of rural harmony and beauty. In examining current forces of change and seeking ways in which to conserve the landscape, it is fascinating and salutary to compare the issues previous commentators have identified and the prescriptions they espoused.

Perhaps the earliest most noticeable change in the landscape came with the parliamentary enclosures, mainly from 1750-1850, which altered great tracts of central England. In Essex enclosure of common fields was confined to the north-west of the county, and enclosure of other common land was limited mostly to former heaths. Quite apart from the changes in land tenure and social relations that enclosure brought, the process introduced quite new textures into the landscape. The open fields and the heaths and commons, areas of open rough grazing which supported a wide range of husbandry and other activities, were replaced by a distinctive, planned pattern of quickthorn hedges which largely ignored earlier landscape features. As Tom Williamson and Liz Bellamy have pointed out (1987):

> 'although the hedge is now eulogised in England, and symbolises the countryside we all have the right to enjoy, not so long ago it was hated by large sections of the people as a symbol of tyranny and despotism. To many the hedge meant enclosure, and a system of property which disregarded not only the rights of the people, but also the traditional way of life which had formerly protected those rights. Many looked back to the time before enclosures as a golden age of rural harmony and happiness.'

They quote William Cobbett's *Rural rides:*

> 'I learnt to hate a system that could lead English gentlemen to disregard matters like these! That could induce them to tear up "wastes" and sweep away occupiers like those I have described! Wastes indeed! Give a dog an ill name. Was Horton Heath a waste? Was it a "waste" when a hundred, perhaps, of healthy boys and girls were playing there of a Sunday, instead of creeping about covered with filth in the alleys of a town?'

A common of the type described by Cobbett would not readily accord with our 20th-century view of a traditional rural idyll. Surtees, used to 'grass, grass, grass, nothing but grass for miles and miles', also complained about the new hedge: 'real sportsmen take no pleasure in leaping!', but in time hunting practice, as many a sporting print shows, adapted to the new landscape.

The industrial revolution produced dramatic changes. The advent of the railways, in particular, caused great consternation in the 19th century. W G Hoskins vividly describes the scale and effect of such changes. In *The making of the English landscape* (1955) he illustrates this with a passage from Dickens' *Dombey and Son* which describes the mayhem of the construction process:

> '...deep pits and trenches dug in the ground; enormous heaps of earth and clay thrown up; ...a chaos of carts, overthrown and jumbled together, lay topsy-turvy at the bottom a steep unnatural hill.'

Wordsworth and Ruskin were both ardent campaigners against the spread of railways. In 1844 Wordsworth was aroused by the proposal to build a railway from Kendal to Windermere. Hoskins writes that Wordsworth's 'two long letters to the *Morning Post* marshal every conservative argument against the proposal':

> 'Is then no nook of English ground secure from rash assault?'

In 1883 Ruskin wrote in a letter, 'You may always put my name–without asking leave–to any petition against any railway anywhere' (quoted in Waterson 1994).

The National Trust was formed, initially, to protect landscape from change rather than to preserve and exhibit buildings. In 1895 the Trust was given an area of open cliff above Barmouth with the donor's wish 'to put into custody of some society that will never vulgarise it, or prevent wild Nature from having its own way... I wish to avoid the abomination of asphalt paths and the cast iron seats of serpent design' (Waterson 1994).

Richard Jefferies (1904) wrote about many of the changes apparent in his lifetime. The jealous guarding by the gamekeeper of pheasant and trout, to the detriment of many other birds and animals; the arrival of agricultural machinery, such as threshers and steam ploughs, which brought with them the beginning of hedgerow removal and a less populated countryside. He also regretted the replacement of tiles with slate which he found 'an offence, nothing less' as well as reminding us how life in the countryside could be at once idyllic and quite brutal.

Clough Williams-Ellis, with *England and the Octopus* (1928), tried to prick the nation's thick-skinned conscience, railing against the spread of towns and other insults to the countryside. His 'Devil's Dictionary' identifies some of the threats: Advertisements, Aerodromes, Broadcasting Aerials, Borough Engineers, Bungalows, Electric Power Distribution, Golf Courses, Petrol Pumps and Soldiers. Amongst these banes he includes Archaeologists and Antiquaries, writing:

> 'These, like elephants, are generally useful but sometimes extremely dangerous. Their gimlet eyes have a special and peculiar focus. Flint arrow-heads and the Old Stone Age are apt to look larger, more interesting and more important to them than Georgian town-halls or the twentieth century. They seem frequently to have perverted standards of value, preferring what is merely rare to what is beautiful'.

Williams-Ellis went on to warn against the public 'considering local antiquaries as *ipso facto* authorities on architecture and amenity, and general arbiters of taste'.

Patrick Abercrombie, a contemporary, took a less iconoclastic line. He recognised that the countryside, created as it is by the action of man is the richest, most vivid piece of history that we possess. The new process of 'country planning' was the perpetuation of a well-established practice but the agent was now the local authority rather than the great estate. His concerns (1934) included: afforestation; the car and resultant pressures such as ribbon development; the expansion of leisure and 'the horrors of the fully exploited beauty spot–whose very name suggests its fate: gramophones, roundabouts, cock-shies, automatic sweet machines, tea booths, picture postcards, touts and crippled mendacity'; 'badly textured, worse lettered and worst coloured advertisements'; and the initial spread of the electricity companies' national grid with, he thought, a consequential decentralisation of industry.

Abercrombie debated alternative planning principles. 'Country' preservation and the zoning of activities, he considered an admission of failure. Pope's idea that 'Whatever is right, is right' and the concept of functional design being acceptable anywhere, he felt were *laissez-faire.* The 'local materials' solution, which argued that only old sorts of materials and old methods of building should be used so that nothing new might appear was 'devoid of courage' and 'based on the fallacy that the English countryside is a museum piece'. All three methods, 'localisation of certain forms; mechanisation of certain parts (as by the aqueduct, viaduct and steel bridge in the past and in the pylon to-day); and the continuance of traditional building' had their roles to play and could not be ignored. Control, under the new Town and Country Planning Act, while it might not create first-class design could prevent outrage. To counter the worst excesses of these approaches he concluded that the principles needed to be exercised with skill and artistry and with a full knowledge of the processes at work.

In 1955 Hoskins raised our awareness and helped us read the historical elements in the landscape. He had his perspective on contemporary landscape change. Chapter 10 of *The making of the English landscape,* entitled 'The landscape today', is strong stuff:

> '...especially since the year 1914, every single change in the English Landscape has either uglified it or destroyed its meaning, or both'.

Hoskins identified the decay and fall of the country house and its parkland, the loss of hedgerows in East Anglia, and is particularly scathing about the misuse of the countryside by the armed forces. He describes airfields flayed bare, where above them

> 'drones, day after day, the obscene shape of the atom-bomber, laying a trail like a filthy slug upon Constable's and Gainsborough's sky. England of the Nissen hut, the "pre-fab", and the electric fence, of the high barbed wire around some unmentionable devilment; England of the arterial by-pass, treeless and stinking of diesel oil, murderous with lorries...England of high explosive falling on prehistoric monuments of Dartmoor. Barbaric England of the scientists, the military men and the politicians: let us turn away and contemplate the past before all is lost to the vandals'.

Lionel Brett (1965) found that 'the things that worried our parents–ribbon development and indiscriminate advertising–have almost (though not quite) stopped'. His concerns were with the protection of areas of tranquillity, for its own sake, against overhead power lines and the failure of all parties, planners, builders, architects and market forces working towards a corrupted public taste, to meet the challenge of providing new housing. In terms of a landscape ideal he follows Humphry Repton's edict that the countryside should exhibit 'a just sense of general utility', a balance between beauty and function. He also sees the local authority as the successor to the landed gentry but finds that the provision of amenity is often outweighed by expediency. He wants elected members of local government to be aware 'of the English landscape and townscape as a historical and evolving work of art and science'. If such people can't be found he proposes high-status co-opted boards to counter crude solutions to technical problems. Such boards 'would not need to be guided by temporising and essentially immature directives such as green belts, areas of outstanding natural beauty, listed buildings and so on, because it would see and feel its county, with all its landscapes and all its buildings, as a living whole'.

By the 1970s concern was widespread that identifiable processes of change in the landscape had reached such momentum that, unless checked, the consequent damage to the countryside would be irreparable (Fig 56). Essex County Council held a conference and the published proceedings, *The Essex countryside–a landscape in decline?* (1972), identified some of the issues involved and looked forward to how the landscape might appear at the end of the century. The outlook seemed bleak but the paper proposed a new framework for countryside planning and its implementation.

Fig 56 Three successive views of the same (imaginary but typical) Essex landscape in the course of post-Second World War redevelopment

The major concern was loss of tree and hedgerow cover mainly through agricultural rationalisation and Dutch Elm disease. Four other concerns were also identified: the intrusive spread of farm buildings; the proliferation of overhead cables, pylons and poles; the impact of new roads without effective planting to soften their imprint on the landscape; and development on the perimeter of towns and villages.

Despite this gloom, various opportunities to reduce the scale and impact of adverse change were identified. It was important to work with, rather than dictate to, farmers and landowners. Some hedgerow loss was considered inevitable but equivalent areas of new woodland could be encouraged with a scheme of grants. Linear woodland could be encouraged on the edge of settlements. Valley floors, often poor land subject to gravel extraction, could be developed in combination with the rationalisation of public rights of way into new linear landscapes ideal for 20th-century recreation. The idea was to replace the 19th-century landscape system, combining food and timber production and meeting the needs of recreation in a 21st-century landscape, and achieving a similarly balanced system to meet a new rationale. The most fundamental change in attitude brought about by this quite radical approach was that the farming community, represented by the Essex Farmers Union, took it seriously.

John Hunter developed some of these ideas further in *Land into landscape* (1985). He also had his view of where the future lay. New landscapes such as those created in the Tennessee Valley Project and the Zuider Zee polders were heady stuff for landscape planners and architects but the opportunities for such radically new starting points were rare. 'In existing long-established landscapes a far subtler approach is necessary that begins with an understanding of their evolution and evaluation of the patterns and features already there; with such knowledge, the legacy of the past, often irreplaceable in biological and historical terms, can enrich the landscapes of today in a process of adaptation and carefully considered change.' He also warns of the harm perpetrated by experts championing solutions on the basis of their own blinkered interests.

So where are we now? We have learnt to love hedges. The railways Ruskin so abhorred have developed a 'heritage' of their own. We are rather fond of serpentine benches. 'Tea Shoppes' and ribbon development are thankfully rare. The rate of loss of hedges has been reduced and stubble burning stopped. Public rights of way, being matters of law, are very resistant to rationalisation.

Approaching the year 2000, the recent threats of wall-to-wall golf courses and out-of-town shopping centres have risen and receded. Farming practice is still the principal defining mechanism in the wider landscape. Subsidies are creating a landscape of their own. Arable crops are grown on unsuitable land, only supported by liberal applications of fertiliser and pesticides. Because of efficient machinery, rarely is ploughed land left bare long enough for us to appreciate the browns, tans, ochres and russets of weathering soil. Set-aside has replaced arable rationalisation. Mad cows and subsidised sheep are departing fringe pasture leaving it to develop bracken, scrub or rank grass instead of meadows, rich in wildflowers.

Despite subjective concern about loss of habitat, where such a thing can be measured objectively the facts are quite revealing. In the Dedham Vale the area of grassland in 1840 was 66%, in 1930 68%, in 1957 it had fallen to 57% but in

1991 it had risen to 70%. Woodland cover has also increased since Constable painted the landscape, in the early 19th century, even though much of this is in poplar and bat willow plantations. John Hunter has shown there is evidence the extent of arable in parts of Essex is now similar to that in the 14th century (Hunter 1999).

The water authorities backed away from the attitude that all rivers should be seen as agricultural drains kept free of any vegetation that might impede maintenance regimes. Overhead wires are still a concern, although now we hardly notice the national grid. Wind and gas-powered local generating stations are perhaps a price worth paying if they reduce further expansion of the grid. A community forest is beginning to grow in that part of south Essex most devastated by quarrying, tipping and elm disease. In expanding woodland cover the grain of the landscape is respected and ancient field patterns used as inspiration. Ancient landscapes, country lanes and historic parks and gardens all have a measure of protection. Archaeology is given a proper respect in the planning process in the light of 'PPG16', *Planning Policy Guidance: archaeology and plannning* (DoE 1990).

Ignoring the ironies of the gradual acceptance of change, a recurring theme is that, to plan properly for the countryside, full knowledge of what elements, in combination, determine its form must be freely available to all who have an influence in shaping the landscape. A heightened awareness of the full context and value of a site is an essential precursor to proper consideration of any planning matter. Landscape character description and analysis, underpinned by knowledge of the landscape's history, helps to define and maintain local distinctiveness. The Sites and Monument Record ensures that nothing of archaeological value is unnecessarily disturbed.

It is to be hoped that the Cressing Landscape Conference, and the publication of these papers, contributes in a significant way to our understanding of the Essex landscape and the forces of history that have shaped its character, complexity and charm.

Fig 57 Hatfield Forest, a remarkable survival and a model for 'new landscapes'

Bibliography and Abbreviations

Abercrombie, P, 1934 *Country planning and landscape design*, London: Hodder & Stoughton

Aberg, F A (ed), 1978 *Medieval moated sites,* London: CBA Research Report **17**

Addyman, P V, [et al], 1963 'Two medieval sites near Sedbergh' *Yorkshire Archaeol J* **41,** 27-42

Ainsworth, S, Cocroft, D, Everson, P, & Ryan, P, 1991 'A fragmentary grave cover and the site of Woodham Walter church' *Essex Archaeol Hist* **22,** 170-3

Allen, J R L, 1997 'The geoarchaeology of land in coastal wetland: a sketch from Britain and the North-west European Atlantic-North Sea Coast' *Archaeol J* **154,** 1-54

Andrews, D D, 1986 'Old Copped Hall: the site of the Tudor mansion' *Essex Archaeol Hist* **17,** 96-106

Andrews, D D (ed), 1993 *Cressing Temple: a Templar and Hospitaller manor in Essex,* Chelmsford: Essex County Council

Andrews, D D, Robey, T, Ryan, P & Tyers, I, 1994 'The Granary at Cressing Temple' *Essex Archaeol Hist* **25,** 79-106

Anon 1913-28 *Feet of Fines for Essex, Volume 2: 1272-1326,* Colchester: Essex Archaeological Society

Anon 1929-49 *Feet of Fines for Essex, Volume 3: 1327-1422,* Colchester: Essex Archaeological Society

Aston, M, Austin, D, and Dyer, C (eds), 1989 *The rural settlements of medieval England,* Oxford: Blackwell

Austin, D, 1985 'Doubts about morphogenesis' *J Hist Geog* **11** (2), 201-9

Bailey, M, 1989 *A marginal economy? East Anglian Breckland in the later Middle Ages,* Cambridge University Press

Barford, P M, 1988a 'After the Red Hills: salt-making in Late Roman, Saxon and medieval Essex' *Colchester Archaeological Group Annual Bulletin* **31,** 3-8

Barford, P M, 1988b 'Fired clay objects', in D Bond, *Excavations at the North Ring, Mucking, Essex* (East Anglian Archaeology **43**), Chelmsford: Essex County Council, 37-41

Bassett, S R, 1982 *Saffron Walden: excavations and research 1972-80,* London: CBA Research Report **45**

Bedwin, O (ed), 1996 *The archaeology of Essex: proceedings of the 1993 Writtle Conference,* Chelmsford: Essex County Council

Bell, M, 1989 'Environmental archaeology as an index of continuity and change in the medieval landscape' in Aston *et al,* 269-86

Benton, P, 1867-8 *A history of Rochford Hundred* (reprinted 1978 with additions by L E Jerram-Burrows), Shoeburyness: Rochford Hundred Historical Society

Beresford, M W, & Hurst, J G, 1971 *Deserted medieval villages,* London, Lutterworth

Booth, D, 1995 'Blenheim Park on the eve of "Mr Brown's improvements"' *J Garden Hist* **15** (2), 107-125

Bradley, R, & Gordon, K, 1988 'Human skulls from the River Thames, their dating and significance' *Antiquity* **62,** 503-9

Brett, L, 1965 *Landscape in distress,* London: Architectural Press

Britnell, R H, 1983 *Agriculture in a region of ancient enclosure, 1185-1500,* Nottingham Medieval Studies **27,** 37-55

Brooks, H, & Bedwin, O, 1989 *Archaeology at the airport: the Stansted Archaeological Project 1985-89,* Chelmsford: Essex County Council

Brown, A E, & Taylor, C C, 1989 'The origins of dispersed settlement; some results from fieldwork in Bedfordshire' *Landscape History* **11,** 61-81

Brown, N, 1987 'Hadleigh, Chapel Lane', in D Priddy (ed) 'Work of the Essex County Council Archaeology Section, 1986' *Essex Archaeol Hist* **18,** 82-103

Brown, N, 1988 'A Late Bronze Age enclosure at Lofts Farm, Essex' *Proc Prehist Soc* **54,** 249-302

Brown, N, 1996 'The archaeology of Essex c.1500-500 BC' in Bedwin, 26-37

Brown, N, 1997 'A landscape of two halves: the Neolithic of the Chelmer Valley/ Blackwater Estuary, Essex', in P Topping (ed) *The Neolithic landscape* (Neolithic Studies Group Monograph **2**)

Brown, N, & Glazebrook, J (eds), forthcoming *Research and archaeology: a framework for the Eastern Counties, 2: research agenda and strategy* (East Anglian Archaeology occasional paper), Norwich: Scole Archaeological Committee for East Anglia

Buckley, D G (ed), 1980 *Archaeology in Essex to AD 1500,* London: CBA Research Report **34**

Burrows, J W, 1909 *Southend-on-Sea and district: historical notes,* Southend-on-Sea: J H Burrows & Sons (reprinted 1970, Wakefield: S R Publishers)

Camden, W, 1607 *Britannia, or a chorographical description of the flourishing kingdoms of England, Scotland and Ireland: ...Essex* (1695 edition reprinted 1971, Newton Abbott: David & Charles)

Campbell, B, 1981 'Commonfield origins–the regional dimension' in Rowley, 112-29

CChR: Calendar of Charter Rolls

CCR: Calendar of Close Rolls

CFR: Calendar of Fine Rolls

Chapman, J, & André, P, 1777 *A map of the County of Essex* (reprinted 1970, Chelmsford: Essex Record Office)

Christy, M, 1907 'Salt-making', in *VCH Essex,* vol **1,** 445

Christy, M, & Dalton, W H, 1928 'On two large groups of marsh-mounds on the Essex coast' *Trans Essex Archaeol Soc* (New Series) **18,** 27-56

CIPM: Calendar of Inquisitions Post Mortem

Clark, D L, 1970 *Beaker Pottery of Great Britain and Ireland,* Cambridge University Press

Clarke, A, 1993 *Excavations at Mucking, Volume 1: the site atlas,* London: English Heritage

Clarke, C P, 1993 'Collins Creek', in P Gilman (ed) 'Archaeology in Essex 1992' *Essex Archaeol Hist* **24,** 209

CLR: Calendar of Liberate Rolls

Coles, B, 1990 'Anthropomorphic wooden figurines from Britain and Ireland' *Proc Prehist Soc* **56,** 315-34

Colvin, H M, 1963 *The history of the King's Works: the Middle Ages, Volume 2,* London: HMSO

Coones, P, 1992 'The unity of landscape', in L Macinnes & C R Wickham-Jones (eds) *All natural things: archaeology and the Green Debate,* Oxford: Oxbow Monograph **21**

Corke, D, 1986 *The nature of Essex: the wildlife and ecology of the county,* Buckingham: Barracuda Books

Cox, B, 1976 'The place-names of the earliest English records' *English Place-Names Soc J* **8,** 12-66

CPR: Calendar of Patent Rolls

Cracknell, B E, 1959 *Canvey Island: the history of a marshland community,* Leicester University Press: Department of English Local History Occasional Papers **12**

Cromarty, D, 1966 *The fields of Saffron Walden in 1400,* Chelmsford: Essex Record Office

Crowe, K, 1996 'The early medieval settlement on Canvey Island' *Essex J* **31** (1), 12-17, 26

Crummy, N, 1982 'Mersea Island: the 11th-century boundaries' *Essex Archaeol Hist* **14,** 87-93

Crummy, P, Hillam, J, & Crossan, C, 1982 'Mersea Island: the Anglo-Saxon causeway' *Essex Archaeol Hist* **14,** 77-86

Crump, B, & Wallis, S, 1992 'Kiddles and the Foulness fishing industry' *Essex J* **27** (2), 38-42

Crump, R W, 1981 'Excavation of a buried wooden structure at Foulness' *Essex Archaeol Hist* **13,** 69-71

Darby, H C, 1971 *The Domesday geography of Eastern England,* Cambridge University Press

Darby, H C, 1977 *Domesday England,* Cambridge University Press

Day, S P, 1993 'Woodland origin and "ancient woodland indicators": a case-study from Sidlings Copse, Oxfordshire, UK' *Holocene* **3** (1), 45-53

DB: Domesday Book (Rumble 1983)

De Brisay, K W, 1978 'The excavation of a Red Hill at Peldon, Essex, with notes on some other sites' *Antiq J* **58,** 31-60

Defoe, D, 1724-6 *A tour through the whole island of Great Britain* (reprinted 1971, Harmondsworth: Penguin)

Defoe, D, 1724 *A tour through England and Wales, divided into circuits or journies, Volume 1* (1928 Everyman edition reprinted 1962, London: Dent, Dutton)

Delderfield, R B, 1981 'The woodlands of south-east Essex: Report 1 Three woods of Thundersley and Hadleigh' *South-East Essex Archaeol,* 9-23

Delderfield, R B, 1982 'The woodlands of south-east Essex: Report 2 West Wood' *South-East Essex Archaeol,* 14-23

Delderfield, R B, & Rippon, S, 1996 'The origins of ancient woodland and a fishpond in Pound Wood, Thundersley, Essex' *Essex Archaeol Hist* **27,** 322-4

Devoy, R J N, 1979 'Flandrian sea-level changes and vegetational history of the lower Thames Estuary' *Phil Trans Roy Soc* London B285, 355-407

DoE [Department of the Environment] 1977 *Audley End, Essex,* London: HMSO (10th impression)

DoE [Department of the Environment] 1990 *Planning Policy Guidance: archaeology and planning (PPG 16),* London: HMSO

DoE [Department of the Environment] 1994: *Planning Policy Guidance: planning and the historic environment (PPG 15),* London: HMSO

Drewett, P L, 1975 'The excavations at Hadleigh Castle, Essex, 1971-72' *J Brit Archaeol Assoc* (3rd series) **38,** 90-154

Drury, P J, 1976 'Braintree: excavations and research 1971-76' *Essex Archaeol Hist* **8,** 1-143

Drury, P J, 1978 *Excavations at Little Waltham,* 1970-71, London: CBA Research Report **26**

Drury, P J, 1983 ' "A Fayre House, Buylt by Sir Thomas Smyth": the development of Hill Hall, Essex, 1557-81' *J Brit Archaeol Assoc* **136,** 98-123

Drury, P J, Rodwell, W J, & Wickenden, N P, 1981 'Finds from the probable site of a Roman villa at Dawes Heath, Thundersley, Essex' *Essex Archaeol Hist* **13,** 66-8

Dyer, C C, 1990a 'Dispersed settlements in medieval England: a case study of Pendock, Worcestershire' *Medieval Archaeol* **34,** 97-121

Dyer, C C, 1990b 'The past, the present and the future in medieval rural history' *Rural History* **1,** 37-49

Dyer, C C, 1996 'Rural settlements in medieval Warwickshire' Trans Birmingham *Warwicks Archaeol Soc* **100,** 117-32

ECC SMR: Essex County Council Sites and Monuments Record

Edelen, G (ed), 1994 *'The description of England': the classic contemporary account of Tudor social life, by William Harrison,* New York: Folger Shakespeare Library

Edwards, A C, 1975 *John Petre: essays on the life and background of John, 1st Lord Petre, 1549-1613,* London: Regency Press

Edwards, A C, 1994 *A history of Essex* (5th edition), Chichester: Phillimore

Edwards, A C, & Newton, K C, 1984 *The Walkers of Hanningfield: surveyors and mapmakers extraordinary,* London: Buckland Publications

Emmison, F G, 1961 *Tudor Secretary: Sir William Petre at court and home,* London: Longmans

Emmison, F G, 1976 *Elizabethan life: home, work and land,* Chelmsford: Essex County Council

English Heritage, 1997 *Sustaining the historic environment: new perspectives on the future,* London

English Heritage & RCHME [Royal Commission on the Historical Monuments of England], 1996 *England's coastal heritage: a statement on the management of coastal archaeology,* London

ERO: Essex Record Office

Essex Archaeology 1995, **12** (supplement to *Essex Chronicle*), Essex County Council Planning Department

Essex County Council 1972 *The Essex countryside–a landscape in decline?,* Chelmsford

Essex County Council, Kent County Concil, English Heritage & RCHME [Royal Commission on the Historical Monuments of England], forthcoming *An archaeological research framework for the Greater Thames Estuary*

Farmer, J, 1735 *The history of the ancient Town and once famous Abbey of Waltham,* London

Faull, M L, & Moorhouse, S A, 1981 *West Yorkshire: an archaeological survey to AD 1500,* Wakefield: West Yorkshire Metropolitan County Council

Fawn, A J, Evans, K A, McMaster, I, & Davies, G M R, 1990 *The red hills of Essex: salt-making in antiquity,* Colchester Archaeology Group

FF: Feet of Fines for Essex (Anon 1913-28; Anon 1929-49; Kirk 1899-1910; Reaney & Fitch 1964)

Fisher, F J, 1934-5 'The development of the London food market 1540-1640' *Economic Hist Review* **5,** 46-64

Fox, H S A, 1981 'Approaches to the adoption of the Midland system' in Rowley, 64-111

Fox, H S A (ed), 1983 'Dispersed settlement' *Medieval Settlement Research Group Annual Report* **31,** 39-45

Fox, H S A, 1989 'The people of the Wolds in English settlement history', in Aston *et al,* 77-101

Fraser, C M, 1968 *The Northumberland Lay Subsidy Roll of 1296* , Newcastle-upon-Tyne: Society of Antiquaries

Fullmer, S, 1781 *The young gardener's best companion for the thorough practical management of the pleasure ground and flower garden,* London

Gelling, M, 1984 *Place-names in the landscape: the geographical roots of Britain's place-names,* London: Dent

Glasscock, R E, 1975 *The Lay Subsidy of 1334,* London: British Academy

Glazebrook, J (ed), 1997 *Research and archaeology: a framework for the Eastern Counties, 1: resource assessment* (East Anglian Archaeology occasional paper **3**), Norwich: Scole Archaeological Committee for East Anglia

Glover, B W, 1990 *Steeple Bumpstead: evolution of the parish through 20 centuries,* typescript in ERO

Godfrey, W H, 1955 *The English almshouse, with some account of its predecessor, the medieval hospital,* London: Faber & Faber

Going, C, 1996 'The Roman countryside' in Bedwin, 95-107

Going, C, 1997 'Roman' in Glazebrook, 35-45

Gray, H L, 1915 *English field systems,* Cambridge, Massachusetts: Harvard University Press

Greenwood, P, 1982 'The cropmark site at Moor Hall Farm, Rainham, Essex' *London Archaeol* **4** (7), 185-93

Haggard, H R, 1905 *The poor and the land,* London: Longmans

Hancock, M, & Harvey, S, 1986 *Hadleigh: an Essex village,* Chichester: Phillimore

Hart, C, 1957a *The early charters of Essex: the Saxon period,* Leicester University Press: Department of English Local History Occasional Papers **10**

Hart, C, 1957b *The early charters of Essex: the Norman period,* Leicester University Press: Department of English Local History Occasional Papers **11**

Harvey, P D A, 1989 'Initiative and authority in settlement change' in Aston *et al,* 31-43

Harvey, S P J, 1979 'The evidence for settlement study: Domesday Book' in P H Sawyer (ed) *English medieval settlement,* London: Edward Arnold, 105-109

Harvey, S P J, 1987 'Taxation and the economy', in J C Holt (ed) *Domesday studies,* Woodbridge: Boydell Press, 249-64

Helliwell, L, & Macleod, D G, 1969 'Excavations at High Street, Hadleigh: brief provisional report' *Essex J* **4,** 29-30

Helliwell, L, & Macleod, D G, 1980 *Rayleigh Castle: documentary evidence and report on excavations 1959-1961 and 1969-70,* Southend: Rayleigh Mount Local Committee

Heygate, W E, 1859 *Sir Henry Appleton; or Essex during the Great Rebellion,* London: J T Hayes

Hill, J, 1757 *Eden, or a compleat body of gardening,* London]

Hinton, D A, 1990 *Archaeology, economy and society: England from the 5th to the 15th century,* London: Seaby

HMC [Historic Manuscripts Commission] 1893 9th report

HMC [Historic Manuscripts Commission] 1897-9 *Castle Howard,* 15th report, Appendix VI [42], 143

Homans, G C, 1941 *English villagers of the 13th century,* Cambridge, Massachusetts: Harvard University Press

Hoskins, W G, 1955 *The making of the English landscape,* London: Hodder & Stoughton (and 1977 edition, Harmondsworth: Penguin)

HRO: Huntingdonshire Records Office

Hunt, J D, & Willis, P, 1975 *The genius of place: the English landscape garden 1620-1820,* London: Elek

Hunter, J M, 1985 *Land into landscape,* London: Goodwin (2nd edition 1993)

Hunter, J M, 1993a 'The age of hedgerows on a Bocking estate' *Essex Archaeol Hist* **24,** 114-117

Hunter, J M, 1993b 'The historic landscape of Cressing Temple and its environs' in Andrews, 25-35

Hunter, J M, 1994a 'Medieval and Tudor parks of the middle Chelmer valley' *Essex Archaeol Hist* **25,** 113-118

Hunter, J M, 1994b 'Littley Park, Great Waltham-historical survey' *Essex Archaeol Hist* **25,** 119-24

Hunter, J.M, 1995 'Settlement and farming patterns on the mid-Essex boulder clays' *Essex Archaeol Hist* **26,** 133-44

Hunter, J M, 1999 *The Essex landscape: a study of its form and history,* Chelmsford: Essex Record Office

Hussey, C, 1967 *English gardens and landscapes 1700-1750,* Country Life

Jefferies, R, 1904 *The life of the fields,* London: Chatto & Windus

Jones, W T, 1980 'Early Saxon cemeteries in Essex' in Buckley, 87-95

Kennett, D, 1984 'Early brick buildings: a question of size' *Brit Brick Soc Information* **33,** 7-12

Kielmansegge, Count F von, 1902, *Diary of a journey to England, 1761-2,* London: Longmans

King, H W, 1863 'Notes on recent excavations at Hadleigh Castle' *Trans Essex Archaeol Soc* **4,** 70-81

Kirk, R E G, 1899-1910 *Feet of Fines for Essex, Volume 1: AD 1182-AD 1272,* Colchester: Essex Archaeological Society

Lake, R D, Ellison, R A, Henson, M R, & Camroy, B M, 1986 *Geology of the country around Southend and Foulness* , London: British Geological Survey

Lennard, R, 1945 'The destruction of woodland in the eastern counties under William the Conqueror' *Econ Hist Rev* **15,** 36-43

Linehan, C D, 1966 'Deserted sites and rabbit warrens in Dartmoor, Devon', *Medieval Archaeol* **10,** 113-44

MacCarthy, F, 1994 *William Morris, a life for our time,* London: Faber & Faber

McIntosh, M K, 1986 *Autonomy and community: the royal manor of Havering, 1200-1500,* Cambridge University Press

Meddens, F M, 1996 'Sites from the Thames Estuary, England, and their Bronze Age use' *Antiquity* **70** (268), 325-34

Min Acc I: King 1863

Min Acc II: Sparvel-Bayly 1878

Morant, P, 1766-8 *The history and antiquities of the County of Essex* (2 vols), London

Murphy, P, 1988 'Plant macrofossils' in Brown, 281-93

Murphy, P, 1989 'Carbonised Neolithic plant remains from The Stumble, an intertidal site in the Blackwater Estuary, Essex, England' *Circaea* **6** (1), 21-38

Murphy, P, 1994 'The Anglo-Saxon landscape and rural economy: some results from sites in East Anglia and Essex' in J Rackham (ed) *Environment and economy in Anglo-Saxon England,* London: CBA Research Report **89**, 23-39

Murphy, P, 1995 'Mollusca' in Wymer & Brown, 142-5

Needham, S P, 1993 'The structure of settlement and ritual in the Late Bronze Age of south-east Britain' in C Mordant & A Richard (eds) *L'habitat et l'occupation du sol à l'Age du Bronze en Europe; Actes du Colloque International de Lons-le-Saurier, 16-19 Mai 1990,* Editions du Comité des Travaux historique et scientifique: Documents préhistoriques **4**, 49-69

Newton, K C, 1960 *Thaxted in the 14th century,* Chelmsford: Essex Record Office

Newton, K, 1970 *The manor of Writtle: the development of a royal manor in Essex c.1086-c.1500,* Chichester: Phillimore

NMR: National Monuments Record (RCHME)

Nurse, B, Pugh, J, & Mollett, I, 1995 *A village in time: the history of Newport, Essex,* Newport: Newport News

OS [Ordnance Survey] 1843 One-Inch Series (1st edition)

Pollitt, W, 1935 *The archaeology of Rochford Hundred and south-east Essex,* Southend Museum

Pollitt, W, 1953 *Southend before the Norman Conquest,* Southend Museum

Pope, A, 1731 'An epistle to Lord Burlington' (ed H Davies, 1966, Oxford University Press)

Potter, S, Renton, D, & Ryan, P, 1986 'Deserted settlement earthworks at Purleigh' *Essex Archaeol Hist* **17,** 107-119

Priddy, D (ed), 1983 'Work of the Essex County Council Archaeology Section, 1982' *Essex Archaeol Hist* **15,** 119-55

Priddy, D, & Buckley, D G, 1987 *An assessment of excavated enclosures in Essex together with a selection of cropmark sites* (East Anglian Archaeology **33**), Chelmsford: Essex County Council, 48-80

Priestley, H E, 1984 *A history of Benfleet: the early days,* Castle Point District Council

Pryor, F, 1992 'Current research at Flag Fen, Peterborough' *Antiquity* **66** (251), 439-57

Pryor, F, 1996 'Sheep, stockyards and field systems: Bronze Age livestock in eastern England' *Antiquity* **70** (268), 313-24

Rackham, O, 1976 *Trees and woodland in the British Landscape,* London: J M Dent (2nd edition 1990)

Rackham, O, 1978 'Archaeology and land-use history' in D Corke (ed) 'Epping Forest-the natural aspect?' *Essex Naturalist,* NS2, 16–75

Rackham, O, 1980a 'The medieval landscape of Essex' in Buckley 1980, 103-107

Rackham, O, 1980b *Ancient woodland: its history, vegetation and use in England,* London: Edward Arnold

Rackham, O, 1986a *The history of the countryside,* London: Dent

Rackham, O, 1986b *The ancient woodland of England: the woods of south-east Essex,* Rochford: Rochford District Council

Rackham, O, 1989 *The last Forest: the story of Hatfield Forest,* London: Dent

Rackham, O, 1993 'Medieval timber economy as illustrated by the Cressing Temple barns' in Andrews, 85–92

Rackham, O, 1994 *The illustrated history of the countryside,* London: Weidenfeld & Nicholson

Ray, J, 1690 *Synopsis methodica stirpium Britannicarum* (1724 edition reprinted 1973, London: The Ray Society)

RCHME [Royal Commission on Historical Monuments, England], 1923 *An inventory of the historical monuments in Essex, Volume 4,* London: HMSO

RCHME [Royal Commission on Historical Monuments, England], 1995 *Thames Gateway: recording historic buildings and landscapes on the Thames Estuary,* London: RCHME

Reader, F W, 1911 'A Neolithic floor on the bed of the Crouch River and other discoveries near Rayleigh, Essex' *Essex Naturalist* **16,** 249-64

Reaney, P H, & Fitch, M, 1964 *Feet of Fines for Essex, Volume 4: AD 1423-AD 1547,* Colchester: Essex Archaeological Society

Reaney, P H (ed), 1935 *The place-names of Essex,* Cambridge University Press: English Place-Names Society vol 12 (2nd edition 1969)

Rippon, S, 1991 'Early planned landscapes in south-east Essex' *Essex Archaeol Hist* **22,** 46-60

Rippon, S, 1996a 'Essex *c.* 700-1066', in Bedwin, 117-28

Rippon, S, 1996b *The Gwent Levels: the evolution of a wetland landscape,* London: CBA Research Report **105**

Rippon, S, 1997 *The Severn Estuary: landscape evolution and wetland reclamation,* Leicester University press

Rippon, S, forthcoming 'Exploitation and modification: changing patterns in the use of coastal resources in southern Britain' in A Aberg & C Lewis (eds) *The archaeology of coastal landscapes,* Oxford: Oxbow

Roberts, B K, & Wrathmell, S, 1998 'Dispersed settlement in England: a national view' in P Everson & T Williamson (eds) *The archaeology of landscape,* Manchester University Press, 95-116

Roberts, B K, & Wrathmell, S, forthcoming *An atlas of rural settlement in England*

Roden, D, 1973 'Field systems of the Chiltern Hills and their environs' in A R H Barker & R A Butlin (eds) *Studies of field systems in the British Isles,* Cambridge University Press

Rodwell, W J, 1965 'Canvey Island' in D Wilson & H Hurst (eds) 'Medieval Britain in 1964' *Medieval Archaeol* **9,** 213

Rodwell, W J, 1978 'Relict landscapes in Essex', in H C Bowen & P J Fowler (eds) *Early land allotment in the British Isles: a survey of recent work,* Oxford: British Archaeological Reports, British series **48,** 89-98

Rodwell, W J, 1979 'Iron Age and Roman salt-winning on the Essex coast' in B C Burnham & H B Johnson (eds) *Invasion and response: the case of Roman Britain,* Oxford: British Archaeological Reports, British series **73,** 133-75

Rodwell, W J, 1993 *The origins and early development of Witham, Essex: a study in settlement and fortification, prehistoric to medieval,* Oxford: Oxbow Monograph **26**

Rodwell, W J, & Rodwell, K A, 1985 *Rivenhall: investigations of a villa, church and village, 1950-1977,* London: CBA Research Report **55**

Rodwell, W J, & Rodwell, K A, 1993 *Rivenhall: investigations of a villa, church and village, 1950-1977, Volume 2 specialist studies.,* London: CBA Research Report **80**

Round, H, 1903 'The Domesday survey' in *VCH Essex,* Vol **1**, 333-598

Rowley, T (ed), 1981 *The origins of open-field agriculture,* London: Nicols

Rumble, A, 1983 *Domesday Book: Essex,* Chichester: Phillimore

Rutter, J, & Carter, D, 1767 *Modern Eden,* London

Ryan, P M, 1989 *Woodham Walter, a village history,* Woodham Walter: Plume Press

Ryan, P M, 1993 'Cressing Temple: its history from documentary sources' in Andrews, 11-24

Ryan, P M, 1996 *Brick in Essex from the Roman Conquest to the Reformation,* Danbury: P Ryan

Ryan, P M, & Andrews, D D, 1993 'The walled garden at Cressing Temple' in Andrews, 105-116

Ryan, P M, Stenning, D F, Tyers, I, & Andrews, D D, 1997 'New House Farm and Hungry Hall, Cressing: the disintegration of the Cressing Temple estate or the Great Rebuilding?' *Essex Archaeol Hist* **28,** 156-64

Scaife, R, 1995 'Pollen analysis' in Wilkinson & Murphy, 43-51

Scarfe, N V, 1942 'Essex', in L Dudley Stamp (ed) *The land of Britain: the report of the Land Utilization Survey of Britain, Part VIII: south-east England,* London: Geographical Publications

Schama, S, 1995 *Landscape and memory,* London: Harper Collins

SM: Southend Museum find number

Sparvel-Bayly, J A, 1878 'Records relating to Hadleigh Castle' *Trans Essex Archaeol Soc,* New Series **1,** 86-108

Spence, J, 1820 (edited J M Osborn, 1966) *Observations, anecdotes and characters of men*

Spurrell, F C J, 1889 'On the estuary of the Thames and its alluvium' *Proc Geol Soc London* **11,** 210-30

Strachan, D, 1995 'Aerial photography and the archaeology of the Essex coast' *Essex J* **30** (2), 41-6

Strachan, D, 1996 *Blackwater Estuary Management Plan (BEMP) area: proposed archaeological programme,* Chelmsford: Essex County Council

Strachan, D, 1998 'Intertidal stationary fishing structures in the Blackwater Estuary' *Essex Archaeol Hist* **29,** 282-90

Stroud, D, 1975 *Capability Brown,* London: Faber & Faber

Toller, H, 1980 'The Orsett Cock enclosure' *Britannia* **11,** 35-42

Toynbee, J M (ed), 1903 *The collected correspondence of Horace Walpole*

Tusser, T, 1573 (edited W Payne & S Herrtage, 1878) *Fiue hundred points of good Husbandrie,* ch 35, v 15

Vancouver, C, 1795 *General view of the agriculture in the County of Essex,* London: Board of Agriculture

VCH [Victoria County History]: H A Doubleday & W Page (eds), 1903 *The Victoria history of the County of Essex,* vol **1,** London

Vincent, S W, & George, W H, 1980 *Some Mesolithic sites along the Rivers Blackwater and Crouch, Essex,* unpublished typescript [in ERO]

Wallis, S, & Waughman, M, 1998 *Archaeology and the landscape in the Lower Blackwater Valley* (East Anglian Archaeology **82**), Chelmsford: Essex County Council

Walpole, H, 1780 *A history of the Modern Taste in gardening* (originally part of *Anecdotes of painting in England,* written 1771)

WAM: Westminster Abbey Muniments Room

Ward, J C, 1987 'Richer in land than in inhabitants: south Essex in the Middle Ages, c.1066-c.1340' in K Neale (ed) *An Essex tribute: essays presented to Frederick G Emmison,* London: Leopard's Head Press

Ward, J C, & Marshall, K, 1972 *Old Thorndon Hall,* Chelmsford: Essex Record Office

Warner, P, 1987 *Greens, common and clayland colonization,* Leicester University Department of English (Local History Occasional Papers, 4th Series, **2**)

Warren, S H, 1911 'On the correlation of the prehistoric "floor" at Hullbridge with similar beds elsewhere' *Essex Naturalist* **16,** 265-82

Warren, S H, Piggott, S, Clark, J G D, Burkitt, M C H, & Godwin, M E, 1936 'Archaeology of the submerged land-surface of the Essex Coast' *Proc Prehist Soc* **2.2,** 178-210

Waterbolk, A T, & Van Zeist, W, 1961 'A Bronze Age sanctuary in the raised bog at Bargeroosterveld, Drenthe' *Helinium I,* 5-19

Waterson, M, 1994 *The National Trust–the first hundred years,* London: BBC Books

WD: Westminster Domesday survey, in Westminster Abbey Muniments Room

Welldon-Finn, R, 1972 'Changes in the population of Essex 1066-86' *Essex Archaeol Hist* **4,** 128-33

Wilkinson, T J, 1988 *Archaeology and environment in south Essex: rescue archaeology along the Grays by-pass 1979-80* (East Anglian Archaeology **42**), Chelmsford: Essex County Council

Wilkinson, T J, & Murphy, P, 1986 'Archaeological survey of an intertidal zone: the submerged landscape of the Essex coast, England' *J Field Archaeol* **13** (2), 177-94

Wilkinson, T J, & Murphy, P, 1995 *Archaeology of the Essex Coast, Volume 1: The Hullbridge Survey* (East Anglian Archaeology **71**), Chelmsford: Essex County Council

Wilkinson, T J, & Murphy, P, forthcoming *Archaeology of the Essex Coast, Volume 2,* (East Anglian Archaeology)

Williams-Ellis, C, 1928 *England and the Octopus,* London, Geoffrey Bles (reprinted 1996, Council for the Preservation of Rural England)

Williamson, T, 1986 'The development of settlement in north-west Essex: the results of a recent field survey' *Essex Archaeol Hist* **17,** 120-32

Williamson, T, 1988 'Explaining regional landscapes: woodland and champion in southern and eastern England' *Landscape History* **10,** 5-13

Williamson, T, 1993 *The origins of Norfolk,* Manchester University Press

Williamson, T, 1995 *Polite landscapes: gardens and society in eighteenth-century England,* Stroud: Alan Sutton

Williamson, T, & Bellamy, L, 1987 *Property and landscape–a social history of land ownership and the English countryside,* London: George Philip

Willis, P, 1977 *Charles Bridgeman,* London: Zwemmer

Wiltshire, P, & Murphy, P, 1998 'An analysis of plant microfossils and macrofossils from waterlogged deposits at Slough House and Chigborough Farms' in Wallis & Waughman, 172-96

Woodward, H B, 1903 'Geology' in *VCH Essex,* vol **1**, 1-23

Wymer, J J, & Brown, N R, 1995 *Excavations at North Shoebury: settlement and economy in south-east Essex 1500 BC-AD 1500* (East Anglian Archaeology **75**), Chelmsford: Essex County Council